FL puts guillotine Fitzroy's neck

FAREWELL SCHWABBY

$100m. MCG PLAN

Life after footy

OUTGOING AFL chief executive Ross Oakley today said money was no object in his search for a new job.

Mr Oakley, who re-signed yesterday, said job satisfaction was his priority, hinting that he might have earned more money had he stayed in the corporate world 10 years ago.

Mr Oakley declared he had no interest in joining the media or returning to insurance, preferring to "step out of the limelight".

A CLUB IS BORN

Since his controversial appointment 10 years ago as the head of the AFL, Ross Oakley has turned the sport into a flourishing business with a series of successful initiatives. **ROD NICHOLSON** reports

WHY I QUIT

     **And then there were...**

THE PHOENIX RISES

The Slattery Media Group Pty Ltd
1 Albert St, Richmond
Victoria, Australia, 3121

© Ross Oakley 2014

First published by The Slattery Media Group Pty Ltd 2014

All images reproduced with permission.

All rights reserved. No part of this publication may be reproduced, stored in a retrieval system or transmitted in any form or by any means without the prior written permission of the copyright owner. Inquiries should be made to the publisher.

® The AFL logo and competing team logos, emblems and names used are all trade marks of and used under licence from the owner, the Australian Football League, by whom all copyright and other rights of reproduction are reserved. Australian Football League AFL House, 140 Harbour Esplanade, Docklands, Victoria, Australia, 3008.

National Library of Australia Cataloguing-in-Publication entry

Author: Oakley, Ross, author.
Title: The Phoenix Rises / Ross Oakley with Jonathan Green and Geoff Slattery.
ISBN: 9780987420596 (hardback)
Subjects: Oakley, Ross.
               Australian football–History.
               Football players–Australia–Biography.

Other Authors/Contributors:
               Green, Jonathan, author.
               Slattery, Geoff, author.

Dewey Number: 796.336092

Group Publisher: Geoff Slattery
Editors: Geoff Slattery and Katie Purvis
Creative Director and Design: Kate Slattery
Printed and bound in Australia by Griffin Press

Every effort has been made to verify the source of the photographs in this book. Inquiries should be made to the publisher.

slatterymedia.com

THE PHOENIX RISES

ROSS OAKLEY OAM
with Jonathan Green & Geoff Slattery

visit *slatterymedia.com*

DEDICATION

To my family, all of whom put up with the scrutiny of unwanted public attention throughout my 10 years at the AFL

To my children, Melanie and Gregory, wonderful loving siblings who both supported me wholeheartedly without complaint

And to Christine, my wife of 46 years, a beautiful lady;
my rock, always by my side when you were needed.
You sacrificed your love of teaching to fulfil your AFL role and for this Australian football will be eternally in your debt.

THE PHOENIX RISES

CONTENTS

Foreword by Mike Sheahan:
The man for the moment....................9

1 Death watch....................13
2 The commission is born....................37
3 A visionary departs....................48
4 The commission's early challenges....................53
5 A reality check....................64
6 An alliance of sworn enemies....................70
7 My early days in football....................84
8 Boys' club to business enterprise....................88
9 Two-man band....................103
10 A faltering start to a national competition....................115
11 The television rights dilemma....................126
12 An interrupted holiday....................137
13 A new ball game....................148
14 A new marketing era....................160
15 Around the grounds....................184
16 State of the clubs....................202
17 Up yours Oakley....................216
18 Mergers and acquisitions....................237
19 From sadness to glory....................262
20 Coming of age....................275
21 Leaders of the pack....................299
22 Reflections....................315

Acknowledgments....................319
Index....................321

FOREWORD

by Mike Sheahan

The man for the moment

It was a decade that featured the immortal names of Matthews, Ablett, Lockett, Dunstall, the Maddens, Flower, Williams, Watson, Quinlan, Healy, Glendinning; and a host of others.

No wonder a DVD of the highlights of the time was titled *The Electrifying '80s*.

Off the field, the more appropriate adjectives for the Victorian Football League of the 1980s weren't quite as positive, as exciting. Dramatic, divisive, disturbing and desperate were far more appropriate. Throw in turbulent and you should get the full picture.

The great game was in disarray in the commercial context in the 1980s. It was in need of a searching review and a major revamp.

Ever so slowly, the ailing Victorian Football League addressed its issues and introduced measures that saw it evolve into the Australian Football League, with the name change formalised for the 1990 season.

Actually, it didn't evolve: it was driven into its national incarnation by economic necessity and a small band of men with vision and commitment; men who saw beyond club loyalties and acted in the best interests of the code—a major departure from the days when club-appointed directors ran the VFL according to the wishes of their club, often their own narrow view and, just as often, petty jealousy.

The decade of the 1980s produced the ham-fisted relocation of South Melbourne to Sydney, the first independent commission, and the introduction of West Coast and the Brisbane Bears to the VFL competition. It was a watershed period, a transition from what we knew (and what was eroding the fabric of the game at the highest level) to what *had* to happen if the game was to survive and flourish, as it most certainly has done.

While names such as McCutchan, Nathan, Hamilton and Aylett were immortalised by their contribution as administrators, it was the commission and Ross Oakley who steered football through stormy seas during much of the '80s. Seas so rough, the future of clubs such as South Melbourne/Sydney, Fitzroy and Footscray (Western Bulldogs) hung in the balance, while several other clubs were bankrupt in the true sense, propped up by their siblings.

No wonder John Elliott, then president of Carlton, and sympathisers canvassed and explored the idea of a virtual super-league. That stunning move came in the early '80s and it was deadly serious. Football in Victoria was deep in trouble.

In 1985, attendances for the season totalled 3,113,255; the downward spiral was undeniable. After record crowds of 3,830,231 in 1981—after a period of dominance by heavyweight clubs Carlton and Collingwood—the attendance figures fell for four years straight.

Not a moment too soon, a string of measures, including the reluctant introduction of a commission, started the desperately needed overhaul.

The change was made complete when the commission looked outside the game for the man to drive the competition on a daily basis. They overlooked Alan Schwab, seen as the natural successor to the departing Jack Hamilton, and invested the future in insurance company executive Ross Oakley.

Oakley may have been a former St Kilda player—and a high-quality one at that—and a Hawthorn board member, but he was an "outsider" by comparison with Schwab, who, like Hamilton, had risen from a modest start in football to a position of authority and power.

Schwab almost got the job on the basis he was a "footy man" (and he probably deserved it because of his service, according to his backers), but Oakley's broader CV and the promise of fresh ideas swayed the more powerful members of the commission. History says it was the correct decision.

Oakley was the man for the moment. He was the ideal public face for the VFL—an ex-player with a strong corporate history and a willingess to defend the tough decisions, often at a significant cost to himself and his family in terms of public criticism and overt hostility.

He was easy to work with, too. While he had a healthy ego, he could park it when and where necessary. He could adapt or backtrack when he heard a superior argument, and he could take counsel from those he respected. Not all CEOs are entitled to say the same.

Oakley was also better than most at fighting the fight, no matter how public, how emotive the issue, and then moving on. It was a lesson for many of us. He knew not to overstay, too, faithful to his pledge that 10 years was roughly the limit in such a demanding, high-profile role.

Consider the make-up of the current competition: 10 Victorian clubs, eight others from four other states; the mind-boggling dollars generated by the broadcast-rights agreement; the array of high-class stadiums throughout the country; the massive public interest—and you can't reasonably come to any other conclusion. Oakley was, indeed, the man for the moment.

This book reminds us in rich detail how the transition unfolded—and of the constant drama that beset those early days. It is a painstaking exercise of interviews with key participants, of hours and hours poring over minutes of dozens of critical meetings, of reflections formed and strengthened by time.

I was media director at the VFL from 1985 to 1989 and saw the most turbulent period in the game's history unfold in front of my eyes. This book has allowed me to revisit that era—and to learn much more—via Oakley's timely contribution to football's literary history from his unique vantage point.

Mike Sheahan, June 2014

CHAPTER 1

Death watch

To look at the AFL today, you'd never know just how close it came to falling apart at the seams just 30-odd years ago; how vested interests, profligate spending and lack of vision combined to put a clamp on a game that, fortunately, never lost the passionate support of its fans.

Now, it's the dominant sporting body in the country, presiding over one of the world's great sporting codes. Money, power, a commanding national presence—not to mention on-field brilliance—the AFL competition has it all: a national code with a growing audience in every corner of the continent. Match-day attendances, revenue, media coverage and player conditions all continue to improve, year on year.

The AFL's most recent broadcast agreement, locking in free-to-air TV, pay TV and digital rights is an extraordinary thing—a $1.253 billion five-year deal all but unimaginable for those of us who scavenged for small change from a bunch of arrogant and self-assured broadcasters just 25 years ago. Today, wisely managed and with an eye firmly on its future, the AFL juggernaut seems all but unstoppable.

A lot had to fall into place for this to happen. But the modern AFL is proof that with endeavour, energy, commitment and resources—controlled by an independent commission overseeing a coherent strategic plan—right will win out. Somehow, it all came together; the many and varied strands needed to build the modern AFL have been knitted into a proud banner.

But there was a time, through the shaky 1980s, when it all hung very much in the balance.

This is the story of how an organisation, managed by vested interests and all but on its knees, stumbled through the big ideas, big decisions and key strategies that together would lead to its salvation. As it happened, the things that Australian Football needed to construct in a blind hurry to survive its darkest hour—to save its neck—were the very things a burgeoning new world of multi-platform media, an entertainment-hungry public and a host of national brands wanted: a professionally managed game with a devoted army of fans and an awareness of its commercial possibilities *and* its potential to grow from parochial outposts into all parts of the country.

The devotion of the fans had always been part of the fabric of the game. The awareness of the game's commercial possibilities was the problem: could the Victorian Football League (VFL) manage these opportunities calmly, taking into account the League's highly competitive and inward-looking clubs and their one-eyed supporters, neither of whom wanted change? And could a national competition, developed from the Victorian model, draw in teams from the introspective West Australian and South Australian leagues?

Fortunately, it could. The result: football's crisis—its near-fatal moment—became the basis of its greatest period of change.

The VFL might have been the nucleus of Australian Football and far and away the most popular of the state-based competitions (much to the chagrin of the passionate followers of the code in SA and WA, who had, for so long, seen their best players travel east), but despite its standing and history, by the early 1980s the Victorian game was withering away through debt, well-meaning but misdirected management and the blind self-interest of clubs forever warring against each other.

This was also a time of hubris, a time when there was no tomorrow. The game, they thought, would always survive, and the clubs with it, no matter how flamboyant and flighty their financial management was. Few in the administration of the game—at any level—were thinking of the greater good. Footy might easily have wound up where it had started: in the muddy sward of suburban grounds, confined to state-based competitions, compressed into single cities and the traditional game-day clutter of Saturday afternoons, played out before dwindling weekly attendances, the field of play populated by gifted amateurs.

A few in the Anti-Football League—a noisy minority who wondered how a mere game could garner so much media space, and so much passion—might have cheered, but the wider football world would have seen its loyalty to club and game betrayed by an administrative structure that couldn't take the rusted-on faith of the fans, a faith and love built over generations, and couldn't define—and mine—its commercial worth; an administration that couldn't see a way to build that blind enthusiasm into something that would not only sustain the suburban clubs of Melbourne, but also had the potential to grow into a force that could dominate Australia's sporting culture.

As the 1980s wound on, attendances were stagnating. Half the clubs under the proud banner of the VFL were little more than bankruptcies in waiting, with some already under observation and investigation by state authorities. Conditions were primitive—at some grounds they were close to confronting, not just for the fans but for the elite players forced to slog through mud-heaps.

It's not so long ago, but it remains a world apart from the sleek administrative machine AFL football has become, or even the slowly developing head office it would be my privilege to run for a decade some years later. Back then, decisions on the total management of the game had to be stamped "approved" by a dozen club-appointed directors. The close-held interests of the clubs had reduced the capacity of the central administration—led by president Allen Aylett and general manager Jack Hamilton—to make the necessary and visionary decisions that could build the greater game and feed its long-term potential. Self-interest ruled supreme.

For years the club representatives of this compromised VFL board had slowly digested the bad news, seen the raw numbers—of crowds and overall revenues that had peaked with subsequent dire financial circumstances—and finally come to understand that the game was at a crossroads. Big decisions needed to be made. Cases for and against various versions of national expansion had been debated vigorously (publicly and privately), as had the arguments for new—independent—administrative structures, new methods of commercialising the game, better brand management, better administration at club level, and more ways to fund the game beyond the rapidly falling gate receipts. There were submissions and consultancies, papers and reports, subcommittees and expert panels, and all of these were accompanied by prevarication and indecision.

The penny had dropped by the early part of the 1982 season, and by August of that seminal year, Aylett saw the need to call a special meeting of the VFL board and club presidents. This was no jolly get-together, but a meeting in which Aylett put all the cards on the table: the ever-increasing gap between the rich and poor clubs and the uncertain future of many, the pressures on attendances, and the flaws in the game's decision-making process. The crisis in clubland had hit the central administration. Changes, said the president, had to be made.

By then, Aylett, the central administration and the more alert board members were well aware of the gathering strands of catastrophe. Attendances were no more than holding their own and had been drifting at around the same numbers since World War II. Club memberships were held by a minuscule, financially insignificant but devoted elite.[1] Ground facilities were appalling in a world suddenly replete with dozens of other entertainment options. Players were being paid beyond the capacity of their clubs to support their growing salaries, and costly poaching between clubs was rife. The game itself remained strong, although its players were still

---

1 Total club membership in 1984 was 96,827 (12 clubs, average 8068), with Collingwood leading the way with 16,313. In 2012, membership totalled 707,621 (18 clubs, average 39,312), with Collingwood still on top at 72,688.

largely amateurs, with even the highest paid fitting training around full-time jobs. Club administration was still in its formative years, well short of the slickness of today. Aylett knew the time was right to get the business of football away to a new beginning, but the clubs, hampered by conservatism and their insular suburban views, remained hesitant.

Aylett was an agent of change and energy. In his youth, he'd been a champion footballer for North Melbourne, played first-class cricket for Victoria and set up a flourishing dentistry practice. But it was his post-sporting career commitment to aggressive and radical changes at his old club that had confirmed his status as an ambitious visionary, and ultimately a successful leader and change merchant. Aylett was the first of the "executive" club presidents, and would drive the North Melbourne administration, and the total club, to unprecedented success. It was Aylett more than anybody who saw the value in charismatic leadership, appointing Ron Barassi as senior coach in 1973 while also exploiting a short-term law that allowed 10-year players to switch to the club of their choice. North Melbourne pinched the best, and in 1975 won its first flag under the dominant duo of Aylett and Barassi, assisted by a young up-and-coming administrator, Ron Joseph.

When he stood for president of the VFL in 1977—seeking to replace businessman Sir Maurice Nathan—it was a case of a young new world leader, in Aylett (then 43), against a more conservative candidate from Hawthorn, Phil Ryan (then 62). Aylett won a classic backroom battle and took, with that victory, a mandate for change. The League's administration also saw new blood at the top, with former Collingwood premiership full-back and long-time VFL employee Jack Hamilton replacing general manager Eric McCutchan, who had been in the job since 1956.

The Aylett-Hamilton team moved quickly to impose their vision on the game and how it should be managed. Not only did the duo conduct weekly broad-ranging media briefings and create a new, open administrative structure, they also worked hard to evaluate the state of the game and provide solutions that would take it forward. The new administration quickly appointed a corporate planner, John Hennessy, to assess all parts of the game and its processes, and a licensing and marketing agency, Active Marketing, headed by Jim McKay, to monetise the League's brand via an aggressive marketing and licensing program. These appointments might seem passé with the benefit of hindsight, but they were adventurous and forward-thinking for the time. It was, after all, only in 1977 that the VFL Grand Final had first been televised live—and for the princely sum of $100,000.

There were, of course, battles within battles around the VFL board table, and within the administration. Aylett's personality was to lead from the front, to treat the role of president as an executive position. Like all visionaries, he was impatient when he saw the need for change, and he drove the League's administration with a passion. At the core of the Aylett vision was a national competition: he wanted to establish a truly national game, with the 12 VFL clubs as its foundation. This was one battle the president was determined to win. The clubs and their board needed some convincing—as did Hamilton, a man with a much quieter, less confronting *modus operandi*, and the fans, who were well content with a 12-team competition on suburban grounds every Saturday from 2.10pm.

This was a time when the term "ground rationalisation" entered the lexicon; when the notion of Sunday football became a political football; the VFL had plans to better utilise VFL Park and expand its capacity to 160,000 seats (hence the saucer shape of the stands to cater for this massive crowd), and when the League proposed that clubs be considered "franchises" and that the game license its values—its brand—to corporate sponsors, licensees and marketers. Most of these matters were fully in the hands of the administration; what was not was the League's wish to switch the Grand Final from the MCG, the people's ground, to Waverley. It could be argued the VFL had every right to plan its own future and to play its marquee games in its own stadium, but this did not account for the affection of the community for the MCG, and the fact that football had underwritten the past and present of the great stadium; and it was clearly the Labor

Government's wish—led by Premier John Cain—to ensure the League would continue to be the most significant tenant at the MCG.[2] To say relationships between the VFL on the one hand and the state government and the MCG Trust on the other were strained is to dramatically understate the situation.

This was not a time for freeloaders: it was a time for a focused administration to recognise the asset value of the total game and to find new ways to draw revenue. It was also a time when South Melbourne had been driven to Sydney, off the back of gross financial failure, with limited financial support and facilities that were falling down around the players and spectators. It was a time of high emotion. The game was on a knife edge.

Aylett's mid-1982 crisis meeting did not resolve to act immediately. In fact, it was not until well into the following year that plans were put in place to formally evaluate the state of the game and its future, in the short and long term. Aylett had his views on what should happen to the game he loved and had served so well. Keen to present his version of the game's future and to continue to put pressure on the directors for change, he prepared a document and landed it on the board table on 16 February 1983. The League had been in discussions with the international business consultancy McKinsey & Co. for some little time to provide an independent view of its state of play, and two weeks after the Aylett report was submitted it actually appointed McKinsey to "investigate and report on 'The Decision Making Processes of the League'".[3]

In his excellent 1986 autobiography, the tellingly titled *My Game*, Aylett reflects on his decision to act unilaterally: "Thank God I took the positive steps to get my recommendations on the public record. As time passes, those recommendations will be seen in a positive light when historians review what has happened ... since my report."[4]

His report was stark and confronting, and all these years later a thorough

---

2   The League's plans were stymied by the Cain Labor Government. Although the relationship between the game and the League has had its moments, a deal to play the Grand Final at the MCG for 40 years was sealed in 1989.

3   VFL Board minutes, March 1983.

4   Allen Aylett with Greg Hobbs, *My Game: A Life in Football*, Macmillan, 1986, p. 225.

reading of the 25-page document provides a fascinating insight into the stress of the time, the urgency for change, and the apparent belief that only a rocket under the board could effect change. Aylett wrote from the heart:

> Unless we are prepared to honestly and critically look at the future of our game today, and are able to adapt our administrative process to find real lasting solutions, we may be denying our children and our children's children the right to play VFL football.
>
> It is not hard to conclude that unless our structural problems or player payments, player transfer regulations, grounds, club finances and the overall viability and structure of our competition are looked at seriously, and some real, ongoing solutions are found, our present competition will not exist in its present form for much longer.
>
> The VFL has a basic choice facing it: either it demonstrates it can manage itself efficiently and effectively, or control will pass out of its hands.[5]

The Aylett paper was not just about fear-mongering. It presented three choices for the board to consider: stick with the status quo; modify processes of decision-making to produce "real solutions" while retaining the board as the final arbiter; or replace the board with "an independent person or Commission".

Aylett concluded:

> In my opinion, the VFL clubs are capable of exercising and must be entrusted with the responsibility of deciding what is to be done, i.e. formulating the policy and objectives to determine where the VFL is going in the future. However, because of individual club loyalty and emotion in certain areas, clubs are not totally capable of deciding how to best move in the chosen direction.
>
> I am recommending a system of independent commissions, appointed by the VFL Board to assume responsibility for making final strategic decisions in those key areas where clubs' emotion would be present.[6]

Aylett's "commissions" were, in effect, consultancies. The "vast majority

---

5 Report to the VFL Board of Directors by Dr A.J. Aylett, President.
6 Ibid.

of policy and strategy decisions would continue to be made by the VFL Board", he recommended—a point that sounds rather at odds with the need for independence and the need to break free of the chains imposed by the self-interest of the clubs, but in reality describes well the wide spread of power contained within the board in that era.

The Aylett report also took a pragmatic approach, recognising that the board would wish to retain ultimate control but needed a dig in the ribs to be alerted to the reality of the situation, outside the constraints of club loyalties and vested interests.

Aylett's views were well considered and on the edge of radical, while mindful and respectful of the role the board and administration had played through generations of change. His report was more about tweaking than crashing through.

The three Aylett "commissions" (in this current era all part of the administrative structure of the vast AFL) would be responsible for providing recommendations to the board, in a timeline of nine months, on:

(a) "structure and finance", including matters of private ownership, introduction of new teams, and VFL assistance to clubs
(b) "players", including transfers between clubs, total player payments, and the role of players in VFL decision-making
(c) "grounds", including the number of grounds, Sunday football, club needs and government policy.[7]

Effectively Aylett was requesting external input to form the basis of a 10-year plan for the League, to be endorsed by the existing board, and for the board—in whatever iterations it might go through—to adhere to this plan. There was much wisdom in his presentation, overview and perspective, but it was quickly overshadowed when McKinsey & Co. presented their document (and a bill for $80,000) to the board in May 1983—although it did have enough impact on the League for Hamilton to be asked to seek a discount on the McKinsey fee, given the detail and scope of the Aylett report.

---

7   Ibid.

The McKinsey report, researched and presented within six weeks, went way beyond the consciously limited brief given by the board, which had decreed that the consultants report only on the VFL's decision-making process. In fact, as Aylett recalled, "The report covered a wide range of issues—financial affairs, future developments (inside and outside of football), some board administrative strategies for consideration, *and* a recommendation to change the decision-making process of the League."[8]

McKinsey & Co. affirmed Aylett's view that the situation was all but dire, noting in its preamble that "unless the rate of growth of expenses can be reduced, the existing gap between revenue and expenses will widen to as much as $5 million per year by 1985. The VFL faces a critical challenge in developing a management process that creates the authority needed to solve the League's current financial crisis and to make the crucial decisions for the long-term future of the League and Australian football."[9]

Former Melbourne Football Club CEO and a member of the first VFL Commission (he served from 1985 to 1987) Dick Seddon, a significant figure through this era, watched it all unfold with a sense of foreboding and expectation. As he recalls in his unpublished memoir of his time in the game: "McKinsey & Co. recommended that the League should change its organisational structure, appoint independent 'ad hoc task forces' (as Aylett had suggested) to address major issues."[10]

The McKinsey report made two key points: (1) that "structural changes to the existing competition are required, and a long-term, phased move to a national competition is desirable", and (2) "to overcome impasses resulting from parochial mistrust, the League should establish two deliberative bodies: ad hoc Task Forces and a VFL Commission".

The McKinsey version of a commission was a long way from today's structure. It decreed that a commission must be independent, but only to the extent that it would "only be activated when task force recommendations

---

8   Allen Aylett, *My Game*, 1986, p. 226.
9   *Managing the VFL for the Long-term Success of the Game: McKinsey & Co. Report*, 1 May 1983.
10 Dick Seddon, unpublished personal notes and memoirs.

gained neither a clear approval or rejection from the VFL Board". A clear decision was either 8-4 in favour or 7-5 against.

This was a move forward, but hardly the structure required to launch the VFL into a new world of administration. McKinsey favoured a "lower-risk" model, presenting a phased solution that would be acceptable to the board. However, as Seddon relates, "everyone substantially agreed with the recommendations".[11]

McKinsey's "high-risk" model, presented but not recommended, noted an independent board would replace the club directors to allow "tough" decisions to be made and "market forces to determine the shape and nature of the competition".[12] In truth, both the McKinsey report and that of Aylett were driven by the need for independent experts to analyse the state of the game and provide powerful solutions to a basically unchanged board. When the McKinsey report was tabled, League minutes reported: "it was noted that no major objections to the report or its aims and objectives had been conveyed by VFL club representatives at a meeting held on 2nd May".[13]

According to Aylett, "Both my report and the McKinsey report agreed that the VFL needed an infusion of independent specialists. But my submission pushed for automatic adoption of these independent specialists' recommendations, after plenty of provision for club input and review. The McKinsey report did not. This was the main difference between the two."[14]

The McKinsey report was adopted—at least in principle—in May 1983. It had to be, as a week later the reality of the state of one club, the Sydney Swans, was presented to the VFL Board. On 11 May 1983, a report by David Crawford of the accountancy firm Peat, Marwick and Mitchell noted the Swans were close to extinct, and the League faced two options, according to the minutes:

---

11   Ibid.
12   *Managing the VFL for the Long-term Success of the Game: McKinsey & Co. Report*, 1 May 1983.
13   VFL Board minutes, May 1983. David Crawford would prove to be a significant figure in the evolution of the AFL Commission, with his 1993 report recommending that the commission be the ultimate manager of the League (see Chapter 19).
14   Allen Aylett, *My Game*, 1986.

1. to permit the Company to proceed to liquidation, which would, in effect, be the end of the Swans Club

2. for the League to support a scheme of arrangement to enable the Club to continue to operate until at least the end of the 1983 season.[15]

Dire indeed. By July, the VFL had agreed to support the Swans' scheme of arrangement, and had extended its funding commitment in 1983 to $1 million.

Also swirling about the game were challenges to its transfer laws. At the same time the laws had been tested in the Supreme Court of Victoria by Sydney player Silvio Foschini, who won the right, through the court, to switch to St Kilda without a formal clearance. The Saints had seen an opening and swooped, with scant regard for the overall competition. Foschini's Sydney teammate Paul Morwood would follow suit, with each playing for the Saints in round four, 1983 without formal clearances and permits. Before the match, Morwood told Seven News, in a statement that showed the reality of the dysfunctional collection of clubs: "Oh, it's open slather now (laughing). So you can go from one club one week to another the next week if you're not on contract. Make some brass out of that one!"[16]

By 5 October 1983 the board was testing the waters of its prescribed new approach, setting up the first McKinsey-recommended task force to look broadly at the future nature of the competition and testing a series of questions that would become key issues of the game's development through the next decade: how many teams, where those teams should be, what grounds would be needed and what would be the strategy for rationalising the grounds then in use, and importantly, a restructuring of the League's transfer rules.

---

15   VFL Board minutes, May 1983.
16   "Foschini and Morwood to St Kilda" [online video], 2009, http://youtu.be/dFAG8pyrAWw (accessed 22 May 2014).

Like most things in those tricky days around the VFL Board table, the birth of this initial McKinsey-prompted task force was troubled; choosing the members was typically controversial and divisive. After much to-ing and fro-ing, the membership was decided by a ballot: Bill Pratt, then chairman of Safeway; lawyer and former Richmond player Neil Busse; legendary Hawthorn player and coach and education bureaucrat (and later AFL Commission chairman) John Kennedy; and David Mandie, a well-known Melbourne businessman and philanthropist and avid Richmond fan, as chair. The task force was rounded out by Victorian MP and one-time Melbourne player Bob Miller, a government appointee.

The Mandie task force would report three times. The first, an interim volume presented on 1 August 1984 that made stringent criticisms of the League's decision-making processes, did not go down well at the board table. The League's minutes reported the disagreement:

> ... it was noted that the Task Force had concluded that "the overwhelming preponderance of evidence received by the Task Force supports its unanimous view that a new management and policy-making structure with clearly defined objectives needs to be created for the VFL and further, the Task Force has concluded that the present decision-making process with the League is fundamentally (sic) deficient".
>
> Directors indicated strong disapproval of the contents of the Task Force interim statement, noting that matters as requested had not been addressed and that the comments in relation to the deficiencies of decision-making were most objectionable.[17]

The board was effectively telling the task force to show more respect to the management of the game, and to stick with the guidelines it had been commissioned to achieve. The task force was also content to be at odds with the board, suggesting its processes were not subject to board approval and that it was an independent body commissioned to provide recommendations, to be well met by the board or not.

At the next meeting, on 8 August, the board had softened its aggressive

---

17   VFL Board minutes, 8 August 1984.

approach and requested the task force continue its work, with its final report expected to be presented in October.¹⁸ The minutes of that meeting also noted that the League had got wind of malcontents in some clubs looking at acting outside the constraints of the League. Aylett reported to the board that "recent speculation that some VFL clubs or officials involved at some clubs were contemplating establishment of an alternative playing competition to the VFL":

> During discussion it was noted that due to various pressures being placed on the League externally, it was essential that the League should appear as a united body in the face of outside scrutiny ...
>
> After considerable discussion, it was resolved as follows:
> At a meeting of VFL Directors and VFL Club Presidents, all 12 clubs resolved unanimously to affirm their commitment to work together in the best interests of the VFL competition and the maintenance of the 12 club competition together with any recommendations of the Task Force subsequently approved by the League."¹⁹

Dysfunction and discontent were now not only rife, but well and truly exposed.

The rumblings within the more powerful clubs in the League had reached the surface, with some key players clearly impatient with the hesitant program of change favoured by the board and the potential of a powerful commission to reduce the potency of a significant clique of the traditionally strong clubs.

Carlton president John Elliott, then at the peak of his powers in the worlds of business, politics and football, was hatching his own plan for the future of the competition. He was planning a breakaway league of 10 clubs that would include the five most powerful Victorian clubs—Collingwood, Essendon, Richmond, Geelong and, of course, his beloved Carlton—and would introduce non-Victorian teams (two from NSW, two from SA) with

---

18 The final Mandie report would not be presented until June 1985.
19 VFL Board minutes, 8 August 1984.

the potential of abandoning a parade of underperforming Victorian clubs.

The Elliott plan was grand: a mix of purging and restructuring, all leading towards a new national competition. It was economic rationalism at its finest. He also saw the need for an administration that was at arm's length from the clubs: his vision favoured a completely independent commission responsible, as in business, for governance. He had a completed constitution for the new league and, with co-antagonist Ian Wilson, president of Richmond, had garnered support for the concept from the Melbourne Cricket Club (MCC), through secretary Ian Johnson, to use the MCG along with Kardinia Park and, of course, his beloved Princes Park. This new league was ready to go.

In 1984, Elliott was a multi-headed powerhouse. He was midway through the expansion of his Elders IXL corporate empire, which had begun a few years earlier when he and some McKinsey partners (yes, Elliott was a McKinsey man, too) bought IXL, an underachieving jam-maker, and turned it into a colossus. He was a man of ideas—another impatient visionary—and ruthless to boot. Over the next 12 months he would flex his financial and backroom muscle, taking control of the venerable brewing company CUB and attempting to 'Fosterise' the world, while emerging as the white knight who would save BHP from a hostile takeover by another titan of the age, Robert Holmes à Court. By 1987 he would be Liberal Party president and would be being talked about—keenly—as a future prime minister.

Elliott's football club thrived on confrontation, based on a firmly held view of Carlton as the untouchable, dominant club of Melbourne. His plan for a new national competition was taken very seriously. It was caucused and muttered about behind closed doors and over long lunches, in the preferred style of football decision-making back then. Plot and counterplot were the name of the game. So advanced were the thinking and the vision that despite the "all for one" resolution of the VFL Board, Elliott was able to convene a clandestine meeting just a month later, on 4 September 1984, at Sefton in Mt Macedon (an Elders IXL conference facility), to discuss a new world for the League. Many club presidents and executives were keen attendees, with dinner and an overnight stay on the cards if needed.

Melbourne's Dick Seddon was there. As he recalls it, "A new breed of club presidents was emerging, who had business backgrounds and who resented what they perceived to be the 'Big Brother' approach by the VFL to the conduct of the League. They felt the VFL was inhibiting free enterprise and the free marketplace."[20]

These men did not seem to understand that a sporting competition could not replicate the dog-eat-dog environment of business and that a free marketplace was not appropriate to sport. Sporting competitions embody the concept of "mutual dependence"—competitors need each other to ensure a vibrant competition.

Seddon continued: "They were prepared to flout the League rules to achieve their own parochial club self-interests, causing a rapid growth in inflation in clubs, leading to the virtual insolvency of some of the weaker clubs. John Elliott believed the solution to this was to form a breakaway super-league, and to discard the financially weaker clubs."[21]

Originally, Elliott's super-league was restricted to a favoured five, but to get more teams and support for the concept, according to Seddon, he widened his net to gradually involve all 12 clubs. Finally, instead of the super-league being a breakaway from the weaker clubs, it was to be a breakaway from the VFL structure and administration.

Seddon recalled that there were light moments in the middle of the very serious discussions:

> I remember a very humorous moment in what was otherwise a very serious occasion. The president of the Geelong Football Club, Kevin Threlfall, kept looking out the window as the fog rolled in, and continually said that he would have to leave, because he had to drive back to Geelong. This was in the middle of Elliott's presentation, which, if implemented, would have massive implications for Australian Football.

---

20 Dick Seddon, unpublished personal notes and memoirs.
21 Ibid.

In the midst of this extremely important moment in the future of the League, all Threlfall was worried about was whether he would be able to drive home or not. It brought the house down.

No commitments were made by those present that night.

Ian Collins, general manager of Carlton and John Elliott's right-hand man, had driven Ron Joseph (general manager of North Melbourne) and myself to Sefton in his car. On the way home, Joseph and I argued with Collins about whether Allen Aylett and Jack Hamilton, who were oblivious to Elliott's plans for a breakaway league, should be informed. Joseph and I endeavoured to persuade Collins that if change was inevitable, reform was better occurring from within, rather than disruptively from without. To his credit, Collins agreed with us.[22]

After this discussion, Collins spoke to Elliott, who was persuaded that Seddon and Joseph were right. Collins told me in 2014 that "Elliott understood well the need for club support for his concept of a truly independent commission after the Sefton meeting",[23] and Elliott confirmed this: "I was comfortable with the VFL administration being part of this new concept if the board was prepared to vest all its power in the hands of a truly independent commission."[24]

Next morning at 10am, Collins, Joseph and Seddon met with Aylett and Hamilton and briefed them on what was happening. Collins then organised a meeting between Elliott, Aylett and Hamilton during the next week. Aylett was a little put out by the proposal because he thought they were supporting Hamilton rather than him with the structure that had been proposed, but, as Collins relates, "that was not so because up until that day they had not even included the VFL in the deal".[25]

That evening, after the meeting with Aylett and Hamilton, at a regular meeting of the VFL Board (attended by members of the Mandie task force, as observers), Aylett informed the board that he had been "briefed

---

22   Ibid.
23   Ian Collins, interview with the author, 2014.
24   John Elliott, interview with the author, 2013.
25   Ian Collins, interview with the author, 2014.

by various representatives of VFL clubs … of a meeting conducted on the previous evening at Mt Macedon".[26]

Aylett reported that the matters discussed at the Mt Macedon meeting were essentially what was being considered by the task force, as well as a board-appointed subcommittee[27] convened to consider governance and structural matters (including the potential of a national competition), and that a document had been prepared by those at the Elliott meeting and it "was intended to make such a document available to the VFL Task Force".[28]

Seddon described the meeting: "After the board's initial surprise that, firstly there were proposals for a breakaway league, and secondly, it had progressed so far, they realised the seriousness of the situation and were very positive in agreeing that urgent action was required, and they would co-operate with any reasonable proposals to save the League."[29]

The minutes had a softer view: "During general discussion it was noted that Directors appeared of the view that matters reportedly discussed by the previously referred to club representatives had not been the subject of discussion at club level and that views expressed were not necessarily those of clubs as a whole, and perhaps only those present at the meeting at Mt Macedon."[30] It was stressed that the meeting was unofficial, and unconnected to club policy—thus the reference to "club representatives" rather than directors or presidents. A resolution followed that "no action be taken in relation to the meeting of club representatives".[31] Clearly the VFL directors had not been informed by their club presidents, or whoever attended the Elliott meeting, about the gathering.

With the cat now well and truly out of the bag, Elliott presented his vision to the board at an emergency meeting of the League on 12 September 1984,

---

26   VFL Board minutes, September 1984.

27   The subcommittee was comprised of Tony Capes (Footscray), Leon Wiegard (Fitzroy) and Ian McPherson (Collingwood).

28   VFL Board minutes, September 1984.

29   Dick Seddon, unpublished personal notes and memoirs.

30   VFL Board minutes, September 1984.

31   Ibid.

noting that his material had input from the Collingwood president, Ranald Macdonald, and "other club representatives".

The presentation was detailed and lengthy, and was offered off the back of what Elliott described as "the weakening financial position of VFL clubs, explosion in player payments, and problems with the application of the Trade Practices Act, failure of the League's decision-making process ... due to club parochialism, growing government intrusion, and doubts regarding the capacity of the VFL Task Force to identify and address these areas of concern".[32]

It wasn't until I read the minutes of this historic meeting that I had a full understanding of how important this presentation was, and how Elliott had galvanised support from club officials, even if some of that support had come outside official processes.

Elliott's proposal as recorded in the minutes of that board meeting[33] all but describe the current AFL. The key points were:

- the establishment of a four-man board that would include a commissioner and three other members, with the commissioner having, effectively, autocratic powers, tempered marginally by the other members whose role "constitutes an Appeal Board function to decisions made by the Commissioner"
- that a national competition be formed, made up of the 12 VFL clubs (including the Swans out of Sydney) and two each from SA and WA
- that matches be played on Friday evenings, Saturday, and Sunday and Monday evenings with a view "to maximising television revenue opportunities"
- that all players be contracted with the VFL and then subcontracted to clubs. This point was never adopted by the commission, for obvious reasons. The League did not want to be the employers of the players and accept all the responsibilities that go along with these contractual obligations. Indeed, it was more appropriate for the clubs who managed the players' day-to-day activities to be their employers, with the League

---
32   Ibid.
33   Ibid.

overseeing the detail of the contracts (a fundamental of the Total Player Payments package that was to come later).

Elliott agreed that "there were a number of problem areas which would require identification and addressing ... including whether the required substantial increase in television rights to ensure the viability of such a competition would be available, whether the proposed changes were achievable for 1985, whether market surveys to determine public reaction to such a national competition amongst football supporters in all four states concerned would be desirable and whether the Players Association or players in general would be prepared to support the contract arrangements ... to enable the competition to get off the ground."[34] The subcommittee investigating governance was asked to attempt to resolve these matters.

On 26 September, the subcommittee reported that it did not believe such changes as recommended by Elliott could be put in place for the 1985 season, and that the public should be "assured that the 1985 competition would proceed without any uncertainty or lack of confidence".[35] It was noted that the matters raised in the report *could* be implemented for the 1986 season,[36] and that Alan Schwab, the man ultimately responsible for football matters at the time, be given the authority and opportunity to review and evaluate all issues raised.

The following week, on 1 October 1984, the second (interim) Mandie report was tabled, and on 7 November, "after long and careful consideration it was resolved "that the VFL Board endorse in principal the Task Force recommendation that the existing VFL Board of Directors structure be replaced by the appointment of a full-time Commissioner and four part-time Commissioners to conduct the administrative affairs of the League on a trial basis".[37]

The outcome had Elliott all over it. His drive and purpose, and that far-reaching presentation to the League directors, had forced the

---

34 Report to VFL Board by John Elliott, 12 September 1984.
35 VFL Board minutes, 26 September 1984.
36 Eventually, new teams—the Brisbane Bears and the West Coast Eagles—were introduced in 1987.
37 VFL Board minutes, October 1984.

administration's hand. Another subcommittee, of Tony Capes (Footscray), Ron Cook (Hawthorn), Leon Wiegard (Fitzroy), Greg Sewell (Essendon) and Bob Ansett (North), was appointed to choose the commissioners. The subcommittee made Ansett, North's president, its chair.

Bob Ansett, the American-raised son of airline pioneer Sir Reginald Ansett, was another corporate star very firmly in the public eye. He was the hard-talking entrepreneur behind Budget Rent a Car, a man who fronted his own highly visible TV campaigns and would be North Melbourne's president for 13 years (1977-90) and a similarly aggressive change merchant for the club as his predecessor, Aylett. Even for such an energetic high-flyer, taking hold of this brief was a tough challenge. As he recalled it in conversation in 2013, "It took a lot of courage, but there was an understanding that things just had to change. The financial side was important, but it was much more than that. Much more significant to overcome was the parochialism of the board."[38]

There's no doubt he was right on that one. Parochialism and club loyalty were the long suit that each club representative took to the VFL Board as a club-appointed, non-elected director.

Through this period I was a member of the Hawthorn board. Our president from 1980 to 1987, Ron Cook, took a seat at the VFL table and would rise to vice-president (1982-85). Cook was typical of the clubmen running the VFL. As Jake Niall wrote in *The Age* following Cook's death in 2004, "[Ron Cook] was devoted to Hawthorn in various capacities— recruiter, club secretary, selector, committeeman, under-19s player, vice-president, president, VFL vice-president, VFL club delegate and organiser of [club] sausage sizzles—in an association that stretched over six decades."[39]

For Cook and all men like him, it was club first and foremost. Never in my five years as a Hawthorn director do I remember a serious board discussion about the problems faced by the League or how it might find a remedy, or whether we needed to change our ways to fit in. We were

---

38   Bob Ansett, interview with the author, 2013.
39   Jake Niall, "Ron Cook, Hawthorn father figure, dies aged 74", *The Age*, 5 December 2004.

immune to the League's issues—or so we thought. Truth was if we had thought about it we were dead in the water, weighed down by the emerging realities of the pressures on the game and by the underperformance of at least half the VFL clubs. But we never did think about it, or bring it to bear. Hawthorn was prosperous and a winning team, in the midst of its greatest era. That's all that mattered to us, and that was typical.

Wiegard, a successful businessman, sportsman, broadcaster and raconteur, was Fitzroy's director at the time (his brother Keith was president of Fitzroy from 1981 to 1984). He recalls a typical pattern from VFL Board meetings:

> I remember distinctly, we used to have our VFL meetings at night—a five o'clock start, and you'd go through till 7.30 or something. And then you'd prepare for dinner at VFL House. A few wines, and I used to run a trivia thing. That was how friendly all the clubs were.
>
> But in between the time of the meeting and the dinner everybody would rush to the phone and tell their clubs how to beat whatever rules or changes had just been agreed on at the meeting. Everybody was so interested in their own club. So you had to measure up these two things … the club and the competition and it was, in the end, unworkable, because everyone was club first and how to beat the system.[40]

It wasn't just the state of the League that was swept under the table at club level. Even as a Hawthorn board member I didn't know some of the club deals that were going on behind the scenes. We were talking with WA star Gary Buckenara from Subiaco, for example, and other players during that time, but the board as a group had no idea how the deals were done or what the deals were. We'd try to get the information, and Cook, who pretty much did it all, would just say, "Don't ask me, guys. You don't need to know this. If you know then someone might ask you, and you might have to tell the truth. You don't need to know it. But we'll get Buckenara, don't worry."[41]

---

[40] Leon Wiegard, interview with the author, 2014.
[41] Gary Buckenara played 61 games for Subiaco from 1979 to 1981 before playing 154 games for Hawthorn from 1982 to 1990, and later coached Sydney (1992-93).

That "need to know, best if you don't" culture was common to all clubs. Win at all costs, whatever it takes.

It was this sort of thinking that Ansett would have to confront in choosing the personnel to fill the new commission—a move still eyed with considerable scepticism around the VFL Board table.

Here, as everywhere, there were motives and subplots. For Wiegard, a presence on the subcommittee was strategic, and his thinking gives a window into how the VFL Board operated, even as it resolved to move forward. As he puts it, the business of establishing the ground rules for the new VFL Commission was no different from any other deliberation around the VFL Board table—he was there for his club as much as for the greater good: "You just had to be there; it was important to just be in the room. And you had to work out the numbers so that you could get something for your own club out of whatever decision was being made. Make sure you got something out of it in your interest. Even the commission, once it was formed, you could get something out of the commission, you know, by holding back your vote for a while."[42]

He also saw a great truth that for a struggling club like Fitzroy, the only hope was to secure the future of the League itself: success would trickle down. The commission was the only way forward. An effective commission was pretty much Fitzroy's last best hope, and hope was pretty much all Fitzroy had: at about the same time as the VFL considered the appointment of a commission, Fitzroy revealed an operating loss for 1983-84 of $661,000, a staggering sum by the standards of the time and a figure that would add to accrued losses of more than $1 million.

Fitzroy had been struggling for years, without a home ground since it had left Brunswick Street after the 1966 season. The once-proud Lions, a foundation club of the VFL in 1897 and the League's most successful in its early years, would be the exploited tenants at Princes Park (1967-69, 1987-93), Junction Oval (1970-84), Victoria Park (1985-86) and Whitten Oval (1994-96). They had also flirted with a money-making hope, playing

---

42   Leon Wiegard, interview with the author, 2014.

home games at North Hobart in 1991 and 1992, with little to show for it. Within a dozen years Fitzroy would be gone, merged with the Brisbane Bears, after an AFL-sponsored marriage with Footscray was scuppered by the passion of the Bulldogs supporters.

But that—a passionate, unyielding period that would change my life—was still to come.

CHAPTER 2

The commission is born

So here they were, these football men in the first days of the summer of 1984. There was no smell of liniment, no raw edge of adrenaline, no hot pies, no putrid scent of muddied turf—just men of purpose gathering in the third-floor boardroom of VFL House, Jolimont Street, in the shadows of the MCG on the night of 12 December 1984. It was a moment in that tiny enclave of Jolimont as big as any Grand Final, even if only a handful of people were privy to it.

This was the night the board would vote to wield the shears it would ultimately use to neuter itself, for it was this meeting that would not only seek the board's approval to implement the Mandie report, but also to name names courtesy of the Ansett recommendations, having previously accepted the Elliott paper. The speed and pitch of the game's death spiral meant that the board knew it had no choice but to surrender all but its last shreds of power.

The meeting began, as they always did, at 5pm—a convivial schedule that allowed time for the meeting, then dinner and drinks. The absence of Carlton president John Elliott sucked some of the cigarette smoke and bombast out of the room; Blues general manager Ian Collins was his stand-in. Elliott's influence over proceedings would still be strong, but it would be North Melbourne's Bob Ansett who would take the limelight.

The windows of the boardroom faced southwest across the railyards towards the Old Scotch Oval (now enveloped by Rod Laver Arena and the National Tennis Centre) to the city fringe beyond. President Allen Aylett was chairing from the head of a large table inlaid with the state's football trademark and symbol of past dominance, the Big V. It was to be a bittersweet night for Aylett. His number was up, with what he must have wanted in his heart—to steer the League to a national competition as its chairman—about to be confirmed.

Unusually for the time, the Ansett subcommittee had acted swiftly. At the board meeting of 21 November 1984, Ansett had tabled the subcommittee's recommended terms of reference for the appointment of the VFL's inaugural commission, noting it favoured "retention by the board of all policy and strategic decisions".[1]

The board had requested the subcommittee recommend the nominees for the five commissioners to be appointed within 21 days, while confirming the subcommittee's recommended choice of Jack Hamilton as full-time commissioner-elect. It was a lightning-fast timeline for such a huge challenge: to deliver to the board a construct for placing power over the game into independent, non-aligned hands.

They hadn't spent too much time choosing a name for Ansett's game-changing project: it was called the "VFL Board Special Sub-Committee". Its report was first order of business on the neatly typed and copied agenda papers spread around the Big V of the boardroom table on that seminal night of 12 December 1984: "Mr R. Ansett as Chairman of the VFL Board's Special Sub-Committee advised that the sub-committee had given detailed consideration to the proposed amendments to the League's Articles of Association and Rules and also the Terms of Reference for the operation of the proposed commission."[2]

And there it was:

---

[1] VFL Board minutes, 21 November 1984.
[2] Report of VFL Board Special Sub-Committee, presented to VFL Board on 12 December 1984.

1. (a) The VFL establish a Board of Commissioners to be called "The Commission".
   (b) The Commission comprise five Commissioners, one full-time and four part-time; the full-time commissioner to be called "the Commissioner" and the part-time Commissioners to be called "the part-time Commissioners".
   (c) The Commission have such powers as the League may from time to time delegate to it on the basis that any delegation of power may be revoked or made subject to conditions at any time by a resolution passed by a simple majority at a meeting of the League.[3]

Well, that all made perfect if cautious sense. The Ansett subcommittee squibbed it on one point, but perhaps it sensed the political reality of the boardroom:

(d) Initially, the League should delegate to the Commission for a period of one year all powers exercisable by the League other than the specific major powers referred to in the draft resolution annexed to these minutes.[4]

The subcommittee also put forward the names of the four men to sit on the first commission: Graeme Samuel, Peter Scanlon, Peter Nixon (all newcomers to football administration) and Dick Seddon, once CEO of Melbourne and a long-time club delegate on the VFL Board.

Behind the scenes there had been some agitation over the candidates. Even on the night, Carlton's Collins piped up to ask whether alternative names could be considered beyond those about to be proposed by the subcommittee. The short answer was no, with Ansett noting that to submit other names would be insensitive to those who "may subsequently not be appointed by the League".[5]

---

3   Ibid.
4   Ibid.
5   VFL Board minutes, 12 December 1984.

The trust of the board—and the subcommittee—in Hamilton was noted in the fine print: "resolutions brought before the Commission shall be decided according to the vote of the Commissioner, unless all of the part-time Commissioners unanimously vote against the resolution".[6] The board was clearly considering Hamilton to be a benign dictator, although the recommendation was later changed to "three of the four" part-timers rejecting the position of the commissioner.

The board did note "that after an initial period it would be proposed that the powers of the Commission could be widened in due course".[7]

Effectively it would be a 12-month trial; after two years of competing reports, due consideration and nervous steps while treading on the brink of financial collapse and facing legal challenges left, right and centre, the subcommittee's solution, as endorsed by the full board, was to put a toe in the water. But OK, at least the structure was changing to a form that put some authority into the hands of reforming and independent commissioners—a step towards removing the vested interests of the club delegates. Such a structure had the long-term potential to stop the bleeding and save the game.

But exposed in the fine print was the conservative nature of the game's administration. The board was prepared to be "half-pregnant" and allow the commissioners notional authority, but the list of what the commission could *not* do was extensive, and in its way utterly extraordinary. It was a commission on P-plates. The board had confirmed the need for change but allowed for the brakes to be applied if, by some unlikely chance, the new commission did not fulfil its expectations.

According to Attachment No. 1(a)[8] to the board papers of that fateful evening:

> That the Victorian Football League entrusts to and confers upon the Commission all of the powers exercisable by it with the restriction that the Commission may not unless otherwise expressly authorised by the League exercise any of the powers of the League:

---

6   Report of VFL Board Special Sub-Committee, presented to VFL Board on 12 December 1984.
7   Ibid.
8   Ibid.

(a) to admit any Club to or expel or suspend any club from the VFL competition;

(b) to amalgamate or join any other league;

(c) to take over the administration of any additional football club;

(d) to vary the basis of participation by clubs in the VFL competition;

(e) to vary the football grounds of any clubs or to approve the move of any clubs out of Victoria;

(f) to provide financial assistance to any Club (other than by payment of advances of final dividends expressly authorised by the Board of Directors) or to guarantee the obligations of any club;

(g) to vary the basis upon which players are entitled to play for clubs in the VFL competition;

(h) except as expressly authorised in any budget approved by the Board of Directors, to purchase or dispose of any capital asset with a cost of more than $50,000;

(i) except as expressly authorised in any budget approved by the Board of Directors, to borrow any money otherwise than for the ordinary purposes of the League or to give any security for any such borrowing;

(j) to undertake any major capital works (including major works in relation to existing assets of the League);

(k) to determine the distributions made to clubs;

(l) to exercise any of the powers of the League in owning or operating any television or radio station;

(m) to appoint the representatives of the League on the National Football League of Australia Limited or Australian Football Championships Pty Limited; or

(n) to amend or introduce any rules and regulations or player rules of the League or to amend the laws of the game.

The casual observer could be forgiven for wondering what exactly the new commission was actually authorised to do: certainly its hands were tied when it came to having direct impact on the key issues confronting the game in 1984. But despite the restrictions its confirmation, and the variation to the League's articles, was a huge step forward—a step short of the sort of powers proposed by Elliott and the Mandie task force in its first and second reports, a step short of what was truly necessary, but a step ahead of what Aylett and the McKinsey report had suggested. It may have been a short step, but it was a step at least. (The final Mandie report, due on 5 December 1984, was not delivered until 5 June 1985 after the Ansett subcommittee had selected the new commission.)

The big news the next day was not the confirmation of an independent commission—a fait accompli for the voracious media—but the names of those who had been given the responsibility to bring some business sense and commonsense to the game's operation. *BIG FOUR FOR VFL* was the front-page banner heading on the next morning's edition of *The Sun*. Michael Davis and Michael Roberts were the reporters, and the story took out the entire page:

> Two leading businessmen, a football club chief and a former federal minister last night were given the job of leading the VFL out of the wilderness.
>
> They are former National Party MP, the Hon. Peter Nixon, 56, merchant banker Graeme Samuel, 38, Elders-IXL executive Peter Scanlon, 39, and retiring Melbourne Football Club chief executive and former solicitor Dick Seddon, 49.[9]

All but one of these names had been the unanimous choice of the subcommittee: Ansett had argued hard for one-time North Melbourne hard man Albert Mantello to take the commission seat eventually occupied by Seddon. Mantello's day would come.[10] Seddon won his seat off the back of the great work he had done in researching much of the basis of the draft and salary cap, and his experience at club level (it was Seddon who had brought Ron Barassi back to Melbourne in 1981—the return of the messiah!).

---

9   Michael Davis and Michael Roberts, "Big four for VFL", *The Sun*, 13 December 1984.
10 Mantello took Dick Seddon's place on the commission in 1988 and served until 1992.

The part-timers would be paid a splendid $7500 a year, a return probably commensurate with the less than stratospheric scope of their new powers. The figure was notional anyway, as most of the commissioners did the job for nothing. As *The Age*'s chief football writer, Ron Carter, wrote:

> The Commissioners certainly will not have control of the VFL competition itself. They will not be able to say which clubs are included or excluded. That power will remain with the VFL directors.
>
> Mr Hamilton said, "It is easier to talk about what powers the board has retained rather than that given to the Commissioners. The board will retain control over policy and corporate strategy and also over the actual competition of the VFL."
>
> Mr Hamilton said the commissioners had a very important role to play in the future of football and their role would be reviewed.[11]

The Sun reported:

> Mr Hamilton agreed the board had given the Commissioners less power then recommended by the first Mandie task force report, set up to examine all aspects of VFL football.
>
> "The Task Force had them totally autonomous," he said. "The League has not been prepared to do that, but this will be reviewed in 12 months.
>
> "It isn't going to happen overnight. It's an enormous step for the 12 clubs to appoint an independent Commission. The powers will be reviewed and they may well be increased."[12]

In truth, the issue of commission powers was a compromise formed to satisfy the various club interests around the VFL Board table. Aylett had announced his intention to retire from the board on 5 December once the new administrative structure was in place, and that he would be making public comments as to his views on the changes once his tenure had finished. He was true to his word. Two days after the board meeting that appointed the commission, he cut loose in the press.

---

11 Ron Carter, in *The Age*, 13 December 1984.
12 Michael Davis and Michael Roberts, "Big four for VFL", *The Sun*, 13 December 1984.

AYLETT: BIG FOUR LACK POWER was *The Sun*'s back-page headline on 14 December. The new commission was constrained by compromise, said Aylett: "The situation's no different from what it's been for some time." *The Sun* reported:

> Dr Aylett said the Commission should have been given power to make independent decisions, "rather than be the halfway house it is at the moment".
>
> "It will take longer to come to the rescue (of the game) now than we had all been hoping for."
>
> Some clubs, including Carlton, have indicated they agree with Dr Aylett in wanting the Commission to have far more wide-ranging powers from its inception.[13]

That was still a year away. For now, the commissioner and his part-time colleagues would need to get a feel for the possibilities of their new office and for the issues that confronted the code.

It was to be more of a learning curve for some than others.

Of all the part-timers, Samuel was the least grounded in the game. He still looks back on his appointment as a VFL commissioner with a sense of mild amazement:

> My involvement actually started by accident. Back then I was working with Macquarie Bank, and I had a call from Lindsay Fox, who was involved with St Kilda. He said, "Look, can you come and talk to us about St Kilda and how we might be able to, you know, try and sort out St Kilda's mess?"
>
> Together with Robert Johanson, who was with me at Macquarie, we put together a bit of a screed, which actually focused a bit on St Kilda but also focused on the competition itself. And we went out and saw Lindsay, and we talked it through. Nothing much came of that.
>
> Then one Sunday morning, Lindsay rang me at home and he said, "Graeme"–I remember the conversation vividly–he said, "Do you want

---

13   "Aylett: big four lack power", *The Sun*, 14 December 1984.

to go on the VFL Commission?" I said, "Yeah, sounds all right." He said, "Good." Bang–that was it.

And then the next day, I went into the office and frantically asked the guys, "What the hell's the VFL Commission, and can you tell me the names of the teams in the VFL?" Right. "And what their nicknames are—you know, who are the Bulldogs?" That's as much as I knew about football at the time.

So Lindsay put my name forward, and the next thing I remember is that there's an interview in the VFL's boardroom. I'd swotted up by then. I do remember Ron Cook saying to me, "Now, you do like football?" I said, "Of course. Of course I do, yeah." And I was thinking, "I hope he doesn't ask any more questions", because I had no idea.[14]

Samuel would form a pretty good idea soon enough.

Scanlon had been recommended by a friend, Kevin Luscombe, when asked by Ansett for advice, but the committee had no idea of his football background. His father, Jack, played 67 games for St Kilda between 1930 and 1936 and captain-coached Coburg in the Victorian Football Association (VFA) from 1937 to 1939. Peter had been a top amateur footballer playing for Coburg amateurs, and represented Victoria many times. Interestingly, for his honours degree in commerce his thesis was on the economics and administration of the VFL.

Nixon, on the other hand, had been approached by Hamilton (with the rest of the selection committee in tow) to canvass his interest. Through his friendships with Aylett and Aylett's predecessor as League president, Sir Maurice Nathan, he did have an understanding of the issues the League faced. Hamilton pointed out that the commission would have an advisory role with the board on many substantive issues. He asked for a definition of "advisory" as he had had experience with this flawed concept in government, where decision-making did not mesh with acceptance of responsibility.

As he recalls, "It was clear that the presidents were loath to actually hand over power and for my part I was not prepared to join the commission

---

14 Graeme Samuel, interview with the author, 2014.

under those circumstances and withdrew from the meeting."[15] They were shocked.

A week or so later he was approached again with a proposition that the commission begin as proposed even though reform could be difficult initially and it was expected power would start to transfer after a trial period of some months. Nixon accepted a place on the commission on these terms.

At the new commission's first meeting it became obvious that it was to have little power, so a process of lobbying with the clubs was started—to no avail. Nixon spoke again to the selection panel about the assurances he had been offered, and eventually a breakthrough was achieved.

On the same day that *The Sun* reported Aylett's misgivings over the new powers of the VFL Commission, *The Age*'s Trevor Grant reported that four VFL clubs had failed to comply with a state government request to provide details of their financial situation. He wrote: "In what is seen as a stern government warning to club administrators about their legal responsibilities, the attorney-general, Mr (Jim) Kennan, wrote to seven clubs on 24 October asking them to supply details by the end of November of their financial accounts, and declare that their directors had not breached the Companies Code."[16]

The seriousness of the situation was now public. The walls of consequence, of uncontrollable repercussion, were closing in. The commission would soon have its hands full. Scanlon remembers: "I arrived to take my position on a commission that was clearly on 12 months' trial and facing Corporate Affairs, who were contemplating moving against several clubs for trading while insolvent. Indeed, eight of the 12 clubs were in trouble. Many of them had listed intangibles in their balance sheets, including a value for their share of VFL assets, to which they had no entitlement. They were in fact 'pyramiding' as there was debt in the VFL balance sheet and in their own balance sheet that was all fed by the one income stream."[17]

---

15   Peter Nixon, *The Peter Nixon Story: An Active Journey*, Connor Court Publishing, 2012, p. 263.
16   Trevor Grant, in *The Age*, 14 December 1984.
17   Peter Scanlon, interview with the author, 2014.

Welcome to football administration.

Twelve months after that first VFL Board vote of 12 December 1984 it would reconfirm its commitment to the idea of a VFL Commission. And this time, on 4 December 1985, it would pump up the powers of the commissioners to a point where they might just have an outside chance of beginning on the imposing mountain of work that lay between the VFL and a sense of sustainable, expansionary, successful future.

In the commission's ideal future view, this would mean fewer Victorian-based clubs—10 of them in the suburbs of Melbourne. It would mean new clubs in new territories and a fierce determination to be national, a code without borders. It would mean new deals for media rights and sponsorship, the end of suburban grounds, the end of suburban ambitions for a national game. It would also mean the removal of emotional and conflicted decision-making at the board table, which were processes that led to sub-optimal decisions.

All this rolls off the tongue easily, but it would turn out to be one hell of a job for the commission. I didn't know it yet, but it would also be the job for me.

CHAPTER 3

A visionary departs

The appointment of Hamilton ended a lengthy struggle for power that had been played out over perhaps 18 months. It was a complex battle that had pitted Hamilton against his notional boss, Allen Aylett.

Dick Seddon notes that the first signs of division had come when Aylett presented his report into the League's administrative troubles to the board in February 1984, ahead of the officially commissioned McKinsey document two months later: "Jack Hamilton thought Aylett was planning to get the position of chairman of the new commission, which may have jeopardised Hamilton's chances of securing a role in the new order; so he actively campaigned against him."[1]

At the next board meeting, on 28 November, Aylett announced his intention to resign as VFL president and said that he would not seek a position as a part-time commissioner and would formally terminate his involvement with the League "at the decision-making level".[2] Seddon recalls the moment: "It was a sad end for someone who had sacrificed so much for football, but that was the brutal nature of the sport."[3]

The directors, conservative to the last, concurred with the subcommittee's

---

1   Dick Seddon, unpublished personal notes and memoirs.
2   VFL Board minutes, 28 November 1984.
3   Dick Seddon, unpublished personal notes and memoirs.

choice of Hamilton over Aylett as the new chief of the commission. There was a sense that Aylett would pursue change with too much zeal; Hamilton, the clubmen reasoned, would wield a steadier, less ambitious hand on the tiller. Aylett just didn't have the numbers on either the Ansett subcommittee or on a board that was still hedging its bets and clinging to its authority over the game. He was so strong, so dominant; people were happy for him to be working away and doing things around the game so long as ultimate control rested with the board of directors.

And now? That balance was shifting.

I suspect that the board was worried that Aylett would go off gung-ho, pursuing all his pet projects, including licensing the brand, pushing the game to all parts of the country—all the things we take for granted in the new century. Better to go for consistent, reliable old Jack. They could coerce Jack—even tell him to do it a certain way and Jack would go and do it. He would, more often than not, respond to the political pressure applied. Peter Nixon recalls: "They were scared of what Aylett might do in charge of a new commission. Aylett was very progressive and had upset many people, while Jack had many friends in the game, and around the board table."[4]

Peter Scanlon admits he was surprised at the board's decision: "I just don't know why Hamilton was selected over Aylett, but the call had been made before we arrived. I do know that Jack was seen as someone who would protect the football culture—they loved using the term 'football people', which was code for football's old boys' club. Jack was there to protect this concept."[5]

Yet Aylett was a true "football person" by any sense. He was a great footballer and a great club president, and had surely shown his mettle as the League's president. However, he was not a status quo person, whereas Hamilton was.

Perhaps it was no more than theory anyway. The commission had been structured with a full-time chairman and it would have been impossible for Aylett to take on the job given his thriving dental practice, which,

---

4   Peter Nixon, interview with the author, 2014.
5   Peter Scanlon, interview with the author, 2014.

he acknowledged, had suffered somewhat from his "part-time" role as president of the VFL. He told me he had recently introduced some new marketing concepts into his practice and they needed additional time and attention, which a full-time role at the VFL would not allow.[6]

So was he really a candidate for a full-time job? If the directors had created a part-time chairman's role, he may have been motivated to fight for it. Journalist Mike Sheahan, who had seen the machinations from the media side and from the inside, feels the move to a full-time commission chair was a deliberate strategy to remove Aylett's candidacy![7]

To step back from the position of head honcho to playing a part-time role was, one would expect, also not attractive to a man used to doing it his way. In 2014 Aylett said to me, "While I was asked to be a commissioner I was never a candidate for a full-time role, as my business had suffered during my time as president. I knocked back the part-time commission role because I had been in football for what seemed like an eternity, having played at an elite level for so many years, been president of North Melbourne, and then spent nine years trying to change and save the League. There was no shock for me—I was done!"[8]

As Scanlon relates, "This [the appointment as chairman] put Jack [Hamilton] in a very powerful position. He was the supreme politician moving around the clubs, but this was the first time that he could move away from the politics and actually work on the real substance of football. Football [administration] was much more about politics than it was about substance at that time. Jack had a wonderful sense of humour, his one-liners were legendary, but he worked out quickly that being political with the new commissioners was a waste of time. It was now time for some substance. I couldn't say that he embraced it with great enthusiasm, but he did do it with a sense of humour and a realisation that things had changed."[9]

Aylett's departure was the end of a role at the top for one of the game's

---

6   Allen Aylett, interview with the author, 2014.
7   Mike Sheahan, interview with the author, 2014.
8   Allen Aylett, interview with the author, 2014.
9   Peter Scanlon, interview with the author, 2014.

true visionaries—a man one future chairman, Ron Evans, said in the early 2000s could well be known as "the father of the national competition".[10] It was a cruel irony that this came at the same time as the first foundations were being laid for the sort of League Aylett must have imagined; compared to Hamilton, he was far and away the more talented man.

Hamilton was a real old-time football person; according to Scanlon, he had a lot of nous, and well-developed street smarts, but he was not very inventive. Good mates with everyone, that was Jack. His quick wit at meetings could put a rather heated situation at ease. That nature was one of the reasons he had survived for so long (he had joined the League as an office boy in the early 1950s while still a Collingwood player). He had the sort of skills that the directors wanted for the League's first full-time commissioner. He would not be shaking any branches.

Scanlon told me, "He refused point blank to ever bring another executive into a commission meeting, no matter how many times we asked. He would explain that he held his job because of his control of the information flow. He was an intelligent and logical man and once he had the sense that the new people he was dealing with had the game at heart, he got rid of the politics and vested interests. And even though he thought some of the things we were thinking about were sacrilege, he would begrudgingly, over a bottle of wine, accept that things were changing."[11]

In the end, it was a role that he would keep for only a year, and there's no doubt in my mind that at the end of that first 12 months, as the commission set itself to take a more serious grip on the future of the game, Jack was struggling with the new agenda before him. He didn't have the corporate skills or imagination to keep up, especially with the likes of Peter Scanlon, Graeme Samuel, Dick Seddon and Peter Nixon—they were smart cookies and didn't stand for any nonsense, or anything less than the best. They would not tolerate the old way of doing things; they were there to get things right and get things done.

---

10   Speech to Grand Final function, 2005. Allen Aylett would return to administration as chairman of North Melbourne from 2001 to 2005.

11   Peter Scanlon, interview with the author, 2014.

And in his heart of hearts, Jack wasn't sold on the rapid expansion of the competition, nor the apparent downgrading of Waverley Park, with a firm focus being placed on the MCG as the game's premier ground. Scanlon recalled these misgivings: "I had many discussions with Jack, and it was not that he thought the switch in mindset was wrong, he just couldn't cope with a decision that rendered in vain all the work that had been put into the Waverley ground by Sir Kenneth Luke, Eric McCutchan and Jack over the years—work that they thought would break the stranglehold the MCC held over the League."[12]

In December 1984, that conservative approach was in his favour: the VFL Board wanted to hasten slowly. The simple creation of a commission was a big enough step, never mind a commission that might actually change the structure and purpose of the game's administration in a dramatic way. That was the perceived risk with Aylett. Not with Hamilton.

---

12   Ibid.

CHAPTER 4

The commission's early challenges

Things weren't standing still in the world of footy. After Allen Aylett's retirement, Jack Hamilton, who had effectively been appointed months earlier, had taken charge of the new commission-driven administration once its structure was formally adopted by the VFL Board in February 1985.

The commission hit the ground running. As Graeme Samuel recalls it, "We were appointed in December of 1984 to take up office in February '85; but in fact, we got embroiled very quickly in some significant issues, particularly matters which related to Geoffrey Edelsten and the Sydney Swans in January '85."[1]

The national ambitions of the VFL would be a preoccupation of the commission for much of the decade (and still are for the League, for that matter). The Swans had been based in Sydney since 1982, but four years down the track the move—a cornerstone of the League's expansionary vision—had massive problems. Jim Main sets the scene in his chronicle of the Swans' journey, *Shake Down the Thunder*:

---

1   Graeme Samuel, interview with the author, 2014.

> The Swans entered 1985 in a holding pattern. They still faced financial difficulties, despite VFL assistance, and new coach John Northey had to work on a shoestring budget. However, even before the start of the new season, the VFL was discussing a radical plan to solve what was now its greatest problem—the club's survival ...
>
> In January 1985, the club's management committee discussed the concept of private ownership, and on February 6 the VFL considered the same question. However, that night also marked the formal beginnings of the somewhat independent VFL Commission. The matter therefore, was now out of the hands of the other 11 clubs. The new VFL Commission assumed responsibility, effectively determining whether it would allow its brave new venture into private hands.[2]

That of course was not entirely correct, as while the commission took over effective negotiations, the club-dominated VFL Board retained the power to make the final decision off the back of any commission recommendation.

As it turned out, the question of the Swans' private ownership would test the power and standing of the new commission. It would also test the relationship between the part-time commissioners and Hamilton, the only full-time commissioner, on the one hand, and the limits of the commission's authority over the VFL Board, on the other. These would be key and formative issues for the new administration.

In a competition loaded with financial basket cases, the Sydney Swans were a special example, requiring special treatment. The Sydney outpost represented the game's future—an experiment no longer, but a business that *had* to succeed if football was going to flourish beyond state-based borders.

"You've got to go back a bit from there," says Samuel.

"Before we arrived, in 1982, the board made a wonderful decision, strategically brilliant," he says sarcastically.

"'We're going to enter a foreign territory called Sydney,' said the board.

---

2   Jim Main, *Shake Down the Thunder: From Ugly Duckling to AFL Premiers—The Story of the Sydney Swans*, Geoff Slattery Publishing, 2006, p. 98.

'Sydney has had nothing to do with Australian football for a long, long while. It's a city in a state totally committed to rugby league and dominated by rugby league, not just in the media, but throughout the community.

"'What we'll do is, we'll send up a bankrupt team called South Melbourne. We'll rename it Sydney and manage it from Melbourne. Some of the players will train in Sydney and some will train in Melbourne.[3] And we'll give them little money, and no players—that's how we're going to enter this new territory.'

"I mean, of course it was failing; it was destined to fail. That's how we came to contemplate private ownership. The League had no money—it was carrying about $20 million in debt at the time—so this was a way of introducing outside money to help the game survive."[4]

Samuel's co-commissioner Peter Scanlon had an opposing view to the introduction of "foreign" capital into the business of football. "Strategically, private ownership was all wrong," he says. "To understand the system we operated in, you have to understand which, of the VFL and the clubs, is the industry and which is the firm. This is a critical decision you must take before you can take the next step of private ownership.

"Most football people kept saying the clubs are the *firm* and the VFL is the *industry*—and that is incorrect, because the firm is the VFL and the industry is the entertainment industry. The clubs are part of the one firm, not separate entities in terms of the economics of the game, and none of the early reports contemplated this positioning. To introduce private ownership in clubs we were therefore contemplating selling off parts of the one firm, not something that would be contemplated in the business world."[5]

Because of this belief, Scanlon argued long and hard with Samuel. He could not conceive of private enterprise owning a club, but the realities of the time overcame any deeply felt philosophy. Time would prove Scanlon correct, but at that time, there was no time.

"But the VFL was broke," Scanlon added, "and many of the clubs were

---

3   The Melbourne contingent was coached by former Richmond player Peter Hogan.
4   Graeme Samuel, interview with the author, 2014.
5   Peter Scanlon, interview with the author, 2014.

broke, so our only way through was to use other people's money to grow the game."⁶ This decision—to reluctantly allow for private ownership—was agreed to by the clubs at the commission's first meeting with the board, in February 1985.

In the end, a pragmatic decision to allow private ownership would win the day to save clubs and indeed the game, but we were to get our 'firm' back intact some years later!

The idea had been canvassed much earlier: Edelsten had started his push before the commission had been formed, confidently predicting that he would not only take on the Swans but make them a power. That was his declared intention.

The entrepreneurial doctor, he of the grand-piano-equipped, chandelier-strewn medical suites, was a businessman cast in the preferred mould of his times: lavish, loud, and adventurous, as highly leveraged as he was an eager self-promoter.

Edelsten had done his advance work. As Aylett told Main in *Shake Down the Thunder*, "I first met Dr Edelsten ... just after private ownership was first mooted. I went to Sydney to look over his plush medical clinics. As a dentist my motive was purely professional. I have to say I was impressed, not only with the clinics but with Edelsten's entrepreneurial skills. He had genuine marketing and promotional flair and I could not help thinking that he might be the right man for the Swans."⁷

By June 1985 it had been decided formally: the League's preferred option was to pursue private ownership for the Swans. The deal would not only save the Sydney-based club but also bring a financial dividend that would provide a fillip for some Melbourne clubs and buy time for others.

Given his personality and media savvy, Edelsten's bid was the most talked about—but perhaps not the best, at least according to Samuel.

---

6   Ibid. These circumstances sound just a bit like how the Australian Rugby Union (ARU), also broke, introduced the Melbourne Rebels into Victoria nearly 30 years on in 2010 with the financial help of entrepreneur Harold Mitchell, with me as CEO in the club's first season.
7   Jim Main, *Shake Down the Thunder*, 2006, p. 100.

The commission, he recalls, had serious concerns about the proposal and wanted to engage a competitor: "We got launched into the deep end of that issue before the commission had really started. And at that stage, in January of 1985, we had a rapid catch-up, and that's when we started to try and think, 'Is there a better way than Edelsten?' That's how Basil Sellers, John Geraghty, Craig Kimberley, Michael Edgley and the others came in."[8] Scanlon used his considerable influence to interest these friends of his to create some competitive tension in the bidding process.

In the end there *would* be two bids considered, and while the Edelsten offer was a clear winner in the court of public opinion, the counter-offer from the business consortium led by Sellers had a more certain feel to it.

Even by the standards of the time, the high-flying Edelsten looked a slightly risky proposition for this first venture by the VFL into the private ownership of a key sporting franchise, particularly one so far from its foundations in South Melbourne, no matter that those foundations had been shaky to begin with and now were hardly foundations at all. But let's not forget that Australia was in the thrall back then of its business adventurers—the likes of Alan Bond, of America's Cup fame, and Christopher Skase of Qintex. It seemed everything these guys did was front-page news and highly successful. Edelsten was cut from the same flamboyant new-money cloth, with reports at the time outlining his love of fast and expensive cars; he had a stable of Rolls-Royces, Lamborghinis, a Ferrari, a Porsche.

It should be said that the bid was not all about Edelsten. He also had some renowned figures involved in his bid as advisers: the likes of Larry Adler, chair of FAI; Ron Merkel, a well-known QC and future AFL adviser; Brian Ward, a talented solicitor who had acted for many players; Bob Pritchard of America's Cup challenger *Steak and Kidney* fame; Jim McKay of Active Marketing, who had been significant in the growth of the League's licensed-product business; Geoffrey Thomas from the Sydney

---

8   Graeme Samuel, interview with the author, 2014.

Football League; Daryl Smith, president of the NSW AFL; and a pretty good ace in the pack in Swans legend Bobby Skilton.

On reading the minutes of that turbulent time, it seemed that whenever the Sellers team would make an offer, or counter-offer, the Edelsten team would slam more money on the table—a process that went on for some months. At the same time, the commission, either directly or indirectly, was making discreet inquiries about each of the bids and thereby causing delays in the final recommendation being put to the directors. The commission believed this issue required some clarification, as the minutes noted:

> [S]ome criticism has been levelled at the commission in respect of the time delay. The commission was very conscious of the responsibility given and was not prepared to make a hasty decision until all avenues of the investigation had been completed. Whilst a delay has occurred, it has been possible to very substantially increase the offers of both parties. In respect to Dr Edelsten the offer is $1.5 million greater than his first offer, and in respect to Mr B. Sellers the offer has been increased by approximately $400,000.[9]

During that time the commission, and the League's auditors, had canvassed opinion widely, using many of their contacts in media, law enforcement and business to make sure that there would be no whales in the bay once their recommendation was committed to the VFL directors (Samuel recalls a clandestine meeting at *The Age* one Saturday morning with editor Creighton Burns "when we came in through the back entrance"[10]). The minutes record those investigations in subtle, legally tuned language:

> [T]he attached reports received from the League's auditors, Touche Ross and Co., had not been limited solely to financial aspects, but ... other non-financial matters had been addressed ... It was further noted that the commission had undertaken further investigations with appropriate institutions, establishing the bona fide background and capacities of the two respective applicants, to ensure that both

---

9   VFL Board minutes, 31 July 1985.
10 Graeme Samuel, interview with the author, 2014.

prospective owners would be parties satisfactory to the League and the remaining clubs.[11]

I was at the meeting as an observer representing Hawthorn, and it was clear from the narrative, and the slide show, that there were those on the commission who clearly preferred the Sellers consortium, although both Samuel and Scanlon had disqualified themselves from the final recommendation "due to a potential conflict of interest" given their ties to some in the Sellers group.

In the end, the difference in the financial deal, although described to me as "peanuts" by Samuel during the research for this book, was very attractive to the struggling clubs. It was clear they wanted the extra $1 million that Edelsten was offering, i.e. $1.83m versus $2.9m. All that was left was for the club directors to vote.

Whatever the commission's inner thoughts, the numbers were too strong, and the clubs, represented by presidents, general managers and board members, had no hesitation in voting in favour of the commission's final recommendation favouring Edelsten's team. That extra million dollars from Edelsten divided up nicely.

Throughout all the negotiations Sellers had considered pulling out, but after encouragement from the commissioners he was convinced to leave his bid on the table to maintain the necessary competitive tension in the process.

The commission's slide show was not just about money. It was also about the criteria that the commission believed were relevant to its decision-making. They make fascinating reading all these years later:

1. What is in the best interests of football?
- The public must feel comfortable with the decision.
- It will provide long-term stability for the Swans.
- The controller will conduct himself in such a manner as to be consistent with VFL objectives and standards and the personal standards of the leaders of the other clubs.
- Within the rules he will make the Swans competitive.

---

11   VFL Board minutes, 31 July 1985.

- That proper regard will be had to youth football development and community issues.

2. What is in the best interests of the other 11 clubs?
- That they receive an immediate cash injection to keep them solvent.
- That privatising the Swans will not put them apart from the other clubs in the conduct of League affairs.
- Swans do not become a disruptive influence in the competition, either by:
    - poaching other clubs' players,
    - ignoring the rules,
    - attracting adverse publicity,
    - becoming incompatible with other clubs in outlook.
- That there is no possibility of any serious action being taken against controlling interests.
- The controlling interests must be sufficiently financially stable to be able to maintain the requisite level of financial support.
- Endorsement of and abiding by the provisions of the Licensing Agreement.

3. What is in the best interests of the Swans?
- Future becomes assured because existing indebtedness retired and capital base established.
- They become competitive.
- They obtain backing and support of Sydney and NSW.
- They develop football farms in NSW.
- Controller leads in a responsible decent way which is in the best interests of the Swans, VFL and football in general.
- No immediate interference with coaching team management.
- Prior VFL approval to any change in control of the club.
- Members of Swans Football Club to be kept fully informed of all club activities.[12]

As I watched and listened, little did I know how many of those items would land in my lap, and how quickly the optimism of the moment would

---

12   Ibid.

dissipate; but that was for the future. At the moment, the room was clear in its view and supportive of the commission's final recommendation, offered—at least as recorded in the minutes—without equivocation. Any doubts that any of the commissioners might have had were swept away in the moment and in the swathes of cash on the table:

> **Recommendation of the VFL Commission**
> That the VFL enter into an agreement with Dr Geoffrey Edelsten, in the form executed by him, the basis of which has been described to the directors at this meeting.
>
> The $1.4 million repayment of the loan be distributed to the 12 VFL clubs in the normal way. The premium payment of $1.5 million be distributed to the 11 VFL clubs other than the Sydney Swans.
>
> It was then *unanimously* resolved to endorse the recommendation of the commission that the VFL enter into a Licence Agreement with Dr Geoffrey Edelsten in respect to the private ownership of the Sydney Swans in the form executed by him, the basis of which has been previously noted by directors at this meeting, and that the distributions to VFL clubs of $2.9m proceed in accordance with the commission's recommendations.[13]

There it was: the game's first foray into private ownership. Money does talk. Said Samuel: "The board voted straight off: 'Go with Edelsten'. And we were very uncomfortable with that. Jack Hamilton went and rang Edelsten and he said, 'Well, you've won.' And Edelsten said, 'That's good.'"[14]

It all looks so simple in those stark paragraphs, but the minutes through the period—and indeed, on the night the decision was finally made—consist of page after page of discussion, offer, counter-offer, debate, what-ifs and wherebys, since the February meeting of the League that had given the green light to private ownership generally, and specifically to Sydney.

Sellers, waiting for the result at home in Sydney, gave a sense of the drama when he spoke with Jim Main for *Shake Down the Thunder*: "Both groups

---

13   Ibid.
14   Graeme Samuel, interview with the author, 2014.

sweated it out one Monday night in 1985 when the VFL met to decide between us. I held a party at my home in Double Bay and Dr Edelsten held a party at his home, with both groups waiting for a phone call from Jack Hamilton. I took Jack's call at about 10pm."[15] Sellers told me recently that Hamilton said, "Basil, I'm sorry—you have come second in a two-horse race."[16]

Sellers' and Geraghty's and Kimberley's day would come, and no matter where the Swans were, or who was at the helm, Bobby Skilton's loyalties remained forever with the club he had served so well.

As we know, Edelsten's foray into footy didn't end well, although there was plenty of hoopla and the grabbing of top-line players like Gerard Healy and Greg Williams, and Tom Hafey as coach. But by the following July, Edelsten's role as chairman had been taken over by Doug Sutherland, and the next years were surrounded by controversy. For all that, Jeff Browne, the League's legal adviser at the time, believes the decision, with all the facts presented, was the right one:

> Sydney would not have been as successful as it was in those years without the flamboyance of Edelsten. If Sellers' team had got the nod first time around, Sydney would not have achieved the high levels of media exposure and may not have gained the ground it did. To think they would have been more stable and successful under the alternative team is "Melbourne thinking". Sydney needed more sizzle. It needed pizzazz. It needed a flamboyant owner.[17]

That may be so, but Edelsten's reputation was substantially damaged after he filed for bankruptcy in 1987, when he was deregistered as a medical practitioner in 1988 for overservicing, and when he was sentenced to a year in jail in 1990 for hiring a hitman to assault a former patient and perverting the course of justice.[18]

If nothing else, it was a lively opening for the new commission and a

---

15   Jim Main, *Shake Down the Thunder*, 2006, p. 102.
16   Basil Sellers, interview with the author, 2014.
17   Jeff Browne, interview with the author, 2014.
18   "The private wars of Geoffrey Edelsten", *Australian Financial Review*, 18 February 2012.

true learning experience for the commissioners, and also contributed to a growing sense by the board that maybe, just maybe, an independent group *could* have a significant impact on the game's decision-making.

Although I had been a keen observer of this historic meeting, I wasn't paying much attention to all the game-changing machinations leading up to the Sydney decision, nor the swirling crisis surrounding some clubs. Hawthorn was going strongly in the midst of its greatest era, and, to be frank, at that moment I had my own issues, head down at Royal Insurance.

CHAPTER 5

A reality check

The commission was somewhat bloodied by the tactics surrounding the sale of the Sydney Swans. It needed to find its feet and find them quickly, or its impact on the game would be continually overridden by a VFL Board still keen on keeping as much control of the levers as it could.

Football was still a boys' club, a sporting organisation run by a board of clubmen who wanted more than anything for things to go on as they always had. The trouble was they couldn't, but the boys' club mentality made life hard for the commission as it tried to explore—and diligently consider—new ways forward.

Graeme Samuel recalls the difficulties facing the new administration: "Problem was they wanted a toothless commission. They basically said, 'Well, you're there. There you are; we've done this wonderful thing—we've formed a commission. But you have no power.' The Edelsten sale went a long way towards proving that point."[1]

Without the sale of the Sydney Swans, the VFL balance sheet of 1985 would have made sorry reading. As it stood, the League managed a surplus of income over expenditure of $348,600, but that income included an extraordinary item of $1.5 million thanks to the Edelsten bid, giving the

---

1   Graeme Samuel, interview with the author, 2014.

League an annual cash surplus of $1,848,600. It was a healthy enough figure on the face of it, especially compared with 1984's meagre surplus of $69,406, but the underlying picture continued to be grim.

"The competition was broke," says Samuel. "At least half of the clubs were bankrupt, literally bankrupt."[2]

Around the commission table in mid-1985 opinions varied as to the best way forward. As Samuel recalls it, Jack Hamilton took a very simple, old-school line: "Jack would say, 'Look, the problem is Richmond. If Richmond plays well, you've got a lot of supporters, attendances are up. If Richmond's playing badly ...' This was the simplistic, she'll-be-right view that still ran the game, from the full-time commissioner through the administration of the clubs. Success is *just around the corner*."[3]

Driven by Samuel and Scanlon, the commission quickly came to the conclusion that they needed a major study of football, which as part-time commissioners they could not do alone. They sought independent advice, just as the board had done two years earlier with McKinsey & Co. Such a study would also provide some outside expert credibility, which was clearly needed at the time. Under the rules imposed by the League directors, the commission could now spend only $100,000 (it had been only $50,000 in the commission's first year) without seeking board approval. In mid-1985 the commission spent $99,999 and hired the renowned strategic planner Colin Carter, who was a partner of consultancy firm Pappas Carter Evans and Koop, to prepare a critical document outlining the state of the game and the League.

This report, *VFL Football: Establishing the Basis for Future Success*,[4] came to be known as the Blue Report because of its vivid blue cover. Carter worked with both Scanlon, who had a great skill for strategic analysis and formulation, and Samuel to prepare the report, and did a superb job of laying a framework for solving the League's problems.

In October 1985 the commission adopted the Blue Report and its findings

---

2   Ibid.
3   Ibid.
4   *VFL Football: Establishing the Basis for Future Success*, VFL Commission, 1985.

and presented the report under its own name to the board and, through the board, to the VFL clubs. It was a vital blueprint for the game's future, a document that took the discussion of football and its issues away from the generations of parochial orthodoxies and superstitious beliefs that to that point had dominated much of the League's thinking. Never again would a League administrator have to pin the competition's hopes on Richmond's on-field fortunes. Which is just as well.

The report's chapter headings give a sense of its methodical and lateral approach:

> *Chapter A. The first reality:* Attendance levels are being influenced by social changes.
>
> *Chapter B. The second reality:* Melbourne may not be able to afford eleven professional teams.
>
> *Chapter C. The third reality:* Inequalities in popular support will make it difficult for the less supported clubs to survive.

The report went on to make some thoughtful summaries on the state of play, including this one:

> While public concern over the VFL competition has been aired unendingly in the media, sometimes to the exclusion of the game itself, there has been no agreement on the fundamental reasons for the falling attendances or for what seems to be the unstoppable decline of many clubs into virtual financial ruin. This lack of agreement is reflected in the extraordinary range of solutions that have been proposed—less handball, private ownership, lower prices, national competitions, salary caps, improved VFL image and so on ... while every conceivable solution has been proposed, no agreement exists.[5]

And here was the breakthrough thought, the idea that would be a turning point in shaping the future direction of football:

> The underlying causes of the difficulties of the last few years are largely external to the game itself and to its management. In fact, if anyone

---

5   Ibid.

> were to be held "responsible" for the problems of the competition, there would be two culprits, the first being the changing activity patterns in society; the second being the inevitable consequences of change from a near-amateur to a near-professional competition ... The current focus on the game itself (violence, evenness, facilities, prices) or its management (club and VFL competence) are distractions from much more fundamental problems which need to be addressed.[6]

This was lifting the bar on the discussion that had surrounded the game to that point. The Blue Report hit the nail on the head: how could football be considered as separate from the world that surrounded it? That world had changed, and to some extent football had changed with it. But the crisis in the game by the mid-1980s suggested that not enough had changed. The world was slowly but surely moving past football as it had traditionally been organised and managed.

Although football's problems had arisen as a result of a series of external changes, and the Blue Report suggested no one was responsible, my view is that this was an exercise in getting the board onside. It was certainly the board's (and management's) lack of understanding of these issues and their desperate desire to hold on to power that caused them to continue with a structure that did not allow them to manage their way through the problems the game faced.

The Blue Report argued for a series of simple but deeply significant recommendations:

- that several mergers between clubs with relatively weak franchises be encouraged to take place on a voluntary basis
- that the competition should be expanded by the inclusion of Adelaide/Perth clubs
- that the expanded competition should be limited to 14 teams.

It also recommended three actions to bolster League finances:

---

6   Ibid.

- establish financial disciplines through a licensing system
- introduce a player draft system and limits on player list sizes
- maintain extensive income equalisation as a policy but modify gate equalisation to re-establish direct incentives to clubs to grow attendances.

This was a departure from the free enterprise view held by the new entrepreneurial businessmen in control of the clubs as well as several of the new commissioners—that we should not impose such strict controls on the clubs. But more on that in the next chapter.

There would be ground rationalisations, too, in an attempt to boost the attendances of what the report identified as "theatregoer" fans— those who were inclined to follow the best matches in the best comfort— while simultaneously providing clubs with financial incentives to build memberships of hardcore supporters. And the need for a quality campaign of PR was recognised as fundamental to driving the game: spin was now becoming not just a function of the drop punt.

All this to be attempted with no real money to invest in the goals outlined in the report!

"The public image of the competition, particularly its management, is very poor today," declared the commission in its endorsement of the Blue Report. "Since the game relies on mass support, the competition must be promoted favourably in the news. The commission recommends that a public relations program be developed and implemented as soon as possible."[7]

This declaration fortuitously coincided with a chance meeting between Hamilton and Mike Sheahan, then *The Herald*'s chief football writer. *The Herald,* Melbourne's afternoon daily, had tight deadlines, and Sheahan recalls: "Shivering on a tram stop on Toorak Road in Burwood at 6.30am Monday to Friday in the middle of winter to get to work by 7.15am doesn't have a lot of appeal after five or six years."[8] Despite the fact that Sheahan was at the top of his game in the 1980s, he was up for a change. He had always believed that he loved football as much as he loved journalism, and

---

7 Ibid.
8 Mike Sheahan, interview with the author, 2014.

saw a position at the VFL as the ideal mix of both, particularly at this time in his career.

He told me: "I crossed paths with Jack Hamilton one day outside the *Herald* building in Flinders Street as he enjoyed his regular lunchtime stroll into the city. I remember saying to him, 'Why don't you offer me a job?' Jack said, "What do you want to do?" and I said, "Fix up your image."[9]

Sheahan would replace the veteran newsman Ian McDonald, the League's media manager, who would move down the road in Jolimont to Cricket Australia. Hamilton preferred to call Sheahan the VFL's Public Relations Officer, as it seemed a better fit to the commission's recommendation. Sheahan struck a "hard" bargain. The League generously offered him an annual salary of $35,000 plus the use of a car. Sheahan's bargaining got the figure to $40,000!

Hamilton had acted quickly to plug this perceived gap. However, after the release of the Blue Report he became increasingly uneasy about the commission's plans and his desire and capacity to implement them. He discussed his misgivings with his fellow commissioners, advising them that he was probably not the right person to take the game forward and implement the plan.

At a meeting in March 1986, Hamilton advised the commission of his desire to "retire from service with the League on 10 October" of that year, saying his decision was "entirely personal". Commissioner Peter Nixon "paid tribute to Mr Hamilton's contribution to the establishment of the Commission in its formative times and expressed the view that his strength and experience would be greatly missed".[10]

---

9   Ibid.
10 VFL Commission minutes, 19 March 1986.

CHAPTER 6

An alliance of sworn enemies

Mr Justice Crockett of the Victorian Supreme Court nailed it in April 1983. Handing down his judgment in the case of Silvio Foschini versus the Victorian Football League and the South Melbourne Football Club, he spelt out the tricky balance between calculated self-interest and lofty collective objectives that was at the often warring heart of the VFL.

In the case, Foschini claimed a restraint on his trade as a footballer after the League obstructed his desired move from the Sydney Swans back home to a spot with St Kilda. The League had not cleared the move; Foschini went anyway. The League lost the case and had a spot of rethinking to do as a result, in particular on the subject of zoning. As Dick Seddon, the only "club man" on the inaugural commission, tells the story:

> This was a seminal moment in the history of the VFL. It was not the decision itself that was so momentous, because by this time everybody knew that the permit/zoning rules of the VFL were unenforceable, and courts would find in favour of players. What was so momentous was the demonstration by Lindsay Fox, president of the St Kilda Football Club, of how far he was prepared to go to flout the rules of the VFL for the

benefit of his club. The actions of St Kilda in playing Foschini together with another player, Paul Morwood, who was tied to the Sydney Swans, without a permit, were the catalyst for what was to follow.

The VFL instructed Jack Hamilton, Ron Cook (president of the Hawthorn Football Club) and myself to fly to the USA to meet with the four major sporting leagues. They were the National Football League (NFL), Major League Baseball (MLB), the National Basketball Association (NBA) and the National Hockey League (NHL). Our remit was to gain as much information as we could on payment and retention of players, and the way in which they conducted their competitions. The information we returned with would change forever the way the VFL and its constituent clubs did business with their players. The major reforms that flowed from this trip were the licensing of clubs, the salary cap, and drafting to replace zoning.[1]

But there were other insights, too. In his judgment, His Honour gave a neat summary of internal football politics:

The evidence in the present case ranged over a wide area. It disclosed that tactics adopted by a member club of the VFL to allow players, or to cause them to wish, to escape the coils of the VFL rules are not particularly creditable. The VFL is nothing more than a coalition of each of the twelve clubs acting as such through a representative of each club together with a president ...

But a club, when acting as an individual entity, is often seen to discard ... altruism. Pursuit of success is the predominant driving force. Success means only one thing—to be the premier team for the season. Great effort is devoted to raising money—not for its own sake, not in order to make a profit and declare dividends, but for use in achieving a more successful club on the field. To some extent this means expenditure on playing fields, on spectator facilities, on improved administration and on better coaching. But the prime aim is to acquire the best players. In pursuit of this object clubs will bend or break the very rules they so

---

1   Dick Seddon, unpublished personal notes and memoirs.

righteously make when acting through their representative in their more lofty capacity as a constituent club of the VFL. Such is the paradox.²

The VFL was described during the hearing as "an alliance of sworn enemies". There is more than a little truth in the description: it was an uneasy marriage of conflicting interests. Imposing some discipline and a sense of collective accountability on the structure was a key priority from the very first days of the League's new commission.

Seddon, a lawyer by trade, was acutely aware of this manifestation and was driven by a heightened awareness of the consequences of Justice Crockett's alliance of enemies and, beyond that, of the inherent conflicts of interest in the relationships on the VFL Board. He worked very closely with League legal man Jeff Browne to address these issues. Recalling the time, Seddon puts it this way:

> VFL directors came to the board table of the VFL with divided loyalties, one to the club which they represented as delegates, and one to the VFL corporation of which they were directors. Regrettably, VFL directors did not understand their fiduciary relationships, corporate governance principles, and their duty when conflicts of interest arose.
>
> At the very time during VFL Board discussions when a conflict of interest arose for a particular director, where he should immediately disclose his conflict, withdraw from further discussion, and refrain from voting, he would be at his most voluble and persuasive, endeavouring to enlist the support of fellow directors to vote with him in favour of his parochial club interest as against the best interests of the VFL as a corporate entity.
>
> They would do deals with each other, agreeing to vote or oppose various motions for each other in return for support of, or opposition to, a motion that affected their club favourably, or adversely, whatever the case may be.³

---

2   *Silvio Foschini v. Victorian Football League and South Melbourne Club Ltd* [1983] VSC 126 (15 April 1983), pp. 12-13.

3   Dick Seddon, unpublished personal notes and memoirs.

It's not a pretty picture of board behaviour, and certainly not one that features a robust sense of common purpose—never mind corporate governance—or "mutual dependence", which is at the heart of what sporting competitions are all about. Indeed, nearly every decision involved conflicts for all the directors—in truth, it was probably impossible for them to make an unconflicted decision.

The commission was concerned that if effective controls were not in place it would not be able to effect the changes necessary. If mutual dependence as a concept is fundamental to a sporting team competition, as it surely must be, and competitive evenness ensures interest in the competition, then it follows that the League should have policies in place that ensure that teams compete against each other on a reasonably level playing field. Equalisation, therefore (or as they like to call it today, revenue sharing or competitive balance), must surely be embraced as a concept to deliver these fundamental requirements. We needed an all-embracing strategy involving player-talent sharing, income sharing and cost equalisation.

As a result of the fact-finding mission overseas, the League introduced several strategies to deliver the fundamental prerequisites for an exciting and thriving competition. First, foremost and fundamental to delivering this outcome was locking down a new relationship between the League and the clubs through licence agreements. The individual clubs needed to acknowledge that they were franchisees of a game that was administered centrally by a League controlled by a commission with due authority to make decisions on behalf of and in the interests of the code.

Seddon saw this as the commission's initial priority:

> To me, it seemed that franchising was the priority. It had proven to be too difficult to deal with recalcitrant clubs who were serial offenders under the VFL Constitution, so another mechanism was required in addition to the commission. In my opinion that mechanism was contractual obligations, rather than constitutional obligations, because it is much easier in law to deal with a breach of contract than to obtain

a majority or three-quarter majority vote at the board table for
a constitutional breach.[4]

And so it was that the commission set about defining and instituting a more accountable and formal structure around the relationship between the clubs and the League. In a nutshell, we had to impose some discipline to bring order to the relationship with the clubs and allow us to make "for the good of the game" decisions. Seddon again:

> When creating the commission the clubs had reserved most of the powers to themselves, and it was necessary in my view to shift some power away from the clubs to the commission to provide us with some measure of autonomy. In drafting a licensing agreement, particular attention was paid to the triggers that gave rise to the penalties applicable for breaches of contract. Central to this agreement was the obligation of each franchisee to abide by the VFL Constitution, its rules and regulations.
>
> Failure to do so would automatically give rise to a raft of remedies of escalating seriousness, such as fines, loss of premiership points, assignment to the VFL of the stadium lease where the offending club played its home games, and assignment of player contracts to the VFL.
>
> ... An important feature of the licensing agreement was the formalisation of the agreement of the clubs, originally obtained by Jim McKay in the 1970s, for the permanent assignment to the VFL of the club trademarks, including club name, colours, club logo and registered jumper design.[5]

The clubs—surprise!—were not keen. It meant handing over what today we would call their intellectual property. But of course it was more than that: this was emotional property, too. The club colours and emblem were at the very heart of what it meant to be Collingwood or Carlton, or any other club. Never mind intellectual property—this meant surrendering their birthright.

---

4   Ibid.
5   Ibid.

If the commission were to have the necessary authority to administer the League, then the most valuable properties in football—its most fundamental constituent parts—needed to be controlled by the commission and, therefore, the League. There was no point in having a licence or franchise arrangement with the commercial entity of a club if the things that made up that club's identity as far as the supporters were concerned were not also vested in the League. The League had to own the colours, the jumpers, the names.

Remember that the commission had only just been formed and was an arrangement made under the threat, posed by John Elliott, of a rival competition involving the powerhouse teams of the League. Licence deals would give the constitution of the competition some sense of certainty, a layer of protection. If the League owned the pieces of intellectual property that together made up the essence of the football clubs, then it could rest a little more certain that its most valuable properties, the clubs, would not be picked off.

The thought of that Elliott rival competition was fresh. This was a time of considerable uncertainty, with all the volatility that near-bankruptcy and talk of breakaway leagues and private ownership could bring. Anything that the League could bolt down needed to be bolted down, securely and quickly. On top of all that, the licence agreement also gave the commission power to appoint an administrator if a club did get into trouble, which provided a necessary financial discipline.

Under Seddon's supervision, Browne put together what he thought a licence agreement should look like. While Seddon has some pretty clear ideas on what was required, having discussed the concepts with American sport administrators, Browne went about constructing an agreement to suit our particular situation without reference to the US counterparts.

Importantly, the licence agreement included a section where each club gave power of attorney to the VFL in the event of a serious infraction by the club. This meant the commission would have the authority to activate a penalty unilaterally in the event of a breach without having to obtain the consent of the offending club.

Another important cog in the wheel was the introduction of the standard player contract, which all players were required to execute and lodge copies of with the executive commissioner of the League. It was a tripartite contract involving the player, the club and the League. We always wanted the club to be the player's employer, but the contract gave us more control. Each contract contained a clause whereby the player agreed to an assignment by the club of the player's contract to the VFL in the event of a default by the club in any of its obligations pursuant to the conditions of the licence agreement. It locked both club and player to the League, which meant we would be well and truly protected from invaders and would have the necessary control over our constituents.

So, if, for example the Collingwood Football Club committed a blatant and serious breach of the VFL Constitution, rules or regulations, or wanted to leave the League for some reason, the most extreme consequences hypothetically could be a substantial fine; loss of premiership points; loss of its ground and facilities; loss of its name, logo and jumper design; and, importantly, loss of its players. As Seddon relates: "The Collingwood committee could jump up and down all they liked, but they could not use the name of the Collingwood Football Club or its logo or jumper design, they could not play matches at Victoria Park, and they would not have any players. The commission was free to transfer all these Collingwood Football Club assets to another franchisee."[6]

It took Seddon a bit of time to sell the idea of a licence agreement to the commissioners, but eventually they came to understand that it was the best way of stopping clubs breaking away and bringing the competition down. As he tells it:

> When I tabled the agreement at the first meeting of the commission, I did not immediately receive the positive reaction I was expecting. Peter Scanlon in particular was strongly opposed, and to a lesser extent, Graeme Samuel. Peter Nixon was more or less ambivalent, because to some extent he was able to appreciate the value of franchising. As an

---

6   Dick Seddon, unpublished personal notes and memoirs.

ardent Richmond Football Club supporter, he had been given access to the upper echelons at Richmond and some club exposure and insight into the problems facing football. Jack Hamilton, of course, and Alan Schwab, who sat in on commission meetings, were both in favour, because they knew that the introduction of licensing agreements would make their jobs a lot easier.

In retrospect, the strong opposition of Peter Scanlon was not surprising, considering his background and where he had come from. He had worked for John Elliott at Elders, and was his friend. John was the president at the Carlton Football Club and was one of the more maverick club presidents, resenting VFL regulation and any interference in the affairs of his club. Peter was a "free marketeer", as was John. He preferred market forces to determine outcomes, and believed that regulatory interference distorted the natural marketplace, and produced weaker outcomes.[7]

Here was a funny thing, another paradox for modern football: some of the key men driving the restructure of the game were by every instinct and belief men of the free market, and yet they had to acknowledge that the best interests of the game would be served by introducing elements of central control. It was a kind of sporting socialism, if you wanted to describe it that way, but surely the best model for our situation. If the commission did not impose structure from the centre, then the conflicting interests of the clubs would simply pull the League apart. Samuel and Scanlon joke about it now, but at the time what the commission knew it had to do ran counter to their fundamental belief that markets needed to be left to run their own race. Not so for football.

Seddon engaged in a campaign of slow conversion of his commission colleagues:

> I think Peter Scanlon saw me at the outset as being too bureaucratic, and even socialistic, in my endeavours to impose regulations to control the relationships between the VFL and the clubs. He thought my

---

7   Ibid.

> franchising proposal was draconian, overly bureaucratic, unhealthy
> and unnecessary. His views were most likely shared by a number
> of club presidents. However, Scanlon was not unreasonable, and
> could be convinced by a logical proposition. He was one of the
> most excellent strategic thinkers I had ever met.[8]

A licence agreement was also tremendously important to all the League's commercial operations. How could the VFL sell rights to the game's TV coverage, for example, if we didn't have licence agreements providing us with the intellectual property in the individual clubs that were the subject of those broadcasts?

Competition sponsorship was another revenue stream that had to be controlled by the League in order to avoid major conflicts and maximise our income. Of course, the League was perfectly capable of stuffing that up for itself—the Foster's Cup presented by XXXX being a notable example!

It was complicated. At one point, for example, the League had McDonald's as a major partner (remember those big "M" balls?) and, reasonably enough, McDonald's was upset that the West Coast Eagles had a deal at the same time with Hungry Jack's.

The building blocks were coming together to set up the framework of a League that could ultimately look at truly mature concepts such as equalisation, or whatever you want to call it. In 1986, though, the idea of having clubs accept that a levelling of the playing field could be in everyone's interests was only slowly dawning.

With most of the licence agreements signed off in early December 1985 (all but Carlton, which took another 10 days or so) and the standard player contract settled, we were getting everything in place that was necessary to develop the League.

The next steps were the introduction of a full draft system and the salary cap. These needed to work in unison and towards a common goal—clearly a draft without a salary cap wouldn't work as cashed-up

---

8 Ibid.

clubs would be able to influence a draft. Players could get offered side deals and then make it plain they were reluctant, for example, to shift cities. The combination of the two makes it all work. Browne says, "The licence agreement and the draft were far, far more important than the salary cap; indeed, theoretically you do not need a salary cap if you have an effective, uncompromised draft system."[9] The critical two words here are "effective" and "uncompromised".

The draft and salary cap owe a lot to the work of Justice Crockett, with the Foschini case sounding the death knell of the long-established structure of recruitment zones. The idea of a player draft came up as a zone substitute structure and was championed at the commission table by Seddon:

> I had obtained copies of the drafting rules from the NFL, NBA, MLB and NHL, and I had discussed drafting with a number of their key officials. Thus armed, I was ready to begin designing a set of drafting rules for the VFL. I enlisted the help of Alan Schwab, football operations manager of the VFL, and together with Jeff Browne, the VFL legal adviser, we drew up the drafting rules. The first official VFL draft occurred in late 1986 after Ross was installed as chairman, and was a relatively simple affair compared with the way the draft has evolved into the sophisticated operation that it is today.[10]

Clearly it was a case of treading carefully. Mindful that the League's draft arrangements were in part a response to legal sanctions, we were wary of having them challenged legally as in itself the draft was a restraint on the capacity of footballers to ply their trade wherever it suited them. But at that time some restraint was seen as a necessary and acceptable part of administering a competition such as ours. While the League had used a limited form of drafting since 1982 that allowed clubs to select two non-Victorian players each year, Browne was now drawing up a new, all-encompassing system that would be the forerunner to the player draft we know today. He said, "Although our agreement at that time did not

---

9   Jeff Browne, interview with the author, 2014.
10 Dick Seddon, unpublished personal notes and memoirs.

contemplate free agency, it did include three distinct drafts and gave limited access for interstate players, who needed to have played with the respective state competitions. There is no doubt that the business credentials of those appointed to the commission created a sense of leadership that effectively stemmed any rearguard action against the competition's new building blocks."[11]

For around 20 years, until he took up a senior role with the Nine Network in 2005, Browne continued to update and modify the documents as time required them to change. He was a valuable source of information on labour-market reform while mostly managing to keep the League out of court. His contribution in this area was invaluable. As Browne relates, "Our draft rules were a red rag to a bull for players and their association, and were introduced at a time when the New South Wales Rugby League had introduced a draft and were rapidly defeated in court before the next season got under way. Yet we were able to delay action against the draft long enough to be able to gather evidence for six-plus years to support our contention that it would actually even up the competition."[12]

The early draft picks by clubs were not based on perfect intelligence, and too many first-round selections did not make the grade. To improve this situation we developed the Teal Cup (for elite under 18s), in which pre-draft Victorian players competed against each other in the one competition under very good coaches; as a result the success rate improved dramatically. Other states reacted, and the player intelligence collected around the country grew in content, accuracy and importance—all designed to improve recruiters' selection certainty. To think that the early drafts were "effective" is not correct: the draft was a concept many years in the making.

Those early drafts were also nowhere near "uncompromised", as we were constantly introducing clubs to the competition with the need to offer them priority selections in order for them to have a reasonably competitive list of players. We also experimented with priority selections

---

11   Jeff Browne, interview with the author, 2014.
12   Jeff Browne, interview with the author, 2014.

for perennially underperforming clubs to help bring them back to a competitive situation. Interestingly, that benefit was only recently removed as clubs were finding it necessary to abuse the rule that had been set up to help them improve.

The other half of the equation, the salary cap, was introduced to clubs in 1987, and was absolutely necessary because the draft was neither effective nor uncompromised. It completed an important part of our equalisation and cost-containment policy, which was designed to neutralise the ability of the richest and most successful clubs to dominate the competition perennially. Increasing revenue, or reducing or at least maintaining costs, was all the same to the clubs, so the salary cap was something they were keen to embrace immediately.

There was some blowback from the players, but we argued that the cap wasn't a constraint on any individual payment, merely an overall limit under which all those payments could be made. We could therefore argue that we weren't constraining any individual. It put the onus back on the clubs to negotiate with the players under some sort of framework so it was a restriction on the clubs, not a restriction on the players—or at least that's what we argued.

The early player payment numbers were a little surprising. Seddon recalls:

> We set upon selling our concept of the salary cap to the clubs through the VFL directors. To their credit, most directors were receptive to the concept, because I suppose they realised that time was running out.
> We began by offering a moratorium to clubs to disclose their individual total player payments to provide us with a guide to the setting of the ceiling of the cap. We expected most clubs would fit under a cap of $750,000 per annum, but we were a little concerned that Carlton and Essendon would be above that. When the figures came in, as expected Carlton and Essendon were above that at $1,100,000 and $1,000,000 respectively. But the real surprise was Ron Cook's "family club", Hawthorn, who came in at $1,300,000.
>
> It would be unrealistic to set a cap below the Carlton and Essendon

totals and expect Hawthorn to meet it. Similarly, it would not be prudent, especially when an objective was cost containment, to set the cap at Hawthorn's level, as this would encourage the other clubs to spend more than they already were. The solution was to introduce a three-tiered salary cap for a fixed period, with gradual adjustments to achieve the one ceiling over time.

Implementation was to be achieved by each club lodging with the VFL executive commissioner each year certified copies of all their player contracts, containing details of all player payments and benefits, together with statutory declarations from each player and each club declaring that the payments were true and correct and constituted the total payment and benefit the player was entitled to receive. Player payments were to include signing-on fees and all third-party arrangements benefiting the player.[13]

The general cap was eventually set at $1.2 million for 1987 and $1.3 million for 1988 and 1989, with the salary floor set at 90 per cent of the cap or $1.08 million and $1.17 million respectively. (By way of comparison, the 2014 salary cap, known officially now as Total Player Payments, is $9,632,370 with a salary floor of $9,150,752.)

Seddon goes on: "We took constant legal advice on not just the draft, but also on the interplay between these various elements of licence agreement, draft and salary cap. They did need to work in unison and towards a common goal: clearly a draft without a salary cap was not going to work."[14] Particularly in those early years.

Of course, having the salary cap and the rules governing it in place gave the League power to investigate some of the most sensitive inner workings of the clubs, a power it had not enjoyed before. After a few years clubs were "stretching" the rules. We found a rat's nest of intricate deals and arrangements, and initially it was very difficult to unpick existing deals. I think the commission would admit we were a little bit soft early on.

---

13   Ibid.
14   Ibid.

To provide a fresh start we decided on another moratorium: clubs could make a full confession and we'd set things right and move on without consequence.

Essendon came to us and said, "Well, just suppose we were doing this … and what about this, this and this?" And they went away and never came back to own up to anything. Essendon was first cab off the rank for investigation when the moratorium finished, and the first to be penalised. Carlton, on the other hand, confessed everything and got off scot free; Carlton's executive director, Ian 'Collo' Collins, was no man's dill.

Again, the implementation of the salary cap was a tough step for the free marketeers on the commission; they had savage disagreements about it. Seddon had to fight hard, and fortunately he won out. This was why his early presence on the commission was so important. He understood the necessity of a mixed football economy: a little bit of free market, a little bit of socialism.

CHAPTER 7

My early days in football

You can't plan for the twists and turns that life brings you. Life is a winding road that take you to places you'd never have dreamed possible.

My taste for competitive football started in the under 16s at Wesley College. We were by far the dominant team in the Associated Public Schools (APS) competition, boasting players such as Alan Joyce and Mike Butcher, who both went on to play for Hawthorn in the VFL. In my senior school years I played in three premiership teams in a row; each of these teams included five VFL players. In my last year at school, after the APS season finished, the A-grade Amateurs and Wesley's old boys, Collegians, asked me to come and play the last three weeks of their season. We qualified for the finals and then won the premiership. St Kilda's coach at the time, Allan Jeans, came into the rooms after the game and invited me to play for the Saints in 1962.

Over the next five years I played 62 games and kicked 38 goals. I missed many games due to injury, including two Grand Finals—one of them the 1966 Saints premiership. It was my greatest sporting disappointment, and I thought that was that for my days in footy.

Twenty years on, football would call me again. By then I was making a life in business. I was chairman and managing director of the Australian operation of Royal Insurance, a big British-based company. I was set up for a life in the corporate sector and never imagined for a minute that wouldn't always be my lot, my feet well and truly under the big desk.

I had worked for it, though, through an array of very different roles over many years. Out of school, and while I was playing with St Kilda, I worked at BHP, making my way from a junior sales position through marketing and into corporate planning. During these years I did a Bachelor of Economics followed by an MBA, and worked on many interesting projects, including the Sarich orbital engine and a new colour TV system, neither of which saw the light of day. After almost 12 years with the Big Australian, I needed a new challenge. I just couldn't see what could excite me in that vast organisation. As it turned out, this was one of those key moments—one of those decisions that start the twisting and turning.

In 1974 I went to work at Wynns Winegrowers under the astute direction of Ray King. Ray was an ex-VFL umpire, a very good sportsman and a very smart cookie. He has been a highly successful businessman over the years, but as happened in those days he was more renowned as the only umpire to have awarded two half Brownlow votes to two players because he could not separate them! (Imagine Hamilton's dilemma at the counting table on Brownlow night.) He asked me to be the company's marketing director. I spent six years with him, learned everything I could about the wine industry and a good deal about marketing, and then in 1979 was headhunted away to manage AAMI, the car insurance company.

Managing is managing; business is business. Wine to insurance might look like a giant leap, but to me at the time it was a simple matter of pursuing opportunity as well as personal and professional growth. I spent four years at AAMI before one of the directors—Peter Duerden, a Brit who was the chairman and managing director of Royal Insurance—approached me, saying: "I want you to come and run Royal Insurance Australia. I'm going back to England." And so I took that move, because I knew that Royal would offer me a much broader base of insurance, not just car insurance as AAMI was then.

And it was while I was with Royal Insurance that I was asked to consider leading the VFL.

Left field.

Astounding.

But it came at a critical time—a time when I was ready to listen to an alternative and take another of life's improbable twists and turns.

Football had been reaching out to me for some time before that fateful call, which is probably not surprising. Footy has always been so much a part of Victorian culture, so woven into the corporate and social fabric, that you never really leave it. Back before the VFL came knocking I'd already formed a strong link with the Hawthorn Footy Club; an interesting path to Glenferrie Oval had been mapped out via a potent mix of gin and wine.

When I was still at Wynns I'd been talking to St Kilda about a sponsorship, and they said they couldn't get involved because they had Gilbey's (the distillery) as their major scoreboard sponsor down at Moorabbin. Since the 1940s, Gilbey's Australian corporate office had been a dominant presence on the Nepean Highway in Moorabbin, just down the road from the Saints' home ground. It was a natural fit for a club seeking a connected presence in the southeast after moving from the Junction Oval in St Kilda in the mid-1960s.

The local loyalties were strong. The VFL was a competition with deep local and suburban roots, don't forget. Sponsorship was a pretty unsophisticated business back then: give us money and we'll whack a bloody great sign on the scoreboard. Job done.

I said to the Saints, "Just get rid of the Gilbey's scoreboard, and let's do a deal." Nope. St Kilda wouldn't have a bar of it.

I got adventurous then. Never mind my old club loyalties—I just wanted to do a deal linking with a VFL club to promote the virtues of Wynns. One of my senior sales reps, Bob Dows, was a mad Hawk and introduced me to Hawthorn: another fateful moment. Within weeks they were the Wynvale Hawks and on their way to winning the 1976 premiership.

It had cost Wynns $10,000 for the sponsorship and was the beginning of an association that would turn out to be life-changing for me.

It was the start of an innovative relationship with a club that was keen to be different. Success drives confidence and the need to search for new ways, I guess.

Back then, TV stations didn't like giving sponsors any unpaid exposure. It was a real problem extracting that extra value for money that sponsors were after. Although we could put a sponsor's logo on the breast of the jumper if we did the same on the players' streetwear, the TV stations would crop the logo out of the frame and shoot in tight from above the logo.

I said, "OK, what we're going to do is issue all the players with polonecks, and we're going to have a Wynvale logo right around their necks. They can't shoot from the chin up." The TV stations got quite antsy—they hated it, in fact—and asked the players to roll the neck-roll inwards so the Wynvale brand didn't show. The players stuck tight. "No," they said. "We're wearing the club gear. Full stop."

So the Wynvale Hawks got tremendous exposure. For better or worse—and I guess that depends on your attitude to sponsor logos—it was the beginning of a new world. There is an old Wynvale Hawks polo in the Hawks Museum at Waverley Park. A change icon.

When I eventually left Wynns to join AAMI and begin my time in insurance, it was also the beginning for me of a new, more formal relationship with football. Hawthorn president Ron Cook was used to having me in and out of the club as a sponsor and sought to keep me around. "Will you come on the board?" he asked in 1980, and I said, "Yeah, I'd like to do that."

So that was that. And I stayed on the Hawthorn board for five years until I joined the VFL.

CHAPTER 8

Boys' club to business enterprise

It was just past dawn on Tuesday 5 August 1986 when the phone rang. Not the most convenient time to take a life-changing call.

"Ross? Ross Oakley?"

"Mmmnnnph."

"It's Greg Hobbs here, mate—Greg Hobbs from *The Herald*."

Word was out, it seemed. I'd all but made up my mind to leave Royal Insurance and take the top job at the VFL. The deal wouldn't be done officially for some days yet, but the politicking and speculation as to who would be Jack Hamilton's replacement were growing.

The decision had been a few months in the making. Hawthorn president Ron Cook had been the first to suggest to me that something might be in the wind. Hamilton had announced his retirement but wouldn't leave until October, after the 1986 finals series. The board had appointed a subcommittee of three club representatives—Cook, Footscray president Tony Capes, and VFL Director from North Melbourne Albert Mantello—and commissioners Scanlon, Samuel and Seddon to scout for Hamilton's replacement, assess the candidates and make a final recommendation to the board. The recruiting timeline was pretty short.

This was to be a key decision for the commission. The commissioners were keen for the appointment to be different, to be a selection more in line with the future direction they could see for the game and its management. They needed a new VFL chief with a passion for football to satisfy the clubs, but also with a keen sense of management discipline and experience in the corporate world. Preferably, it seemed, they needed new blood as well—somebody from outside the comfort zone of the League and its administrative structure, not one of the old boys' club.

There was a real sense of urgency and opportunity in the commission's work now. The Blue Report had given them and the board a clear sense of direction, and there was new impetus to take bold steps towards the formation of a truly national game. At that stage it was just the Sydney Swans outside Victorian borders. The appointment of a new chief of the VFL had to reflect the purpose of the commission and share its vision.

Cook pulled me aside one evening at Hawthorn and wondered whether, just on the quiet, I might have any interest in the role. That was the way with Cooky: everything was half said, with a bit of a hint, a wink and a nod. But I gathered they were looking for someone with my credentials.

The timing was interesting. I'd been at Royal Insurance for nigh on four years and had just suffered one of the most irritating knockbacks of my corporate career. I'd taken a serious proposal to head office in London, involving some innovative thinking, at least in my view, around life insurance. I was very excited about what I thought was truly a breakthrough idea. Head office agreed but had other issues. "Love the idea," they said, "but think of the precedent: if we allow you to do this in Australia, how long before Europe and America want to do the same thing?" Indeed, I had tried to sell the idea on the basis of Australia being a test market because we were so isolated from the rest of the world.

I was stunned by their response—a great idea knocked back out of hand because of precedent—and came back to Melbourne pretty seriously out of sorts.

And then Cooky had that word in my ear.

Graeme Samuel was next to get in touch. This was becoming serious, and I needed to think long and hard about it because it would be a major shift in my career path. And if I wanted to move back to the commercial world afterwards, it may well close off the option—few people made such transitions in those days. But what an opportunity to be part of the new national thrust. It was every young man's dream. I couldn't knock it back!

A meeting was set up with Samuel and Peter Scanlon at which they pushed me on my ideas on a national competition: where did I see it in the future of the game? As they fished for my views I didn't give much away; indeed, I was a little cagey—particularly with regard to the structure they wanted me to fit into with the long-serving Alan Schwab and his well-established power base (more on this later in the chapter). It was clear they were looking for someone with commercial experience who was committed to national expansion. I warmed to the idea after assurances from them that there would be a well-spelt-out demarcation of jobs and that Schwab would be instructed on who held the senior position.

National expansion had its risks: a large percentage (more than 80 per cent) of Victoria's vocal football public was against a national competition, while more than 60 per cent was against an expanded VFL competition.[1] They felt they would be giving something away rather than getting something much bigger in return. Why change a good thing? But footy had no choice, as I saw it. Going national was clearly the way of the future—the way not just to sustainable survival, but to significant growth.

The commission was down to the last couple of candidates, a pretty short short list, and while the commissioners led me to believe I was their favoured candidate, they gave me no assurances that I would get the job.

The media? Well, the media, and much of the old-boy football world, were keen on Schwab. Under the sort of organisation that had appointed Hamilton to run the League, Schwab would have been a shoo-in for the top job. He was a football "lifer", with a career that had begun when he was employed as a junior clerk at the VFL in 1958. He was a junior in the

---

1   *VFL Football: Establishing the Basis for Future Success*, VFL Commission, 1985.

offices at St Kilda in my playing days there before working his way up to assistant general manager of the Saints in 1965. Two years later, he moved to Richmond as club secretary and then, at the age of 36, he returned to the VFL as manager-administrator. By 1986 he was executive director and Hamilton's right-hand man, responsible for football operations and a good deal more. He had a very solid football pedigree and was a popular figure inside the VFL and among the media.

But I felt I was in a good space with the commissioners in my corner.

I finally got my mind on track at that ungodly hour of Hobbs' phone call. I soon learned that the men and women at *The Herald* had no respect for life in the early morning, and such calls were not uncommon. Shuffling around the bedsheets searching for the phone to talk to them and fit in with the paper's early deadlines would become par for the course.

"Yes, Greg," I said. "How can I help you?"

He got straight to the point: "I have it on good authority from someone close to the process that you're taking over the VFL, and that Alan Schwab's not going to get the top job."

Obviously I had an inkling that he was right, but it was far from a done deal, at least as I understood it. Clearly the commission was moving in a way that the people around Schwab and his campaign were not happy with. Schwab was marshalling the troops—journalists and club people with whom he had a good relationship as a result of favour swapping. This was all part of the game; it was the way of the world in those days.

There was nothing I was prepared to tell Hobbs that morning. "Is that right?" I replied. "Well, I can't comment about that. You can't ring me first thing in the morning, put that to me and expect an answer. I'm not making any comment."

Never let a "no comment" get in the way of the story—a basic journalistic rule, it seems. Greg came back, quick as a whip: "Oh well, I'm running it. It's going to run in *The Herald* this afternoon."

I said, "Well, you better think long and hard about that, Greg."

"Why?" he asked. "If I've got a story, I'll run it."

I thought for a moment. I wasn't going to be bullied. "Well, Greg, look at it this way. If you run it and I don't get the job, I'll sue you for everything you've got because it will damage my position at Royal. If you run it and I do get the job, I'll never give you another bloody story in your life."

I paused, then said, "Your decision, Greg." He hung up.[2]

Greg told me later that he thought long and hard over what he should do that day, pacing among the sports reporters' desks on the cigarette-burned carpet on the third floor of *The Herald* building in Flinders Street. But when the presses rolled for the paper's first edition in the middle of that morning, there it was on the back page, leading the sports section: BATTLE FOR FOOTY'S TOP JOB HOTS UP. The headshot sitting on the shoulder of the piece was of a smiling Alan Schwab.

The story cut to the chase:

> Former St Kilda wingman Ross Oakley is the latest name to enter discussions for Jack Hamilton's job as the VFL commissioner.
> But Oakley, 45, and now a member of the Hawthorn FC board,
> said today that he was not a candidate for the post. When questioned further he said, "It's a very, very sensitive issue and it may well turn out that any premature comments could be damaging."[3]

I don't remember saying any of that, but lack of a quote hasn't stopped journalists before. The cat, it seemed, was wriggling out of the bag.

For me, the timing was awkward. The day of the Hobbs article was the day I was supposed to be meeting my British boss from Royal Insurance, who had flown out to make sure I hadn't taken my recent rejection too hard. The news in *The Herald* would probably give him a pretty accurate sense of how I was feeling. Not that Hobbs would have known any of that.

Later that day I met my boss, and sure enough, he had a copy of the paper under his arm. "What the hell is this?" he said in a very pucker British accent as he unrolled it.

---

2   I later employed Hobbs to edit the VFL's *Football Record*.
3   Greg Hobbs, "Battle for footy's top job hots up", *The Herald*, 5 August 1986. I was actually 43, not 45.

I said, "They approached me when I returned from the UK, which was an opportune time given the result of my board proposal. Yes, I am very seriously considering the position, given my football background."

He was flabbergasted, but deep down I think he was beginning to understand how big Australian Football was in Melbourne.

Hobbs was right on the money in more ways than one. It was the first time my name had been raised as a candidate but it also described the awkwardness faced by the selection committee and the commission in dealing with the Schwab power base and his ambition for the job. Nine paragraphs in, Schwab made his appearance:

> Alan Schwab, who is Hamilton's right-hand man at the VFL in his capacity as executive director, remains the favourite to become the new commissioner.
>
> Strict secrecy surrounds the interview list ... One official admitted that Schwab was not a clear-cut favourite and the opposition could not be discounted.
>
> The pro-Schwab group is presently lobbying strongly to put him in power when Hamilton resigns from the VFL in October. Several officials fear the repercussions if Schwab does not get the job—particularly in football's present climate. They believe it would be unwise to "rock the boat" while the big decisions have to be made over the expansion of football on a national front.[4]

The truth was that the job was never going to be Schwab's, no matter how much the old boys' club pushed for it. The commission, particularly the Samuel-Scanlon push, was determined to replace Hamilton with somebody with significant commercial experience. Football had to be run as a commercial operation utilising proper business practices—of that they were certain.

Although the job seemed to be mine, I may not have been their first (or only) option, as I discovered later when I found a headhunter's file in one of the drawers in Hamilton's desk. It contained names such as Graeme John,

---

4   Ibid.

who was to become a part-time commissioner after my time.⁵

Dick Seddon had also been in touch with former Carlton premiership captain Mike Fitzpatrick, whose name was not on the headhunter's list; Fitzpatrick was then working in New York in a senior role with Merrill Lynch. As Seddon recalls it in his papers:

> The method I adopted to start the search was to make a list of all the VFL players who stood out 10 to 20 years ago as good players and decent types, and who currently were successful in business or the professions. The person I came up with was Mike Fitzpatrick, then 38, not long out of the game, forging a powerful career in government, then in merchant banking.
>
> Mike had won a Rhodes Scholarship and attended Oxford University for three years. On his return he played for Carlton, was appointed captain in 1980 and led them to two premierships in 1981 and 1982. By 1985, Mike was in New York working as an investment banker. He seemed to fit my criteria perfectly.
>
> Fitzpatrick as a candidate did not impress Scanlon and Samuel because he did not receive the endorsement of John Elliott.⁶

Indeed, if Elliott had been asked he would not have been supportive of Mike—as a recent comment suggests: "I felt he was not decisive as he was always wanting a deferral of Carlton board meetings until next month to further consider issues. During my court case some years later, Fitzpatrick moved a motion to have me removed from the board and he did not receive a seconder. I spoke to Mike and suggested that there was no doubt who should exit the board, and he did so several weeks later."⁷

Looking for options, Seddon telephoned Fitzpatrick in New York and asked him whether he would consider the position of executive commissioner of the VFL. Fitzpatrick advised that he was attracted to the possibility but the timing was off: he didn't want to leave his prestigious job and had

---

5   Graeme John, a former South Melbourne player, served on the AFL Commission from 2001 to 2011.
6   Dick Seddon, unpublished personal notes and memoirs.
7   John Elliott, interview with the author, 2013.

settled with his young family in the USA.

Both Scanlon and Samuel make the point that they had never discussed Fitzpatrick's candidacy with Elliott as at no stage was Fitzpatrick available to be considered.

Seddon goes on:

> It is ironic that Mike Fitzpatrick subsequently joined the AFL Commission, and eventually became its chairman, a position he still holds today. He is the fourth chairman, having succeeded Ross Oakley, the first chairman and CEO, then the non-executive chairs, John Kennedy, and Mike's immediate predecessor, the late Ron Evans. Today, Mike and I can laugh at how he has come full circle, from my invitation to consider the possibility of executive commissioner to his current post as chairman of the commission.[8]

No doubt Fitzpatrick's appointment as chairman of the commission puts a different light on Elliott's view of Mike's Carlton days.

Meanwhile, Schwab certainly had his backers through the process. He was Hamilton's reluctant preference, as Seddon put it: "If we could not find anyone better, Alan could probably do the job; although Jack hoped we could find someone better."[9]

Hobbs had another crack a week after his first shot. His next back-page article was headed: *OAKLEY FIRMS IN VFL STAKES*.

The story was still drenched with the machinations running through the corridors: "Football's hottest topic today is not national football—but the political fight being waged to install the next full-time VFL commissioner."[10]

In truth, the state of the game was being discussed behind closed doors, including the ongoing kerfuffle surrounding a VFL licence for the new teams from Brisbane and Perth and how each would be set up. It was hard to believe that in mid-August nothing had been decided. Would Fitzroy play

---

8   Dick Seddon, unpublished personal notes and memoirs.
9   Ibid.
10 Greg Hobbs, "Oakley firms in VFL stakes", *The Herald*, August 1986.

games out of Brisbane? Would a new franchise be established? Everything was up in the air.

Behind the scenes there was a growing sense of urgency. TV rights and the League's naming-rights sponsorship—there was no holder when I took over—were due for negotiation. It was not a good time for the boss to be winding down with just months left to serve.

The bottom line of football remained anything but healthy, and on Friday 8 August the Victorian commissioner for corporate affairs, Gordon Lewis, read the riot act: the 11 Victoria-based VFL clubs had the same responsibility as any other trading entity—they had to be solvent. As Michael Lovett reported in *The Herald*:

> Mr Lewis was commenting on the VFL Commission's decision to allow the clubs to remain in their present form next season.
>
> Since the VFL Commission announced on Tuesday night that the 12 clubs would be part of any planned expansion of the League, doubts have been raised about the legal rights of some clubs to continue trading. It is no secret that some are in the red, some by seven-figure sums …
>
> "It appears there has been some confusion this week on where some of these clubs stand. I will be in touch with the commission in the next day or so to get a clearer picture," said Lewis.[11]

The commission painted that picture in detail in an extraordinary paper presented to the VFL directors and club presidents on 30 July. The 20-page stream of consciousness held nothing back and could not have more starkly defined the parlous state of the game and the forlorn options that faced the clubs if aggressive and substantial change were not taken, and taken rapidly. The document is not just a blunt representation of what was wrong but, on re-reading it all these years later, almost derisory in its condemnation of the game's administration and the excuses mounted for the poor state of the nation. It also paints a picture of the changes that had greatly affected society as a whole during the previous three decades.

---

11   Michael Lovett, in *The Herald*, August 1986.

For example, when discussing the fall in attendances:

> [T]he percent of Melbourne's population who attend the football has declined almost every year for over 30 years. Football's greatest supporters clearly find the fact difficult to stomach and most of the discussion around attendances is downright silly.
>
> It is too simple to say that prices, player loyalty, handball or talk of expanded competitions is the cause of this. Over the past decades the lifestyle of the population has changed. There are more cars, more recreational alternatives, more disposable income, altered family roles and obligations. All of these changes have made regular weekly attendance less likely.
>
> At some stage in their life, most industries go through massive and traumatic change. Suburban movie theatres were changed irrevocably by television; local shops by supermarkets. Twenty years ago, when Geelong, Melbourne and St Kilda last won flags, Australians still travelled overseas by ship, drive-in theatres were in great demand and banks had never heard of automatic teller machines. Traditional bankers tried to ignore ATMs, ships no longer carry our tourists, and drive-ins have all but disappeared.
>
> In each case, the changes were not welcome but proved irresistible. Those who ignored change were likely to be more damaged in the process.
>
> This is precisely the commission's view. The current debate over whether mergers or expanded competitions are good or bad ideas is not the real issue. The critical issues concern the realities we face. The commission has come to the view, not lightly, that whether we like it or not Melbourne cannot continue to support 11 teams. To ignore this, or seek to deny it, is to put at even greater risk that which could be saved. The realities that must be addressed are the impact of the move from an amateur game and the changing society in which we live.[12]

Page after page the commission pushed its case, eventually providing

---

12 "Discussion paper for VFL directors and club presidents from VFL Commission", 30 July 1986.

three options—two of them clearly without hope in their view, and the third painful, but at least with some hope for the greater good. The two "hopeless" options were (1) status quo and (2) allowing private or corporate ownership for Victorian clubs. The commission's favoured option (expansion nationally, contraction locally [North Melbourne and Fitzroy to merge or move to Brisbane], and a reluctant view that "while not satisfied that private ownership is in the best interest of the VFL competition and the football public, it will consider … any specific proposals") was preceded by a dire warning: "The commission has no power to force clubs to a particular course of action and feels deeply for the clubs faced with the awful choices at hand. However, reality must be faced—better now than from a position of ruin in several years time."[13]

The document still makes compelling, almost chilling reading, and none of these conclusions were shielded from me during my discussions with the commission. The reality was that with this knowledge, and with Hamilton soon to leave, the pressure was mounting to make the right choice for his successor. The commissioners were, effectively, playing against time to find a new head with the skill set to manage the game *and* please all parties concerned in the selection *and* keep a hold of the rudder of a ship that was all but sinking.

A new hand on that tiller was clearly a vital consideration, but Seddon was keeping an open mind and considering all likely options. He believed that, although Schwab had credentials for the role, a new broom was required; the League needed a person with football savvy, but more importantly with a sense of management beyond the laws of the game and the politics that had driven footy management for generations. Seddon wrote:

> Graeme Samuel mistakenly believed that I intended to support Alan Schwab, which was absolute nonsense. My preference was for Mike Fitzpatrick, but he was unavailable. Samuel invited me to his home for a private meeting, and threatened me by saying that if I supported Schwab, he would resign from the commission; and that Scanlon would resign also. I was faintly amused that Graeme was naive enough to think that his

---

13 Ibid.

> threat would influence my opinion. I raised the matter with Peter Scanlon, who laughingly dismissed it by saying, "You know what Graeme is like."[14]

Samuel does not recall this meeting but knows he was resolute in his belief that I was the best choice. He does remember a meeting with Seddon where he discussed the leaks that were coming from the commission; it was his and other commissioners' view that it was Dick who was doing the leaking, and he told him it had to stop. Scanlon also recently told me he made it clear to the board members on the selection panel that if Schwab was their choice then he would resign from the commission as he had no time for Alan in that capacity, for lots of reasons: "Schwabby had many attributes, great knowledge of football and club operations, but he was a terrible user of his power—indeed, he blatantly abused his power—and he did not have the discipline to properly represent the League."[15]

On the VFL Board, among the clubmen Schwab had strong support. He'd curried the favour of some: rumour had it that he had promised Ron Joseph at North Melbourne a senior role at the League if Ron could bring North's vote. Ron denies this happened, but confirms they had a close relationship.[16] Nevertheless, the politicking was serious and constant.

"The board representatives were clearly frightened not to appoint Alan because there had been a lot of lobbying going on and he had a lot of knowledge about each of the clubs and their foibles," said Scanlon.[17]

Seddon recalls:

> The subcommittee met at Peter Scanlon's Collins Street offices, and from preliminary discussions it soon became apparent that Capes, Cook and Mantello had come down strongly on the side of Alan Schwab. Scanlon and Samuel were in favour of Ross Oakley, who an executive search firm had unearthed for them, and I had an open mind. I knew Ross Oakley, but his nomination had come as a surprise as this was the first time I had heard of it. I wanted to hear more and further consider his suitability.

---

14   Dick Seddon, unpublished personal notes and memoirs.
15   Peter Scanlon, interview with the author, 2014.
16   Ron Joseph, interview with the author, 2014.
17   Peter Scanlon, interview with the author, 2014.

> Cook started to have a change of mind, and swung round in favour of Oakley, because Cook obviously had some dealings with Oakley at Hawthorn as a director, and previously when Oakley was with Wynns Winegrowers, a Hawthorn sponsor.[18]

Scanlon says, "There was an impasse until Mantello and Capes said, 'If you can get Schwab to stay in his current position then we will support Ross.'"

Seddon goes on:

> Scanlon, who was shrewd enough to realise that the VFL could not afford to lose Schwab because they would be very short on football administration experience, proposed a compromise. He suggested that we make a joint appointment, Schwab being in charge of football and Oakley in charge of everything else.
>
> The subcommittee reluctantly agreed, and Scanlon asked me to accompany him to his home, where he had invited Schwab, so we could jointly sell the proposal to Schwab. When we arrived, Schwab was already there.[19]

It must have been a tense meeting. Scanlon left the room for a moment to fetch drinks and Schwab turned to Seddon with a sense of what was to come. "I've missed it, haven't I?"

Seddon said, "Just wait for Peter to come back in—but look, yeah, you have. But we've got this great idea that will really protect your position in football."

And when Scanlon came back, they described what they were going to do: "Oakley, he's going to be chairman, and you're going to be executive commissioner."

Alan did some fast talking. "So, I'm the CEO?"

"No, no," said Scanlon. "He's the chairman and you're the executive commissioner. You run the football and he'll run the commercial side."

---

18   Dick Seddon, unpublished personal notes and memoirs.
19   Ibid.

And that was the murky situation they put me in when I took the job. Schwab would be left with most of his power intact and great influence over the game, but one spot short of the top position. It was a nightmare that I would have to work with.

I soon had my own conversation with Samuel and Scanlon.

"Look, we want you to be the chairman," Scanlon said. "You'll be running it, but you'll focus on the commercial side and Alan will focus on the football side. We'll call him executive commissioner, so he'll sit on the commission, because the thing is we really need him. We don't want him to leave. He's got so much intellectual property in his head."

I could see the sense of it. There was so much going on that to lose Schwab's knowledge, to have his allies ranged against me, would be a disaster—even more of a disaster than having some pretty muddy lines of responsibility and authority between the two top jobs at the VFL.

Never mind. I could—and would—work that out. I was well aware this was a time of compromise, aimed at positive outcomes. It was about looking to the long term rather than being dragged down by the moment.

As Samuel recalled, long after the event, "We had no choice—it was a balance. Yes, we wanted Ross in the top job, but there was no doubt that many of the old-football types, the old boys' club, were keen for Schwab to just step into Hamilton's shoes. It was the best compromise we could manage, pure and simple."[20]

In retrospect, there was no way Schwab was going anywhere despite my appointment. He enjoyed—indeed, thrived on—his high position at football headquarters and the prestige and lifestyle it provided him.

There was one last hurdle. I went home and told my wife, Christine. She was typically supportive, saying, "Well, if that's what you want to do, that's fine. Move out of the commercial world and into the world of sport. Why not?"

The deal was done.

I wanted the role. I was excited by it, and by the potential of the game.

---

20   Graeme Samuel, interview with the author, 2014.

There *was* a bright future—it just needed more planning and perception and vision than it had been allowed under the club-directed structure that had taken the game to the edge. It also needed some drastic surgery and, as that plaintive cry at the end of the commission's July report suggested, a commission with not just independence but muscle. I had a lifetime of unabated passion for the game of football, its clubs and characters, history and culture, and a real sense that something could be pulled from this muddle that would set the path for football into the future. And I knew I had the confidence of the commissioners, each of them leaders in their fields.

There were problems, to be sure. But our game was also the greatest game in the world. I had not a negative thought. All I could see was a wonderful opportunity—a blank canvas.

CHAPTER 9

Two-man band

For me, it was the best and worst of situations. I was about to land the big job and the once-in-a-lifetime opportunity of stepping into VFL football at a moment when, sure, there were difficult issues to resolve, but there was also a structure forming to make the necessary changes to create something great.

I had been given the job because the commission wanted what I could bring: fresh eyes on the issues, and a corporate rather than a club sense of how the game might be managed. I inherited a right-hand man whose long-held ambition had been frustrated, who had every right to be peeved and, perhaps more importantly, who was as steeped in the club old-boy culture as I was a cleanskin.

As Mike Sheahan recalls, "Schwabby didn't like Oakley. Oakley had taken 'his' job, a job he believed was his by right, and he believed—with some justification—he had been promised. Despite Oakley's background as a player and a club board member, Schwabby (and others) saw him as an outsider, an interloper."[1]

Anyway, all misgivings aside, that was the situation I had to deal with. Greg Hobbs was again first with the story on Friday 15 August 1986, courtesy of someone on the selection panel. *VFL'S PAY DAY* was the back-

---

1 Mike Sheahan, interview with the author, 2014.

page screamer. "$230,000 for the supremos".

A quick glance at the page and you might have been forgiven for thinking Prime Minister Bob Hawke was going to run the VFL: there was his mug shot next to those of Jack Hamilton, Schwab and some bloke called Oakley. Look closer and you could see that the PM was just there for salary comparison: his $125,000 a year against Hamilton's $94,000, Schwab's $100,000 and my $130,000.

Hobbs wrote: "The VFL will pay an overall yearly income of about $230,000 for Ross Oakley and Alan Schwab, the two men who will be given the responsibility of leading the League out of troubled times. Oakley and Schwab will be appointed to the VFL's chief administrative positions at a meeting of VFL directors tonight."[2]

Indeed we were.

Hobbs continued: "Oakley, who will most probably be given the higher-profile post of marketing the VFL, will receive more than Prime Minister Bob Hawke."[3]

I guess journalists have to find an angle, and the comparison between corporate Australia and the PM's salary is a tried and true provocateur. Sheahan, then the League's media director, had hosed down Hobbs from an earlier set of vastly inflated figures he was looking to publish. The final $230,000 in the paper was close enough—a bit underdone thanks to Mike's fast talking, but close enough.

Never mind the newspaper silliness about money, Schwab and I had to talk about how our relationship would work. His first reaction: "We'll run this together and we'll be equal decision-makers."

Nope. That was never going to work.

"No, Schwabby," I told him, "we're not equals." There was no ego in this: it was simply a matter of what would work. Two equal decision-makers at the top of any organisation just doesn't work. I'd been around business long enough to know that there has to be one boss. When executive decisions need to be made, you must have clear direction from one person.

---

2   Greg Hobbs, "VFL's pay day", *The Herald*, 15 August 1986.
3   Ibid.

I put it straight, right then and there, with Schwab: "I'll give you freedom to run the footy department and make decisions there, but if something comes off the rails, or if a big decision has to be made, I'm responsible. I'll seek your advice, but it'll be my role to make those decisions."

We had something close to an understanding by the time the formal announcement was made on Friday 15 August. Not that I was kidding myself—this would be difficult.

I felt at the outset it would be a complex working relationship, and as things turned out I was right to be concerned. Schwab was a seasoned football operator, a man who knew the politics of the VFL inside out. Footy was all he knew, and he was well acquainted with the ins and outs of the VFL, the clubs, the characters and the media.

But while I was relatively young at 43 (I turned 44 that September), I was no spring chicken. I'd run some big organisations and had my share of tough calls and conflict. I never doubted I could manage both the job and Schwab's clearly frustrated ambition. But then, I didn't know him that well!

On the afternoon of the announcement there was a big press conference at VFL House, with Schwab, Hamilton, Graeme Samuel, Albert Mantello and I sitting at the press-conference table as a show of strength and unity between the new and old of football.

Hamilton played it for the laughs, of course, saying, "Looks like they need two people to replace me!" In a sense I guess he was right, although he had conveniently missed the notion that Schwab was not a new employee in a new role—he just had a new title.

Hamilton's one-liner did not understate the extent of the task the League faced. The next few years would require radical change in the game: new teams in new territories, new sponsorship, new media rights, the beginnings of discussion on ground rationalisation, and a host of other issues, some foreseen, many not. (These challenges continue to face every AFL CEO.) The task needed business minds, but also the cooperation of the clubs, and that was what made the commission's decision to appoint an Oakley-

Schwab "partnership" inevitable. It was a compromise that would make it possible to put in place the raft of changes that were no longer a wish list, but a necessity.

As Samuel recalls it: "There was no way round it. Peter Scanlon and I never really had a short list for the job: it was Ross and Ross alone. Schwab was never a contender in our view—he just didn't have the business nous to do what had to be done. And he was too much a captive of the old style of club politics. However, the other side of the coin was that we needed him there to bring the clubs along with the job that Ross had to do. That meant keeping Schwab in the frame."[4]

Which is where he was in the press conference. The inevitable question came from *The Age*'s Trevor Grant. "Ross, tell us," he said, "who's in charge?"

I looked him in the eye and said, "If I was looking at the titles of the two guys who are now going to run the League, I think I'd have a fair idea who was boss."

I left it at that. My card read "Chairman, AFL Commission"; Schwab's noted him as "Executive Commissioner".

"Ross, what are your early priorities?" was the next question. I answered, "To plug all the leaks into the media from the administration which have the prospect of detrimentally impacting our business relations."

It seemed to me that many of the leaks were coming directly from Schwab's office. Little did I know that plugging them was a futile task, but it didn't take me too long to work that out.

Schwab was publicly relaxed about his position, at least according to an interview he gave Hobbs for the Saturday *Herald*. The headline told a different story, perhaps the truth of the matter from Alan's point of view: *SCHWAB: SECOND IS BEST*. Hobbs wrote:

> The morning after the big announcement–and Alan Schwab, the VFL's new executive commissioner, was happy and contented with the decisions of last night. Schwab isn't the top man at the VFL–a position

---

4   Graeme Samuel, interview with the author, 2014.

he sought when Jack Hamilton announced he would retire in October—but he is the next best thing.⁵

It said something about Schwab's carefully nurtured relationship with the football media that the paper's main story the day after the announcement of a new broom for football was more about the future of Schwab than the future of football:

> Despite Oakley's conservative stance with the press regarding his involvement with the VFL [I presume this was code for my reluctance to provide my views at the first press conference], it has been obvious for more than a week that the League would go for both him and Schwab to fill the Hamilton gap.⁶

The article went on:

> Schwab's main role will be in the football area, rather than in the marketing and corporate arena. Schwab, 45, has been lifted in status and salary from his job as the League's executive director. Schwab said today he was happy to be working with Oakley, who he first met at the St Kilda Football Club more than 20 years ago.⁷

And was Oakley happy working with Schwab?

It was simply the hand I was dealt, a situation that I accepted as part and parcel of my new role.

My view would harden over the difficult years ahead. Schwab was difficult, sometimes obstructionist, occasionally undisciplined and always political. He was prone to leak for his own purposes, and sometimes played for his own power and advantage, but he had a great love and passion for the game that endeared him to many in football. Sheahan commented, "Schwabby was very smart, he played people very well, he was charming to the right people, but I did not have the same level of respect for him that some others did."⁸

---

5   Greg Hobbs, "Schwab: second is best", *The Herald*, 16-17 August 1986.
6   Ibid.
7   Ibid. As previously stated, I was actually 43, not 45.
8   Mike Sheahan, interview with the author, 2014.

Jeff Browne, whose legal advice to the League over many years was invaluable and who had worked very closely with Schwab on the rules, had another slant on the situation. He told me recently:

> I was quite close to Schwabby. I enjoyed working on those early projects with him, and he was upset to miss the top job, but you made this arrangement you were thrown into, work. Schwabby was up for a fight, but you never let that happen by keeping the relationship clearly on a professional basis.
>
> I believe that Alan eventually understood the value of someone with commercial business experience in the chair and he then got more comfortable in his role with football and I don't think in the end he resented it, because he was more than comfortable working on the footy side of the business. He loved his footy mates, but was not so comfortable with sponsors and commercial deal-making. The business evolved beyond the way he was used to doing things, almost outgrew him in a sense; when you arrived the old boys' club was dead.[9]

Scanlon also recently related: "While Schwabby made it difficult for Ross early in the piece, it did not take long for Alan to recognise that the sort of work Ross started to do was miles away from what he could do or contemplate. Schwabby told me that he had had no idea what the top job really involved."[10]

When Tony Peek arrived in 1989 to replace Mike Sheahan as the League's media director, he found that "Schwabby understood clubs and he understood footy and the rules, he knew how the clubs would try to rort them if he left loopholes. He understood recruiting and the culture of clubs, what makes them tick, and he was generally pretty well regarded around the clubs. I found him good to work with on club issues and comfortable with his situation. He would often talk about his time at Richmond. However, he should not have developed a liking for wine—this was an issue for him."[11]

---

9   Jeff Browne, interview with the author, 2014.

10   Peter Scanlon, interview with the author, 2014.

11   Tony Peek, interview with the author, 2014.

By way of example, Peek relates an incident when Schwab was in Perth and Peek got a call from a Perth journalist, who said, "I wonder if you could comment on what is reported in Perth today that there would be a second team from WA next year."

Peek was aware that there had been discussion around the commission table but no definitive decision had been made:

> I said, "Who are those comments attributed to?" and the reporter said, "Mr Alan Schwab."
>
> I thought, "What the hell do I do here?" Schwabby had been out for a long lunch, got stopped by a journalist and made an off-the-cuff comment. I remember Oakley and other commissioners tearing strips off him for going too far unilaterally.[12]

Schwab very much represented the style of football administration I had been installed to change. I could see the irony, I guess, that I had to change the culture early on in such an awkward partnership.

And to be honest, there was plenty on my plate in those early days besides focusing on building a relationship with Schwab. The Saturday after our official appointment, Hobbs wrote an article on the state of the game for the Saturday *Herald*, saying: "League football is sick. Not dangerously so, but there is still cause for alarm. It is not the fault of retiring commissioner Jack Hamilton. It is the fault of the system. Whether Ross Oakley and Alan Schwab will change the system is the question. I doubt if they will."[13]

A ringing endorsement. I never spoke with Hobbs about this article, but I always wondered where he gained such a negative view.

There was supposed to be a transition period now, a time of handover between my appointment on 15 August and Hamilton's departure after the Grand Final. I imagined it would be a period in which Hamilton and I would spend a good deal of time together. I was keen to get my head around the issues of the game, to gain an insider's perspective and hopefully

---

12   Ibid.
13   Greg Hobbs, in *The Herald*, 16-17 August 1986.

benefit from the knowledge and experience of the man I was replacing. He had been part of the League's administration for nigh on 40 years.

It was also important to get a sense of the strengths and weaknesses of the staff I was inheriting. Certainly I would form my own views and set out my own expectations, but I thought a "sneak preview" would be of benefit, not just to me but to ensure continuity for the staff, many of whom had worked for Hamilton's VFL for all their time in the game.

What a fantasy. Between my appointment and Hamilton's departure there were only two meetings of any consequence, including a visit to Melbourne's Channel Seven headquarters in which I thought I'd be an observer watching the negotiations of a new TV rights deal. That turned out to be a joke: Hamilton threw me into the deep end of negotiations with station chief Ron Casey without any warning or preparation.

He had set it up perfectly, saying, "I'm going down to see Ronnie Casey at Channel Seven to talk about the television rights, and Peter Scanlon's coming with me. Why don't you come along and just sit in?"

I said, "That'd be good. Thanks very much."

We drove down to Seven's studios in South Melbourne and there was a bit of chit-chat backwards and forwards with Casey, who was a close mate of Hamilton's. Then Hamilton said, "Well, Ross, you're going to be the new CEO—why don't you negotiate with Ron?"

I stumbled around talking about the new expanded League with much increased TV airtime and greater interest in both Queensland and Western Australia, but it was not my finest hour. Scanlon soon jumped in to get us back to the point where the negotiations had been left after a previous meeting.

This was typical of Hamilton, an old Collingwood full-back in action: try out the new guy, make him squirm. I could see his mind ticking away.

Other than that, the transition was unremarkable: there was no transition.

Jeff Browne had a good insight into Hamilton's personality early in Browne's involvement with the League. At the time, Richmond player Maurice Rioli wanted to move to the Swans. He was told that was not possible, and his Perth-based management company proceeded to take out an injunction against the League.

Browne accompanied Hamilton to Perth to deal with it. Hamilton, according to Browne, was not too taken by the young lawyer; he saw Browne as a smart-arse, a new kid in town, and was barely able to put up with him. Browne tells the story:

> As we got off the plane in Perth there were cameras everywhere and Jack and I made our way to chambers without comment. The judge, Mr Justice Muirhead, was extremely well respected. The case was going against us and I tried to condition Jack to a potential loss. I told him, "Jack, I think we are still OK, but we must understand that these cases can easily turn against you. If we do lose we can go back to chambers and talk about an appeal."
>
> Jack just grunted, but when it was clear we were going to lose I said, "When you get outside, do not say anything to the press about the case or the result in order not to inflame the situation. We will go back to chambers and discuss our next move." When we got outside, the media asked Jack if he had any comment, and he said, through gritted teeth, "I've got absolutely nothing to say about the decision of his honour Mr Justice Dickhead."
>
> Then he looked over at me and said, "I didn't say a thing. I did exactly what you told me." It was all about his and my relationship—he took my advice, but not really.[14]

Hamilton had a deserved round of farewell and salutation. When a man serves 10 years at the peak of an organisation as complex as the VFL, he richly deserves at least the plaudits of all in football. He had developed a strong bond with the small but powerful media elite through the Melbourne metropolitan dailies. Hamilton was never a man to leak, but he was always happy to confirm or deny on background.

---

14   Jeff Browne, interview with the author, 2014. Maurice Rioli never played for the Sydney Swans: his hoped-for move was quashed by salary-cap restrictions. He remained with Richmond until the end of the 1987 season, when he returned to his original club, South Fremantle, as captain in 1988 and 1989.

Writing in *The Herald*, Michael Lovett seemed a little wide of the mark when he analysed Hamilton's swansong: "Unlike most company directors who count down the time to retirement day with a series of farewell lunches [and] dinners and, understandably, slacken their workload, the VFL will get its pound of flesh right up until October 10."[15]

The fact was that when I took over in October I had to deal with the new club licences, TV rights (with a good deal of help from Scanlon and Samuel), League sponsorship and the airline agreement. The "real" world of football—the game itself—couldn't keep the off-field events out of the papers. While Queensland and Western Australia were firming as the first unique interstate entries to the League, the powers that be in South Australia were comfortable that a delayed entry into the VFL would not detrimentally harm their long-term cause. They were probably right. Earlier on Schwab had tried to get Port Adelaide involved as the SA entrant through the back door—a move Scanlon says was backed by the commission, but it probably put SA's entry back several years. More on this in the next chapter.

None of these changes would be simple. A handful of the Victorian clubs were determined to resist a WA entry, and there was no ground available in Brisbane for any of the still-battling consortiums to field a team. Teething problems, to be sure. Before September was done, North Melbourne's Bob Ansett would be warning in the media that "A Kerry Packer-type entrepreneur will move into football and form a breakaway league unless the VFL decides to expand the competition."[16]

Hawthorn claimed a notable victory over Carlton in the Hawks' fourth straight Grand Final, and I accepted an invitation from *The Herald* to pen a piece under my own name for the paper's Monday afternoon Grand Final supplement. I wrote:

> For the people charged with the responsibility of determining the future of the game all of us love and cherish, the coming months are

---

15   Michael Lovett, in *The Herald*, 1986.
16   Quoted in *The Herald*, 25 September 1986.

of unparalleled importance.

I believe that it is fair to say that all of us who hold the game dear would like nothing better than to have the competition in exactly the same form as we knew it in the not too distant past, when there was stability of clubs, about public support, about dominance of the minority of clubs at the expense of the majority.

Sadly, those days have passed.

The VFL Commission's extensive research and analysis clearly shows that changes need to be made, that no-change is not an option.[17]

It was something of a manifesto, an important statement two days before a commission vote on the future composition of the competition. That vote would come down to the wire, the League remaining divided over a key element of its future. The healing and the moving forward—well, they would be my problem.

Ready for the challenge, I moved into the big office at the top of VFL House. The task was made difficult by the vacuum Hamilton left in his wake. Not an administrative vacuum in the allegorical sense: there was hardly a thing left in his office, nor in his adjoining filing room. Not a file, not a handover note, not a dossier. No copies of past TV or sponsorship contracts (I'm not sure there ever was a TV contract as such). Actually there was a dossier of sorts filled with the names and CVs of the candidates for my job with comments on their appropriateness. Interesting. Otherwise, a completely clean slate.

How was I to operate when I didn't know where I was starting from?

I sat down and ranged though what I thought would be my priorities and then spoke to Schwab to get some files from him on those matters with which he was able to help me, as he kept good records.

Brenda Testro was Hamilton's PA, and the commission was keen for me to retain her because she knew her way around the issues that were current at the time.

---

17 Ross Oakley, "The season over, the work begins", *The Herald*, 29 September 1986.

I did not hit it off with Brenda; she was one of the old school. I soon found out this was not going to be a long-term relationship when I asked her to do some copying for me in the room next to mine and she rang down to the typing pool (yes, the typing pool) to ask one of the "girls" to come upstairs and do it. The relationship soon ended, as do many new CEO and PA relationships after a change of boss—it is a very personal relationship, and the chemistry must be right.

I asked around the office for advice as to who on the staff could be my executive assistant and received from people like Mike Sheahan and Greg Durham the best advice possible: get Ros Desmond.

Ros stayed with me for my 10 years and was more than a right hand: she was a gatekeeper extraordinaire. She also ran all the commission lunches at matches and other events during the week and managed the commissioners extremely well, particularly the challenging Albert Mantello when he arrived several years later. Nothing was a problem for Ros. She made my job a good deal easier than it might have been.

Ros commented recently:

> I look back now and realise my 10 years with Ross was a very significant period in the history of the AFL. People were very passionate about their football and many resisted the changes to the national competition and were unsure of what it would mean for them. I have many memories of people calling the office in tears because their team was to merge with another, begging the administration to reconsider. Then there were the many abusive calls, sometimes using very colourful language. Had it not been for some hard decisions made by the commission, the national competition would no doubt be very different from what we have today.[18]

---

18 Ros Desmond, interview with the author, 2014. When I resigned in 1996, Ros spent a short time as EA to Wayne Jackson and then found herself in the marketing department. She now works as EA to Jeff Kennett—another challenging role!

CHAPTER 10

A faltering start to a national competition

It'd be fair to say there was a bit to do. The football world was soaking up another Hawthorn premiership, Jack Hamilton was going quietly into the good night of retirement, and I was at his old, large and disconcertingly empty desk.

It wouldn't stay empty for long. Between October and February I needed to complete a reasonably daunting to-do list. Top items: finalise negotiations for the entry of two new clubs into the VFL, resolve the airline agreement and the League's TV rights, and find a major sponsor. As well as keeping the existing clubs afloat, there was work still to be done on the club licensing agreements, particularly fine-tuning the new clubs' agreements; on the salary cap, which, although in play, still had plenty of issues to be resolved; and on the draft, the first of which was to be held just after my arrival.

Alan Schwab had his own share of big jobs to tackle, not the least of which was the match fixure for 1987, which could not be completed until the new teams were finalised. There were also rule adjustments to be made, particularly regarding the salary cap and player rules to provide the new teams with competitive lists, and of course the first draft, which was designed to even up the competition, needed to be organised.

October began with the commission standing firm against a bid by a company called Hecron to acquire the Fitzroy Football Club for $2.6 million.[1] Fitzroy's woes had been constant, and getting worse through the 1980s, as they lurched from one poor decision to another. On-field 1986 had been a good year, with the club making the preliminary final, but off-field the situation remained as it had been when the commission met the club's board the previous December and told the club there were three possibilities for it to continue in the long term. The description of Fitzroy's options is a great insight into the difficult times:

(a) to trade out of its current critical position—which was not possible;

(b) to find a "fairy godmother"—this was a possibility;

(c) to merge with another club—this also was a possibility.[2]

By September 1986, nine months later, Hecron had emerged as the "fairy godmother", willing to offer $2.6 million to take control of Fitzroy. The commission remained firmly of the view that the licence fee payable by interstate clubs ($4 million) was required here, too, and that $2 million of that fee would be payable to the other clubs and $2 million would go to paying down debt. Despite an emotional appeal by Fitzroy director Leon Wiegard at the board meeting of 1 October (Hamilton was still in the chair, with me watching on as the chair-in-waiting) that rejection would "effectively eliminate Fitzroy from the VFL competition",[3] the directors stood by the commission's recommendation—an indication of the growing support for not just the commission's independence, but its growing respect among the clubs.

In principle there was no problem with agreement on the expansion of the League, although all sorts of permutations and combinations had been proffered, considered and repositioned during emotional debates at the table (including a Richmond proposal to play 11 games in Brisbane in 1987).

---

1   Hecron Ltd, formerly known as Hecla Australia Ltd, was a manufacturer of domestic appliances that for some reason wanted to acquire the Fitzroy Football Club. The company was delisted in 1991.

2   VFL Commission minutes, 9 December 1985.

3   VFL Board minutes, 1 October 1986.

A FALTERING START TO A NATIONAL COMPETITION

Eventually consensus was reached to expand the competition by two in line with the recommendations of the Blue Report and the subsequent report of the commission, with the clubs more or less agreeing that expansion was not only inevitable but the only way forward. Maybe not desirable, but inevitable.

What enthusiasm there was was not so much for the introduction of new members to the VFL family; it was more for the licence-fee cash that would follow. That would be $4 million from each of the two new teams proposed, to be divided among the 12 existing teams. It was the whiff of cash, in fact, that proved decisive—a real vote swinger.

The commission proposed that the two clubs Brisbane and West Coast should be admitted. Such a move needed a two-thirds majority vote of the VFL Board, which came at that 1 October meeting, although nothing like certainty had been reached as to the ownership of each, or, in the case of the Brisbane venture, where the team would be playing in season 1987. The commission's original recommendation for the Brisbane licence was for a consortium led by sports promoter John Brown and including impresarios Kevin Jacobsen and Michael Edgley to run the club. This was later withdrawn, and the offer made to a co-venture between the Queensland Australian Football League (QAFL) and a group headed by actor Paul Cronin; this would later morph into the entity led by Christopher Skase and Qintex that launched the club at Carrara in 1987.

The original intention had been to bring in a South Australian club rather than the West Australians, but the process had faltered—in part because of the licence fee required, which the South Australian National Football League (SANFL) rejected while requesting that a possible inclusion in 1988 be left on the table. In fact, in one of my first meetings as chairman, Alan Schwab and I met with SANFL vice-president Bob Lee and general manager Leigh Whicker to discuss the possibility of a composite club playing in the VFL from 1988, and also—in rather a bizarre twist, in retrospect—whether the SA club could be a relocated VFL club. The minutes record the moment: "In response to a question from Mr Lee, it was advised that the VFL could probably favour the relocation of a VFL club to South Australia but would not openly encourage it."[4]

The Brisbane vote passed without too much fuss. The clubs were relatively relaxed about a new club in a new VFL territory—no threat, and plenty of cash to share. When it came to West Coast, the wheels ran off the rails. Remember that WA was a traditional football territory that had been a long-term talent feeder to the VFL. Among some clubs there was not unreasonable anxiety that with its own club in the competition, the flow of skilled players from the west would dry to something less than a trickle and the West Coast side would become an unbeatable, talent-heavy colossus with an entire state's rich football resource to draw on.

As Graeme Samuel recalls it, it was Hawthorn's Ron Cook that broke ranks:

> As we got to the meeting, Ron Cook started a rearguard action to stop the admission of West Coast. And part of the thing in admitting the Eagles was that they had to be given some concessions round recruitment—we had to guarantee a certain amount of success if the process was going to work.
>
> Cook was totally opposed to this. There was to be a vote, and it was looking like it was going to go down. I remember sitting there beside Jack, and the vote was looking like it would be seven-five, and that would mean defeat.
>
> As they were talking around the table, I passed a note to Jack. "Jack, adjourn the meeting"—we needed time. He looked at it and said to the meeting, "Look, can we have an adjournment for a short moment?" So we adjourned.
>
> And then Peter Scanlon and I took Leon Wiegard aside; Leon was opposed at that stage. His club, Fitzroy, was in deep trouble. We said, "Leon, look, if you vote with this, you will get an additional $192,000." I remember vividly the number. "You'll get an additional $192,000 out of it to deal with your immediate loan-guarantee problem." This would

---

4   Minutes of VFL/SANFL meeting, 20 October 1986.

be on top of the licence-fee share clubs would receive, which was $666,000.

We came back into the room, and Jack said, "Right, we're now going to put the matter to a vote." We won by one vote, because Leon voted with us. Well, Cook went berserk. He said, "You bastards! You've bought Wiegard!"[5]

Speak to Wiegard about that night and you get a slightly different take: it was a strategic play by Fitzroy, who saw the merit in supporting the expansion. First and foremost that merit was financial. Fitzroy held back its vote on the West Coast admission not because it objected: the Lions were simply in pursuit of advantage, to see what a little time and pressure might bring for the struggling club.

As Wiegard recalls it:

We went to that meeting with two thoughts in mind: one, it would be good to have the money; and two, we'd better not chuck the moment away, because there might be something we can do, some way to turn it to our advantage. And no one knew what the numbers were going to be.

We voted against it to see what would happen, and sure enough the votes got to seven-five. They then called a suspension and we got some assurances from the VFL about our guarantees on loans for a period of time—three or four years, which we thought would take us into the period of the new development of the funding thanks to an expanded League and licensing.

So that was the whole philosophy. It beat selling raffle tickets.[6]

In part, the West Coast Eagles can thank the faltering fortunes of the Fitzroy Football Club and the decision of the board to turn its back on Hecron for their presence in national football, although the allure of the licence fee would surely have seen the vote turn eventually. That's how the west was won—not through high-minded dedication to the notion

---

5   Graeme Samuel, interview with the author, 2014.
6   Leon Wiegard, interview with the author, 2014.

of a national league, but through the ongoing strength of narrow vested interests and the power of money.

Still, we now had League agreement for the entry of two new teams: the West Coast Eagles and the Brisbane Bears. All we had to do now was negotiate the fine detail and secure the licence fees. That would take some doing, seeing the two clubs already knew they were in. There were so many details to put to bed: Brisbane's first ground option was Boondall, a northern suburb of Brisbane, then Chandler Arena to the east (the commission "did not view the Gabba as a long-term proposal"[7]) and finally Carrara; then the colours, with their initial offering of blue and yellow rejected; then discussion about the quality of players offered by the other clubs to the new franchise; and then the inclusion of Skase in the consortium—and importantly, the money was late and the League had decreed a late interest fee be paid.

The Eagles arrangement was a little easier to manage, although it did come as something of a surprise to me to note that the West Australian Football League (WAFL) had apparently onsold the sub-licence to Indian Pacific Limited (IPL) for $5.6 million, pocketing a nice little windfall of $1.6 million on the way through for the somewhat destitute local clubs. Also on the table was an understanding that should a second licence be issued in WA, IPL had the rights to offer 50 per cent of any shares on offer to the public.

One rather interesting stipulation on each licence agreement was that the League would settle on the fee of $4 million, but the interstate clubs would be liable for their own travel expenses. Yep—join our competition for $4 million, fly to play from the furthest corners of the continent, but pay your own way. *But* only as part of the deal the League had struck with its airline partner.

After some difficult negotiations they bought it, funnily enough.

---

7 VFL Commission minutes, 10 November 1986.

A FALTERING START TO A NATIONAL COMPETITION

With all this in play around Christmas, and the new season looming, the pressure was on. Garry Linnell's book *Football Ltd* gives a sense of the politics whirling around VFL House in my first months in charge:

> The lead-up to Christmas 1986 had hardly been a season of good cheer for the League. Its new commissioner, Ross Oakley, was in the sights of several club leaders. Ian Collins and Ron Joseph were two administrators querying Oakley's credentials and track record. A new airlines agreement had only just been reached and the television rights controversy was about to break.[8]

Air travel was going to be a bigger and bigger part of football, but back in 1986 I'm not sure we could have imagined just how big. The airlines agreement was not too complicated: could they meet the growing complexity of travel times, what discount would they provide for our seats, and how many complimentary tickets would they provide to reduce head-office overheads.

Of necessity, the 1986 three-year deal with Australian Airlines (later to become Qantas) had been a fast-track renewal done in the VFL house style because of the short timeframe available to us before the 1987 season. However, I wanted to make a point during the negotiations leading into the 1989 deal: I wanted a simple open tender process to apply, not the usual "nod and wink" approach. We called for tenders in August 1989. Wally Mariani at Australian Airlines was nonplussed: before I arrived he'd been given a second chance to undercut the bid from Australian's rival, Ansett. Not this time. I made it very clear to the bidding parties that there would be no second dip.

Samuel had been to see Tom Derry at Ansett to convince him that things were being done differently under the new regime and that he could tender without being gazumped. Derry agreed to speak to me and by the end of our meeting was convinced that he would be given a fair chance. The contract eventually went to Ansett, but that didn't stop Australian Airlines from asking for a second dip despite my advice to the contrary and, when it was

---

8   Garry Linnell, *Football Ltd: The Inside Story of the AFL*, Ironbark, 1995, p. 230.

not provided, becoming quite upset at the change in arrangements. Albert Mantello, who had a very good relationship with Mariani, approached me and queried my new approach, saying he felt it was not maximising our deal.

No—things had changed. No more second-dipping, and maybe less first-class contra! I had again made my point on the way I wanted commercial processes around the League to run.

The to-do list was ticking over, more or less. This was a different world for me, though. It's hard to imagine, until it happens, the effect of constant public pressure and scrutiny on your public and private life. My wife and children found it difficult to see their husband and father in the news every day surrounded by the usual media negativity.

Running football is a political activity like few others. It is a job with various constituencies who have great divisions in their interests and expectations. Being the head of the VFL Commission created a pressure I'd never known, with all the expectations of the greater public and the need to be accountable outside of the organisation. And the pace was hectic—it was a seven-day-a-week job. I had run corporations with three times the financial turnover of the VFL, but in these early days I harboured some concern over whether I could manage and grow this high-profile business of football, a cultural phenomenon so important to so many people in our community, and one under more scrutiny, in many ways, than the government.

As it transpired, the business part was not to be my real risk (it would eventually grow exponentially)—it was more about whether I could personally cope. Was I mentally strong enough to run this business and meet all the demands of the fans, the clubs, the corporates and, surrounding all those, the media, 14 hours a day, seven days a week? There was no respite.

This was all new to me. While I had some media experience, it had been nothing like what I now had to face. Unlike politics, there was no honeymoon period. From that first press conference and those pointed questions, it was unrelenting. Everyone needs mental downtime—time to switch off, time away from the coalface—but this business did not allow it, and still doesn't.

There were, and remain, hundreds of members of the media all trying to find or indeed create a football story to meet their deadlines. Unless you actually occupy the job, it is impossible to imagine or foresee the pressure and stress that builds and accumulates in such circumstances. By the end of December in that first year, I was deep into it. As Mike Sheahan recalls, "It was always full on, always a sense—not of crisis, but of never knowing when you walked in the door of the place what would be on that day, where the problem would be."[9]

Tony Peek found it much the same: "When I arrived at the VFL in August 1989 I was immediately struck by the hectic pace of life and the constant phone calls at home. What these young guys today don't realise is that we ran this business with fewer than 60 people and only four on the executive team—Ross, Greg Durham, Schwabby and me, with Kevin Lehmann (finance) and Ian Collins (football) replacing Greg and Alan in the early 1990s. We had no money and we were making groundbreaking decisions every day."[10]

The commissioners were extremely helpful to me, particularly Graeme Samuel, who was able to give me a lot of his time. I had a dearth of top executives with his corporate capabilities on my staff, so I would have been struggling without his assistance.

The commission worked on a consensus basis, and I'm not sure we ever had a vote. We functioned well together and understood where each of us was coming from—and not just that first commission, but every group I worked with. Scanlon later confessed: "I was a little frustrated during those times because you had no management support and as a result you used Graeme to bounce things off, as he was readily available. You would then come to the meetings with strategies and ideas that another commissioner had basically approved, which left me in a 'reviewer' capacity for ideas that had pretty much already been decided."[11]

I can certainly understand Scanlon's feelings on this point, but he

---

9   Mike Sheahan, interview with the author, 2014.
10 Tony Peek, interview with the author, 2014.
11 Peter Scanlon, interview with the author, 2014.

underestimates the value of the creative ideas he contributed to the table. My actions were a function of the time and level of expertise I had available to me on staff; I had to use those non-staff experts who were readily available to me.

Frustrations? Well, that brings us to Christopher Skase.

The entry of the Brisbane Bears to the League had been complex—what in the world of football wasn't?

A pattern of entrepreneurs believing they could make a pile out of new or old footy clubs was developing here: first Edelsten, then Skase; Alan Bond and Richmond would also enjoy a brief flirtation in 1987. This was the late 1980s, and for the entrepreneur who had pretty much everything, a football club gave profile, presence and a sense of flamboyance. My encounters with Skase were a window into the fast-money world of the times, in which very little was as it seemed.

The hard work had been done—assessment of the various syndicates with changing members, changing locations for the team, the QAFL in, then out—and we eventually got the Brisbane deal to the stage of launching the club and, importantly, payment of the licence fee. The function was in Brisbane; Skase was going to speak and the media was going to be there in force. It was a big moment—the creation of a new entity in Australian Football, the bridging of a geographic and cultural divide, a bold foray deep into enemy territory.

At this stage we hadn't seen any of the $4 million licence fee. What were we thinking? That Skase would pay on time? Obviously launching the team officially in advance of the payment was putting the cart before the horse.

I called Skase ahead of the event and said, "You've got to give me the $4 million before we announce this to the media, otherwise it's just not happening."

He was ready for that: "Don't worry—I want to make it a feature of the launch."

Well, that did sound plausible.

On the day, Skase spoke and then called me to the podium. "And we have here the chairman of the commission, Ross Oakley. Ross, I'd like you to say a few words, and I'd like to hand over the licence fee."

I took the envelope, we shook hands and the camera flashes went off and the motor drives whirred. I was keen to show the cheque because it would make a great newspaper photo, so I began opening the envelope.

Skase leaned across. "Gentlemen don't open envelopes in public," he whispered. Well, OK. Weird, but fair enough, I thought. I put the envelope into my inside pocket and went on with my speech.

The first opportunity I had, I raced out to the toilet and ripped the envelope open.

Empty. Nothing in there at all.

So I've made the announcement that he's won the licence, and we haven't got our $4 million. I informed Mike Sheahan on the plane on the way home and he couldn't believe what had happened. An empty envelope! How could a person who wanted to do business with you do such a thing?

It took another month and a few sleepless nights, but we did get the cheque in the end.

CHAPTER 11

The television rights dilemma

We were moving through turbulent waters slowly but surely with the West Coast and Brisbane teams. The League had locked in the money at least—two licence fees worth $8 million, to be shared equally by the 12 clubs.

That left plenty on the to-do list with both new clubs—but there was also a pressing urgency to resolve the issue of TV rights. There was no point combing the office for the just-lapsed contract with Channel Seven Melbourne: there wasn't one. Like so much in football, the deal was not put to paper—or at least if it was, I couldn't find it. The rights arrangement for the telecast of VFL football, held from the beginning of TV by Seven in one form or another (and other stations at various times), seemed to have been done on a handshake.

It was a baffling state of affairs even then, and astounding now when you reflect on the significance of rights agreements across a range of modern media in the financial structuring of football. Nothing could be more important, particularly in that first season of the national competition.

Back then, it was just another handshake between mates. The mates in this $3 million equation had been Ron Casey at Seven and Jack Hamilton, and it seemed like good money for the time. But the deal had expired. Times had changed. The game was getting bigger and the commission wanted more.

Casey was what you might politely call "larger than life". He'd begun his media career in the 1940s as a panel operator at radio 3DB and ended up behind the microphone, becoming a caller of all sorts of sports. His most famous radio moment came in 1968 during a live call from Japan of Lionel Rose defeating Masahiko 'Fighting' Harada for the world bantamweight title. Casey joined HSV7 in 1956 and hosted the legendary *World of Sport* for 28 years. He was just as impressive off camera, becoming studio manager of HSV7 in 1969 and general manager from 1972 until 1987, at which time the station was sold to the Fairfax Group.

TV rights deals with the VFL were Casey's jealously guarded domain. Gary Fenton, Casey's close confidant, had been with Seven since 1969 and was program director of HSV7 from 1976 to 1991; he produced *World of Sport* in the early 1970s and later created the ever-popular *Talking Footy*, which was fronted by Bruce McAvaney and put Mike Sheahan on TV for the first time. In a recent conversation Fenton told me, "Casey was a good bloke—in fact, more than a good bloke—but would play his cards close to his chest, particularly on VFL rights. But then there is nothing wrong with that."[12]

Responding to a comment that there was a view in the football world that HSV7 had gained the rights cheaply, Fenton angrily denied this and said that whoever held that view just did not appreciate how difficult it was to gain national coverage for the VFL at the time. He explained:

> Casey would buy the football television rights from the VFL and then provide them to Seven's Adelaide station, ADN, and also sell them to his Sydney affiliate, ATN, and Brisbane's BTQ, owned by Fairfax. I was at every network meeting between 1976 and 1996 and saw first hand how hard Casey had to work with Ted Thomas, the manager of ATN. He would say, "Ted, we have renewed the VFL rights and we were

---

12 Gary Fenton, interview with the author, 2014.

> hoping that ATN would take the Sydney rights." Ted would hold him to ransom, saying, "Nobody in Sydney cares about the VFL." And then inevitably after some time Ted would add: "Well, I've got the World 18ft Sailing Championships and the Sydney to Hobart, so if I take the VFL you will have to take these two events."[13]

Other than to tell Fenton in casual conversation that Channel Seven had won the rights again, Casey never discussed the contract with him. Fenton reflected: "Casey would wander into my office in the morning and strike up a conversation about one of the programs on air the night before and then, almost as an aside, would say, 'I have renewed the VFL rights'."[14]

Further, Fenton confirmed he could not find a VFL TV contract when he went looking for it as part of the due-diligence process required during the Fairfax takeover—which supports my contention that one never existed.

Back to late 1986. The most recent of the Casey-crafted three-year deals had run down and the VFL had no broadcaster for the 1987 season—a season that would be remarkable as it would see the first clubs added to the League since 1925, when Footscray, Hawthorn and North Melbourne had been admitted. Presumably, negotiations had been delayed to see if the expansion vote would be won. Under these difficult circumstances I was determined to get an increased offering from Seven.

It stood to reason: the competition was raising its national profile, and while Seven was a Melbourne broadcaster, it already on-sold the rights to interstate affiliates. Surely new teams would make this a more attractive and lucrative proposition?

I've mentioned my introduction to the negotiation process—a Jack Hamilton prank that left me stumbling for words. I held the reins now and was ready for my first meeting with Casey. I was fully briefed and up to speed this time—or as briefed and up to speed as I could be without the benefit of any sort of paperwork recording the previous agreement.

---

13   Ibid.
14   Ibid.

Casey's response stunned me: "I'm going to offer you $3.4 million next year." That was it: a 13 per cent increase. No way.

"Well, that's unacceptable," I told him. "Totally unacceptable, given the expanded competition." Casey just gave me a "take it or leave it" shrug.

I told him again: "It's unacceptable."

He said, "OK, well, in two weeks—Friday, two weeks—if you don't accept it, the deal's back to last year's $3 million."

I told him to forget it and that we would be putting it out to tender, and walked out. Casey was full of confidence, but I decided to call his bluff. Just because the VFL rights had traditionally been with Seven didn't mean they had to stay that way. The commission needed an increase because a large part of the justification for going national was increased TV rights money.

I quickly arranged meetings with the local offices of Nine and Ten. There was tremendous initial interest from them—"Oh shit, we've got a chance?" "Yeah, you sure have"—but within a week both networks came back and said their head office wasn't interested.

I was puzzled, to put it mildly. "You're not interested in the VFL when we're expanding to a national format?" Nope. Pass. No interest at all.

I was beginning to suspect that somewhere between Casey's quite unnatural overconfidence and the total lack of interest from his competitors that the fix was in. He made contact, still full of beans, and told me we'd dithered too long. His deadline was up and the offer from Seven was now back to the previous figure of $3 million. How could he be so confident? There was no doubt that football was a big thing for Seven, especially in Melbourne. To lose the rights would do tremendous commercial damage to them, and yet here he was bargaining as if Seven was in an unassailable monopoly position.

The reason was becoming clear to me: there was a "keep off the grass" (KOTG) deal between the TV networks. They'd divvied up the sports-rights possibilities between them in the sort of handshake-between-the-lads deal that was so typical in football. This explained the quick turnaround in attitude from Nine and Ten when the right people were consulted. It also explained why Casey thought he could squeeze down the VFL price with impunity.

When asked about the existence of a KOTG agreement, Fenton said, tongue firmly in cheek, "If there was such an agreement, it was broken so often it didn't matter, and it certainly wouldn't have impacted the VFL agreement."[15] The lack of traction I achieved from the other stations would tend to contradict this claim, although it was true Sydney television management had yet to really embrace football.

It was a head-in-hands moment for me. We had to put our thinking caps on at the commission, and for a moment I felt my lack of industry knowledge keenly. I didn't have the contacts, the resources or the background to do the backroom work between football and the loosely formed networks of the time. I was up against it with the year ticking away and the hugely significant season of 1987 bearing down.

Contract negotiations continued through October and I reported to the commission that tender documents were being prepared for distribution to stations during November. I suggested we should look at a shorter contract period as a result of the changing face of the competition and the media.

The tender documents were duly sent out, with a deadline for return of 27 November. On 1 December I reported to the commission that Channel 10 and Channel Nine were not tendering and that Channel Seven and the ABC had concerns with the tender conditions. Indeed, Seven had indicated "that unless the proposed tender documents were capable of amendment then HSV7 would not tender for television broadcast rights".[16] There was a lot of head-scratching around the commission table, and not only was I looking to rekindle interest with the networks on pretty much any permutation and combination of rights, "it was further agreed that Mr P. Scanlon should make preliminary contact with Mr K. Packer, head of the National Nine Network, with a view to cultivating Mr Packer's interest in this opportunity to become involved in a major Australian sporting enterprise on the basis that the League would appreciate the network's assistance in improving the

---

15 Ibid.
16 VFL Commission minutes, 1 December 1986.

coverage and promoting the game nationally".[17] The way those words were couched will tell you that we were hardly in the driver's seat.

Two options did come forward: one was from Sportsplay, a production and packaging company that provided live sports to pubs via satellite TV (and was interconnected with the web of companies behind the Sydney Swans), and the other came via Peter Scanlon. He said, "Look, there's a mob I know called Broadcom. It's a wholesaler. If we get them involved, they can do all the work—they know everyone in the industry."

I said, "Get 'em in."

I didn't know it then, but all hell was about to break loose, not just with the rights and sponsorship deals, but also with all sorts of twisting and turning related to the ownership of Sydney and Brisbane, and the fine details of the WA deal to launch the Eagles. It seemed there was never a day when a new model wasn't presented to us regarding the shareholdings of the Swans, and what was what in WA. Not only that, but we had received advice that the SANFL wanted to join the League from 1988, and a deputation from Norwood Football Club had announced it was interested in joining "at any time in the future" and that a private consortium headed by Ken Eustace was interested in grabbing a licence to field an SA team.

So the next few weeks leading up to Christmas 1986 would be a steep learning curve for me—a lesson in what a public role heading the VFL was, and how deep the web of media networks ran through the football community. These networks could bring a wall of hostile media down on your head if you threatened their interests.

Which was precisely what I was about to do.

Steve Cosser, the principal behind Broadcom, came to my place at Wheelers Hill to discuss Broadcom's possible involvement in the rights deal. Cosser was a man of energy and talent who was chipping his way

---

[17] Ibid. Nothing came of that prospect at the time, but in the middle of 1987 Nine, through Gary Rice and David Hill, did make a significant presentation to the commission that not only included Nine but also Sky Channel and PBL Marketing. Interestingly, Nine was only concerned at that time in broadcasting night matches and Sunday games. See Chapter 13 for more details.

up in the world, from hawking music cassettes door to door[18] to hosting the ABC's flagship radio news program, *PM*, to a brief stint in the early 1980s as the host of an ill-fated Channel 10 show called *The Reporters*. The show flopped but Cosser walked away the richer for it. That money would eventually form the basis of Broadcom, a firm that was later picked up by a significant investment entity, the Linter Group, a business controlled by the AFP Investment Corporation. AFP's deputy chairman was Peter Scanlon, and a Graeme Samuel trust company also had a shareholding. Interestingly, it was a time of disclosure all round: Peter Nixon and Alan Schwab also declared holdings in AFP, "but ... those interests could not properly be regarded as substantial".[19] With all that before us, the rights deal would be decided by me, Dick Seddon, Schwab and Nixon.

Yes, the degrees of separation needed to be pretty finely judged. That said, Scanlon and Samuel absented themselves from all relevant commission discussions and I was confident there was no conflict of interest. But it was important to dot the i's and cross the t's. The eventual deal we struck with Broadcom would be a game changer.

At the commission meeting on 19 December, I reported that Seven had made an offer of $3 million, the same as the previous year. The commissioners were beginning to realise that the fix was in between the various free-to-air stations, and decided that the Seven offer was unacceptable. Broadcom and Sportsplay had both submitted proposals, but the Broadcom deal was far and away the best option, and we would also be pursuing the ABC as a failsafe for the pre-season competition at least.

Cosser sat himself down at my place on a balmy December evening in 1986, a fateful night for football's future. We were about to get real on the issue of TV rights. I sensed he had been well briefed. This was a foundation moment for the modern competition, a point in the progress of the game that is hard to underestimate. Finally we would price the media coverage of Australian football at something close to a national-competition market rate, and we would begin the process of a cash flow that now underpins

---

18   Garry Linnell, *Football Ltd: The Inside Story of the AFL*, Ironbark, 1995, p. 170.
19   VFL Commission minutes, 19 December 1986.

everything in football, from player salaries to the capacity to nurture the game at its grassroots.

The ball was pretty much in Cosser's court. We had no deal, the offer on the table from Seven was paltry, and the other networks seemed closed to us through the strings held by the old-boy networks.

"So, Ross, I hear you've been having some problems," Cosser said. An understatement for his opening.

We talked through how we would break the KOTG agreement by a divide-and-conquer strategy. He knew all the players and was a good negotiator, but the VFL still had to play a role in the negotiations. Cosser was, to say the least, very accommodating and that night we had the bones of a deal that would bring in a minimum of $24.55 million over the next six years. In the first season—the year of national expansion, 1987—Broadcom would provide $3.5m plus an upfront payment of $1.3m, for a total of $5m compared to Channel Seven's $3.4m (before their withdrawal to $3m). There would be even more upside for us if rights monies took off later in the contract period.

This was clearly from left field, and unprecedented. Broadcom was not able to broadcast in its own right but was a packager of content, and had to negotiate with all the networks across all markets. For all that, I had no doubt that Cosser and Broadcom could walk the walk and fulfil all the commitments they had presented to the commission. It was also my view, and subsequently that of the commission, that Broadcom's offer—although the final amount the League would receive was not guaranteed—was better than the $21 million put on the table by Sportsplay over three years. We felt there were too many "what-ifs" in Sportsplay's potential to deal with the networks, something we knew was never going to be easy.

After discussing the two proposals, the commission endorsed Broadcom's on 24 December—yes, Christmas Eve—awarding the company a six-year deal as a joint marketing venture with the VFL and "noting that Broadcom would be responsible for the production, packaging and sale of VFL football to all television interests and satellite networks".[20] The only downside was that Broadcom could not deliver a Melbourne broadcaster. It could sell the game around the country, but locally we'd still need to deal with Seven Melbourne, we thought. Discussion—brief discussion, I might add—also considered the potential of the VFL producing and packaging its own TV arrangements.

That evening I called Casey and let him know we'd sold the rights to someone else. He insisted on knowing who. I said, "Broadcom, but I do hope Seven can stay involved." Garry Linnell paints a very powerful picture of Casey's response:

> Casey was mystified. Broadcom? The name rang a bell, but only softly. He hung up and walked over to a filing cabinet. There it was. Some young bloke called Cosser had been to see him a few months before, trying to package a weekend business program.
>
> Casey ran his eye down a list of names associated with the company. He saw two familiar ones: Peter Scanlon and Graeme Samuel. He got straight back on the phone to Oakley.
>
> "This is a pretty funny sort of situation," said Casey angrily.
>
> "I know all about Scanlon and Samuel's involvement," replied Oakley. "But they didn't vote."
>
> Casey hung up, seething. That evening on the night before Christmas, he stirred restlessly.[21]

There would be no deal with Seven, though Casey wouldn't go down without a fight. The wheels of the friends of Seven started to turn. Casey's long association with *The Sun* was about to come into play, and the newspaper took up the fight strongly.

We'd picked a pretty big fight with Casey and HSV7 over TV rights and VFL broadcasts. That meant we'd picked a pretty big fight with the Herald and Weekly Times—which, to complicate things further, Rupert Murdoch

---

20 VFL Commission minutes, 24 December 1986.
21 Garry Linnell, *Football Ltd*, 1995, p. 172.

had just acquired, so we'd picked a fight with him as well. In Melbourne media at that time they didn't come much bigger than H&WT, publisher of *The Herald* and *The Sun* and owner of 3DB and HSV7.

But then, was it H&WT and Murdoch we were fighting? Or was there some other dark figure in the frame unbeknown to us?

Fenton tells the story that HSV7 management knew Murdoch was looking to acquire H&WT fairly early in the piece, but also that he would have to on-sell the station. Fenton knew they were in troubled waters. He describes the position:

> When Murdoch bought H&WT in December 1986 he was advised that the broadcasting authority would give him dispensation for a short period of time in order to on-sell Channel Seven to another owner. Casey found himself in a situation where he was virtually in limbo—he basically had no functional owner or board to speak to. Indeed, he was not sure to whom he should report between the time Murdoch acquired H&WT and the station and ultimately when the Fairfax takeover of Seven took place in February.[22]

Then Fenton dropped a bombshell: "Unbeknown to anyone then and now, Murdoch had actually secretly sold the station just before Christmas to an undisclosed buyer. This was despite Fairfax and H&WT having an agreement dating back 20 years that detailed that if either one of them wanted to sell their station, they had to provide a first and last right to acquire the station to the other station. As a result, in February 1987 he had to undo the sale to his secret buyer, because Fairfax threatened to sue him."[23]

So who was this unknown buyer? Fenton tells the story that on Christmas Day he had reason to visit the office and was looking out the window when who should he see but Casey showing a famous media mogul around. It was none other than Robert Holmes à Court who had "bought" the station. But no one knew about it. The sale to Holmes à Court was later

---

22   Gary Fenton, interview with the author, 2014.
23   Ibid.

confirmed by Gerry Carrington, the chief finance officer at Seven, when Fenton asked him what was going on.

Fenton says that during late December 1986, Casey would have been acting under the apparent influence of Holmes à Court in relation to the VFL deal and this was the reason he acted the way he did. It was not Casey's style, he said, to negotiate by holding someone to ransom. Having offered me $3.4m early in December, he had said to Fenton, "They might have to take a cut shortly." That wasn't Casey's style, but the cut was communicated to me.

We went to Christmas with a TV deal, but as with so many of the deals that were swirling about me and the commission, a lot would happen before the switch was flicked to turn on TV's new era.

CHAPTER 12

An interrupted holiday

For a day or two I was happily oblivious to the massive storm brewing about the TV rights. Part of my deal when joining the VFL was that I would take a long-planned two-week family holiday over the Christmas–New Year break. With the Broadcom deal in place and the wheels turning with both the Brisbane Bears and West Coast Eagles, I felt relaxed about stepping out of the office.

The holiday was a bit special, too. I was taking the family on a cruise with friends. We'd booked a beautiful 75ft ketch called *Pingvin* (Swedish for "penguin") that had once been owned by the royal family of Sweden. The heat of the Queensland summer and the sparkling waters of the Whitsundays were calling.

Before I left I had a long talk with Alan Schwab and filled him in on where things were at, but I felt confident that things would be calm enough over the holiday period.

I was delighted with the Broadcom deal. From a position of being held over a barrel by Ron Casey and Seven, it really felt as though the VFL was on the front foot in the TV rights discussion, and the revenue potential was far more attractive than Seven's arrogant offer. More than that, a new model was now in play that would set the scene for an expansionary future based on a growing national rights pool.

Mike Sheahan recalls the shocked faces in the MCG press box at the Test match when we announced the Broadcom deal to the media on Boxing Day. On the eve of my holiday I was reported to have spoken with reporter Martin Blake when he covered the deal for *The Age* (the words were probably ghosted by Sheahan in my absence): "We are moving into a new era with a national football environment and a new media environment and it would have been the wrong thing for football to award the rights to a station like we have in the past."[24]

Blake's piece appeared in *The Age* on Saturday 27 December. It was a measured account, but even he referred to the Broadcom deal as "a slap in the face for the Seven Network". What about *The Sun*, where the Seven Network was family? Well, *The Sun* went to town.

FOOTY TV RIGHTS UPROAR—that was the page-one heading, almost squeezing Pat Cash's Kooyong Davis Cup heroics off the front page.

Almost every paragraph was loaded: "The VFL has awarded its multimillion-dollar TV rights to a Sydney production company in which two VFL commissioners have interests" was the opening of Daryl Timms' report.[25]

"Channel Seven was the only station to tender for the exclusive rights," the *Sun* story trumpeted, ignoring the inadequacy of the Seven bid, "but its offer was rejected in favour of Broadcom—which is a Sydney production and packaging company."[26]

A "Sydney company"—yes, the spirit of football parochialism was alive and well. The suggestion of some sort of commission collusion? That was harder to dismiss. Entirely wrong, but a long way from being a good look the way Timms was telling it.

First quote in the story went to—guess who?—Ron Casey: "The decision to award television rights for the next six years to Broadcom Australia Limited was slammed last night by Channel Seven general manager Ron Casey, who said his station might not televise football next year. He said the

---

24 Martin Blake, "VFL TV rights sold for $24.5m", *The Age*, 27 December 1986.
25 Daryl Timms, "Footy TV rights uproar", *The Sun*, 27 December 1986.
26 Ibid.

VFL had become money crazy and had forgotten about football. Channel Seven has televised the VFL since 1957 and has had exclusive commercial TV rights for seven seasons."[27]

I'd left town the day before, winging it to Hamilton Island to pick up the yacht. Sheahan had placed my quotes into the paper: "VFL Chief Commissioner Ross Oakley said people should not be concerned that commissioners Scanlon and Samuel had interests in the Linter Group. 'It happens every day in the commercial world,' he said. 'There are cross-directorships in business and I've sat on a lot of boards before and constantly I have had directors putting their hands up and saying gentlemen, I must notify you that I have a conflict of interest because I have shares in such and such.'"[28]

Our conscience was as driven snow; as I noted earlier, the commissioners with links to Broadcom had removed themselves from all discussion and decision-making to do with the final outcome. The reality was that it was I who drove the deal, and I who saw all the benefits of the Broadcom relationship and needed Broadcom's help.

To do the *Sun* story credit, the last few paragraphs got right to the point: the Broadcom deal gave us flexibility.

This was a time of great change in the media. Channel Nine was about to be acquired, in a once-in-a-lifetime gift from the Packer family, by Alan Bond. The wrestle for control of the Herald and Weekly Times group had been a daily soap opera, with Rupert Murdoch and Robert Holmes à Court going head-to-head in a deal that would eventually have a considerable impact on the VFL.

The important thing was that allowing Broadcom to on-sell the rights, all to be done in consultation with the League, to many individual stations gave a flexibility to the League that a straight-up sale to Seven would not have achieved—and given what was about to occur with the ownership of HSV7, a business-as-usual deal with Casey would have left us in a hole. As I was quoted in Timms' story, "Obviously we are concerned about

---

27   Ibid.
28   Ibid.

getting locked into a situation where ownership is going to change hands. They might take a different attitude and they might not want football. We believe Broadcom will give us the most flexibility to make the most money. If we don't have that flexibility we won't be able to increase our income."[29]

Prophetic words, given what was about to transpire.

By the time the papers hit the Melbourne streets I was in Hamilton Island. To be honest, there was only so much that could be done about the media reaction to the Broadcom deal. None of the coming hurly-burly would shake my confidence in it, just public perception. In fact, we would be vindicated in very short order indeed.

For now, I wanted to relax and have some decent family time. One thing was certain: the fights and furore of football would still be there when I got back.

We were anchored just off the brilliant-white sandy expanse of Whitehaven Beach; the sun was beaming down, baking the deck, and fish were actually leaping out of the water. It was the closest thing to heaven on earth. But reality was about to strike.

It looked as though the speedboat was moving toward us. Closer and closer—yes, no doubt about it now. Eventually it slowed and pulled beside us. "Is Ross Oakley on board?" the guy behind the wheel called up to us.

It could only be work. I eventually owned up, put a shirt on and made my way back to Hamilton Island—perhaps I would even have to return to Melbourne. Well, not if I could help it.

Back at the resort I hit the phone. Schwab was not a happy man. He was in a bit of a panic, to be honest—and fair enough.

It was now Tuesday morning, and if you read the *Sun*'s front page you could be forgiven for thinking the game was falling apart. War had been declared on several fronts. That was the headline. The paper's prediction was grim: "Football fans are faced with a television blackout of live VFL games next year. The dispute over the VFL television rights has left the ABC

---

29   Ibid.

as the only likely broadcaster of games next season—but it is understood it will only show replays at this stage. And Brisbane Bears syndicate head Paul Cronin warned licences for the Queensland and WA-based teams might have to be reviewed if football was not telecast nationally."[30]

We were on the phone for a couple of hours and by the end of our conversation Schwabby was calmer and more confident. We had the beginnings of a strategy to counter a pretty outrageous press campaign.

The truth is that the Broadcom deal was absolutely in the best interests of the League and the game. And it had saved our bacon. Seven's offer had been absurd, and the other networks were tied down into "keep off the grass" deals. The *Sun*'s story distorted the reality of the relationship—never mind the conflict of interest between the paper and Channel Seven. Yes, there was work to be done, but what was not in the public domain was that Broadcom was really doing what Seven had done for years: on-selling the rights in the best commercial package it could.

Casey sounded off, too. It was "wrong" for the VFL to be dealing with a third party over TV rights, he said. Wrong? Casey's problem was that we'd upset the cosy little apple cart that Seven had been party to for years. "Any money paid for television rights should go to the VFL and not be siphoned off by another party," he said.[31] The hypocrisy of that statement was amazing.

There was blood in the water now, and opponents of the new broom in football were beginning to sense that they could score some easy points. Hawthorn's Ron Cook was being quoted in the media on the basis that he had been the promotions manager of *The Sun* before "astutely" anticipating the government's approval of bingo as a legitimate form of gambling. (He had left the newspaper business to buy up bingo equipment before the approval had been announced, consequently beating the market to the punch.) As Garry Linnell reported it: "Ron Cook, the president of Hawthorn, a former vice-president of the VFL and a football traditionalist, had been sniping at the League for days, mourning the loss of Channel Seven.

---

30   Daryl Timms, in *The Sun*, 30 December 1986.
31   Ibid.

His world was upside down. First there was the decision to go national and allow the Western Australians in. He'd fought a tough fight to prevent that and lost. And now another piece of the game's tradition had gone."[32]

That was so far away from the truth as to be laughable, but Schwab, stuck in unfamiliar territory, didn't see the joke. Neither did I, torn from paradise to discuss events that should have been normal business practice. Nothing in the footy spotlight, however, could ever be considered "normal".

We could see that the League was slowly losing ground in this fight. It was a fight on two fronts: first, to win the public relations battle over the necessity of our new rights structure, and second, to secure a broadcaster for live football in the Melbourne market for the 1987 season. I was sure the first would be no more than the public seeing their game on TV when round one arrived; the second was a tougher task given the intransigence of Seven and the battle for the ownership of the station.

Schwab filled me in on all the newspaper talk in our phone conversation and I indicated what should be said to the clubs (the new clubs, in particular) to water down the impact. I also spoke about the best way to counter the criticism, talking about what our reaction should be and suggesting which of the commissioners in town could make a response on behalf of the commission. I emphasised that we should stick to our agreed approach that the deal was good for football in the long term and vested interests were always likely to react as they were.

On the day Timms' "blackout" story appeared, Graeme Samuel, taking a well-earned break on the Mornington Peninsula, was also sensing the shifting momentum in the PR battle. He made an early call to fellow commissioner Peter Nixon, a man whose capacity to wade into a public stoush and have an impact was the stuff of political legend, and urged him to get involved. Samuel recalls:

> We were losing the fight purely through not getting involved. We were copping a kicking and not kicking back. That just had to stop.
>
> I was down at Frankston and Peter Nixon was in Melbourne, the only

---

32   Garry Linnell, *Football Ltd: The Inside Story of the AFL*, Ironbark, 1995, p. 175.

commissioner around who was capable of speaking to anyone. Ron Casey had just gone absolutely berserk. And not just Ron Casey, but Ron Cook as well. We had to do something.

I called Nixon and said, "Look, Peter, you're the statesman, and the only one in Melbourne at the moment. You go out there and you say what we did and why we did it. We've got to put our side of the story."[33]

Schwab had passed on my thoughts and Nixon hit the phones and offered himself around the media. He sent a strong statement to the TV networks and put in some serious high-level discussions along the newspapers' mahogany row, getting stuck into Cook's position. "I'm very disappointed that Ron Cook has seen fit to criticise the VFL the way he has," Nixon said. "He complains that the clubs haven't been told enough, but there was a meeting before the decision was made that he didn't bother to turn up to. I'm sick and tired of his continued criticism of the commission."[34]

Nixon's intervention was bold. There had been a sense in the football and media worlds that the VFL and its commission were quiet backroom operators, happy to just administer the game and not make any fuss. Well, tough times demanded tough action, and Nixon's attack was a sign of that. We weren't going to simply sit there and take our lumps: the survival and prosperity of the game were at stake here.

It seems Casey took a similar view, but from an opposite perspective. Years later he would recall that Nixon's intervention hardened his resolve not to deal with Broadcom: "We refused to deal with Broadcom. They couldn't get anyone else interested either. I must say I lobbied a bit with the others, although it didn't have anything to do with keep-off-the-grass at all! I saw it as being wrong for there to be an intermediary between football and the broadcasters. I couldn't believe the League had someone to negotiate on their behalf. Nine and Ten agreed."[35]

They all agreed! You bet they did.

It had been a tough tussle, but in the end commercial reality would

---

33 Graeme Samuel, interview with the author, 2014.
34 Peter Nixon, interview with the author, 2014.
35 Quoted in Garry Linnell, *Football Ltd*, 1995, p. 175.

prevail. Wiser and less heated heads within the Herald and Weekly Times group would call a halt to the public feuding and agree to serious negotiation. It may well have helped our cause that H&WT were fighting their own battles concurrent with the blue over football TV rights. As had been prescribed, Murdoch would be forced to cut HSV7 free from H&WT. "A queen of the screen or a prince of print"—that was the choice offered by federal treasurer Paul Keating to media proprietors at the time. We saw it as a very sensible plan given the biased related-entity reporting during the TV wars, and would send our negotiations spinning off in a new direction. But that was, oh, easily two weeks away yet.

For now Nixon had managed, perhaps through family connections with the H&WT chairman, John Dahlsen (he was Peter's wife's cousin), to get a round-table meeting between H&WT, HSV7 and the League upon my return from holidays. We could get down to serious discussion at last.

Nixon, Dick Seddon and I (the only commissioners not conflicted) met in the third-floor boardroom at the Jolimont end of the H&WT headquarters in Flinders Street. The negotiations were tough. Time was obviously against us, with the pre-season competition scheduled to begin in mid-February and the 1987 season being the first as an expanded national league. Before the meeting Casey had approved and then withdrawn a deal to pay $2 million for the Victorian rights in 1987.

In the end—late that night—Seven walked out with a one-year deal for the broadcast rights for Victoria only, for $1.4 million. This did not impact our payments from Broadcom for 1987. Indeed, we were negotiating on behalf of Broadcom, because Casey would not speak with them.

SEVEN WINS FOOTY DEAL was the *Sun*'s headline when it broke the news a couple of days later on 29 January: "VFL Commission Chairman Mr Ross Oakley announced the long-awaited decision yesterday. He would not say how much had been paid, but said the VFL would receive significantly more for the television rights than last season … HSV7 general manager

SAINTS ALL: Great memories of a very happy time with St Kilda, although my opportunity to become a club immortal in 1966 was thwarted when I missed the Grand Final triumph after injuring my knee in second semi-final. As fate would have it, that was my last game of 62. That's me at the start of the second row, with John Bingley on my left. A pretty good crew, this—note the Brownlow medallists Ross Smith and Ian Stewart stuck in the back row, and the great Darrel Baldock and another Brownlow medallist, Verdun Howell, on either side of coach 'Yabby' Jeans.

↑ **GOOD COMPANY:** Getting my kick away as 'Doc' Baldock paves the way, against Collingwood.

→ **HIGH FLYER:** Big leap over Fred Swift, but I can't remember whether it stuck. It certainly stuck in the minds of the marketers at Herbert Adams pies!

← **VISIONARY:** Allen Aylett during his time as president of the VFL. Aylett was perhaps ahead of his time, but left a great legacy that subsequent administrations were able to develop.

↙ **LOGOS:** From the VFL through the early days of the AFL to the logo developed in 1999 under my successor, Wayne Jackson.

↑ **MY FIRST COMMISSIONERS:** One of our regular meetings at Jolimont Road's headquarters. From my left are Alan Schwab, Peter Scanlon, Dick Seddon, Graeme Samuel and Peter Nixon.

RUNNING THE SHOW: Alan Schwab and I discussing any one of a million issues that came before us in those early years.

IMPORTANT FIGURE: John Elliott's impact on the game should never be underestimated. His presentation to the VFL Board in 1984 was, effectively, the blueprint for the commission and the national competition. Here he is with Jon Dorotich (left) and David Rhys-Jones during his long reign as Carlton president.

SWANS ALL: Dr Geoffrey Edelsten, seen here in typical flamboyant style with a group of somewhat underwhelmed players, had a brief moment in the sun as the first private owner of a League club.

TV MOGUL: Ron Casey was a huge figure in the game through the 1960s, '70s and '80s, as his network all but owned the TV rights to VFL footy. That came to a crashing halt in 1987 when we gave the rights to the packager Broadcom, and live TV went to the ABC in Victoria for the first year of the national competition.

SANFL GURUS: Leigh Whicker and Max Basheer before the 1993 Hawthorn v Adelaide elimination final at the MCG. Whicker and Basheer have been significant figures in SA football for generations, and were hearty negotiators on behalf of SA footy before the Crows joined the AFL for the 1991 season.

SIGNIFICANT DAY: It wasn't one of my finest hours, but after this press conference between me, Michael Long (right) and Damien Monkhorst, the League rapidly moved to create the ground-shaping racial and religious vilification code that is still in place today.

Insert: A brochure produced by the League stressing the need for racial equality in our game.

NEW LOOK: After the Crawford report had been accepted by the VFL Board of Directors in 1993, a new-look commission was put in place with John Kennedy as its chairman, on my right. In the back row (l-r) are Ron Evans, Graeme Samuel, Terry O'Connor, Colin Carter and Wayne Jackson (John Winneke was absent).

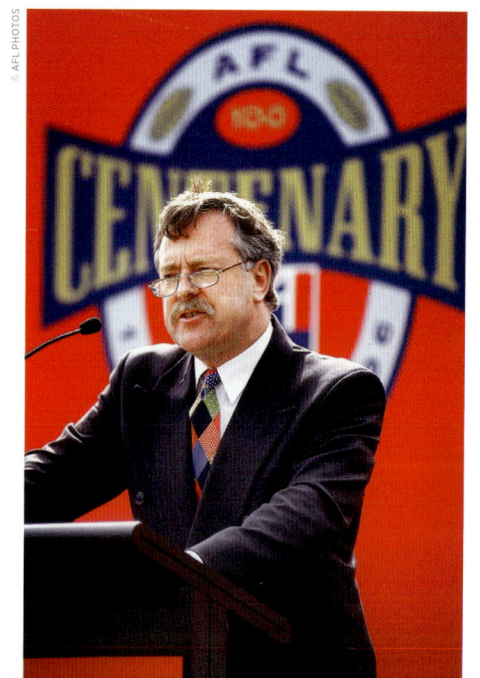

←↑ **CENTENARY FROLICS:** The centenary year of 1996 will always sit fondly in my memory. At left, I speak at a launch event with the year's logo prominent, and above, Tim Watson and I skylark in period costume before the big game commemorating 100 seasons of footy in May 1996.

↓ **ROSS FILES:** Andrew Fyfe's *Footy Show* cartoon about the blackout at Waverley in 1996 was a riff on the then wildly popular TV show *The X Files*. It showed my PA, Ros Desmond, and I as Scully and Mulder investigating, finding a discarded Carlton beanie, beer can and cigarette before discovering the "real" culprit: John Elliott!

EMPEROR OF SORTS: *Herald Sun* cartoonist Mark Knight portrayed me many times over the journey. This one, showing me as a merciless dictator giving the thumbs-down to the Lions, is a favourite, and decorates our stairwell at home.

UNHAPPY LIONS: The Brisbane-Fitzroy merger was far from a happy time for any of us, but these Lions fans were particularly upset, as their banner shows.

FAILED MERGER: Hawthorn president Brian Coleman and Melbourne president Ian Ridley were keen to take up the AFL's generous merger package in 1996, but after an emotional groundswell against the move the nays had it, although the Melbourne members did vote in favour of the merger.

CALLING THE VOTES: It was always a nervous time when the cameras started rolling and the Brownlow Medal vote count was under way. Pictured on my right is the great Jill Lindsay, and on my left, Ian Collins. It's hard to believe, but there was a time when the TV networks didn't see the value in broadcasting this great event.

UP THERE, MIKE BRADY: Mike's contribution to the game through voice, lyrics and music has been enormous. His great song *Up There Cazaly* will outlive us all.

SPECIAL GUEST: *Talking Footy*, the first of so many footy talk shows, was created by Gary Fenton. It was a pleasure to go on it and talk footy with (on my left) Mike Sheahan, Malcolm Blight and Bruce McAvaney.

TANNED UP: *The Age*'s late, great Les Tanner welcomed me to the job as chairman of the commission with a wonderful cartoon showing that it wasn't so much a case of walking on water, but avoiding all the mines that were part of the landscape of footy in those days.

A TEAM FOR THE AGES: We launched the 1991 Foster's Cup at the St Kilda marina, and it seemed a good idea at the time for all of us to act like kids on the winners' podium. From the backline: Peter Nixon, Pat Stone, the late David Austin, Graeme Samuel, Ken Carnie, Robin Huxley, Albert Mantello, Peter Scanlon. In the front: me, Grant Burgess, Barry Capuano, the late Greg Durham, Tony Peek, the late Alan Schwab. I think we had a good day.

AWARD WINNER: Proudly receiving the United Nations Association of Australia's Special Peace Award in recognition of the League's racial and religious vilification code. Presenting the award is Virginia Rogers, chair of the Equal Opportunity Commission of Victoria.

HAPPY DAY: The AFL had become a pretty big show at the end of my time, and we celebrated the 1996 season at the Australia Club. If you get hold of a microscope you'll see me three rows from the back, with commission chairman John Kennedy on my right and the late Jill Lindsay on my left. Of the 90-odd in the photo, only Tony Peek, Michael Lovett, Jennie Loughnane, Ken Gannon, Jodi Collins and Glenda Megson remain on staff.

PROUD MOMENT: It came as a great surprise when a letter arrived in the mail early in 2009 notifying me that I was to be inducted into the Australian Football Hall of Fame. This was particularly gratifying, as it had been a commission initiative in 1996 to set up the Hall of Fame.

Mr Ron Casey last night said his station was naturally pleased to be able to continue its role as the football station in Victoria."[36]

We had a deal—just for the 12 months. That was quite intentional on my part and on the part of the League.

By the end of January, the Nine Network would have been sold, with Kerry Packer getting a cool $1.05 billion from Alan Bond (Packer would buy it back a few years later for around $600 million), and Seven Melbourne was also about to have new owners. Under the edict imposed by the federal government, Murdoch had no choice but to move Seven out of his empire, and on the same day as his papers reported the news of the deal between the VFL and HSV7, they also reported the first of a series of theories on who would pick up ownership of HSV7. First it was Kerry Stokes, then it was Holmes à Court—which, as Gary Fenton described in the previous chapter, had actually happened without anyone knowing.

In the end, though, that prior contractual commitment would win out and by late February Fairfax would own the Seven stations in Melbourne and Sydney. We were midway through the pre-season competition by the time it had all unfolded. The immediate consequence was the resignation of Casey. He was not of a mind to suddenly start playing second banana to network heavies in Sydney.

The Fairfax deal did not come as a complete shock. It was just the sort of turbulence we had been expecting, and the reason we had wanted to make only one-year rights deals with the networks.

I got in touch with Steve Cosser and suggested it might be wise if he made a discreet approach to the managing director of the ABC, David Hill, with Seven's Sydney management team clearly not as committed to the VFL as the previous team. Time was short, and I wanted to have a contingency plan in the back pocket if the new Seven owners decided to walk away from their VFL commitment. We also felt the water with SBS.

How right I was to be looking around. For the moment, Seven was in limbo while the broadcasting authorities considered whether or not to

---

36 "Seven wins footy deal", *The Sun*, 29 January 1987.

approve the acquisition by Fairfax. We didn't know—they didn't know—whether Seven would be calling the football to Victorians when the season proper began. It was a tense time.

That said, the initial response from the ABC was very positive. I was confident that if things fell over with Seven we wouldn't be off the air; indeed, the ABC indicated interest at around $1.6 million for 1987.

Fenton, a man who had played the game at VFA level and loved his football, still held the programming reins at HSV7. I felt certain that if there was any way HSV7 could keep their end of the bargain, Fenton would find it. Not that he would have the final say, of course—that would go to the Sydney-based head of the network, Ted Thomas.

Thomas was notoriously Sydney-centric. It had been his decision in 1985 to dump a certain Melbourne-produced drama, *Neighbours*, in favour of two Sydney productions. Thomas further showed his Sydney-centric colours by confirming his network affiliates' position that he did not rate the VFL.

In late February he asked Fenton what would happen if they dumped the VFL and Fenton said, "Well, I guess if HSV7 didn't have it we would have to come up with other programs, given a lead time of about 12 months."

"What if it was sooner than that?"

"Well, we have a 12-month contract for VFL football."

"What would the viewers of Melbourne think if there was no football on Seven this year?"

"The switchboard would blow up if you dumped the VFL."[37]

There were howls of protest when the Sydney mafia arrived in Melbourne and moved about the offices sacking people. Fenton remembers: "We had a picket line for six months which we had to fight our way through to get to work."[38]

Fenton's advice to Thomas would turn out to be prophetic. Seven was about to walk away from football, and the decision would be a disaster for their local ratings, which collapsed soon after.

But one network's disaster is another network's great good fortune.

---

37   Gary Fenton, interview with the author, 2014.
38   Ibid.

On 13 March, Fairfax got the OK to take over Channel Seven Melbourne. On 13 March, I announced that Seven had walked away from its VFL broadcast deal and that the official Victorian broadcaster of VFL football for 1987 would be the ABC. It was a one-year deal for just under $1.6 million.

Sometimes things just move so fast.

CHAPTER 13

A new ball game

It was going to be a big year for Drew Morphett and Tim Lane—in fact, for all of the ABC broadcast crew about to venture into national footy. Not necessarily a good year—it would end in tears—but for all of that, a big year.

The ABC had the rights to broadcast the VFL in Victoria. Broadcom, that futuristic creature of the new media age, had dealt with a number of commercial stations in the other states and territories while utilising the ABC feed, with each game covered by Broadcom-appointed commentators. The game was being seen across the country, but to say there was much to be done understates the situation somewhat.

As the season's opener drew near, things might have looked a bit up in the air, but the situation would have been worse if we had insisted on holding Seven to its contract, thus locking in an unwilling telecaster and having to put up with key decisions being made out of Sydney. The entire shooting match would have been in turmoil.

If truth be told, it might have been a better thing if the TV arrangements had been a little less seat of the pants. But that was the situation we had to cope with. It's hard to believe when I look back on it, particularly when you look at the way the game is broadcast these days, with highly professional teams, brilliant camerawork, wall-to-wall stats, analysis and, of course, a 24/7 footy channel—not to mention the digital options. Even though some games are on pay TV, the options for viewers now could not have been imagined when we launched the national competition less than 30 years ago.

But for the time, and in the circumstances, the deal we had was good considering the alternative of no deal at all, and just a few short weeks earlier that was precisely what we had—no deal at all.

The old *de facto* rights wholesale arrangement that had been run from Ron Casey's office at Seven Melbourne had been handed over to Broadcom, so in a funny sort of way the fundamentals of the situation were no different from past practice. Seven had always sold the rights round the country, dealing out the League once the initial rights agreement had been finalised. At least we had a more controllable arrangement now—or so it seemed.

That is not to say it was all plain sailing. Broadcom was starting from scratch: no equipment, no commentators. This latter fact presented a career-changing opportunity for one West Australian, Dennis Cometti—a delayed opportunity, as it happened, with Dennis stranded in transit from the west for Broadcom's season-opening production. As Garry Linnell reports it in *Football Ltd*:

> In the opening round, Broadcom's team was due to go live with its first program. The host for the first week, Western Australia's Dennis Cometti, was delayed. The production team turned to (former Seven producer, now Broadcom jack of all trades) Michael McKay.
>
> "You'll have to host this one," said the director. "We've only got a few minutes to go."
>
> "Why me?" asked McKay, as if he wasn't busy enough already.
>
> "You're the only one here wearing a jacket."[39]

That was pretty much the way the season stumbled on: a scramble for gear, crew and facilities. The broadcasts were beset by all sorts of technical glitches, including ABC-TV crews calling games out of radio commentary boxes, a legendary moment when an OB van caught fire racing from Adelaide to Melbourne to fill a gap, fluffed crosses and fumbled calls.

---

39 Garry Linnell, *Football Ltd: The Inside Story of the AFL*, Ironbark, 1995, p. 185.

The only air-conditioning the broadcasters had was fierce winds blowing through the temporary "boxes".

We understood the issues, but there was concern—wringing of hands even—back at the League. We knew the coverage could be salvaged eventually, but the sense around the commission table was that we needed to intervene, and quickly. Could we get the ABC, our key broadcaster in what was still the most important of our TV markets, Melbourne, to lift its game?

With the launch of a national competition, embryonic but still covering all parts of the eastern seaboard, and now into the west, there had never been a more important season for the League. Getting more than a basic coverage of the new teams, and new personalities into the lounge rooms of our key marketplace, was obviously fundamental in what was a sea change in our game. However, in some ways providing at least the level of coverage the public had come to expect in our "home market" was more important for our survival than broadcasts into "foreign" territory around the rest of the country.

We set up a meeting in Sydney for 27 April after the end of round five. Lane, the highly professional face of the ABC team, got the call to attend; he broke his journey home from a Brisbane Bears game on the Gold Coast to do so. It had been a big game for the growing competition, with Brisbane beating Melbourne in a thriller, 12.14 (86) to 12.9 (81). The crowd was a pretty sorry 7451, but that's another story and nothing that had not been expected in these early days of footy in the southeast of Queensland.

Peter Scanlon and I flew up from Melbourne for the meeting at the ABC headquarters. ABC boss David Hill was there, as were football producer Allen Pridmore, Steve Cosser from Broadcom and a couple of others. We were not about to let niceties get in the way of the reality, and said we weren't happy. We told them the ABC's performance had been sub par. Scanlon hit them between the eyes with a list of concerns, as recorded in our report to the commission the following week. He criticised the ABC's directors, camera operators, commentators, and promotion. That just about covered the full spectrum of any broadcast![40]

---

40   VFL Commission minutes, 7 April 1987.

Off such a low base, the meeting went better than we thought it might. Hill agreed that there were problems and that improvements had to be made. Scanlon had one or two pretty strong thoughts, including a fierce set against the work of commentator Peter Gee, the desk-bound, blazer-toting anchor of the ABC coverage. Scanlon called him "Gerry Gee" at the meeting, which was a back-handed "tribute" to Ron Blaskett's ventriloquist doll of that name, but no great compliment to poor Peter, a young man with precious little VFL experience under his belt who had been thrown in at the deep end. Our view was he gave the ABC coverage a vaguely naive flavour. We were both keen to see Drew Morphett, host of the very popular TV show *The Winners*, take a leading role in the coverage.

Hill assured us that things would change, and they did. By mid-year the coverage was much improved and growing ratings were showing the difference.

It was a different story back at Seven. Without the footy the network's ratings were well down and the sharks were circling. One shark in particular: Christopher Skase.

It didn't take a lot of insight into the media business to realise that losing the football would really hurt Seven, or that the station was now networked out of Sydney. Melbourne viewers were voting with their feet and abandoning the channel in droves. This might have been enough to force Fairfax's hand, but other factors collided with the falling ratings, meaning that some sort of change was inevitable.

New cross-media laws introduced by the Hawke-Keating Government in late 1986 made the venerable print company Fairfax's departure from TV ownership a matter of time; it was a clear case of losing either the TV network or its newspapers, and at that stage, pre-internet, there would have been little discussion around the board table.

By July 1987 Skase had put a $780 million offer for the Seven Network on the table. Ultimately the acceptance of this deal would spell the end of the line for the ABC's 12-month dalliance with live VFL broadcasts, but there was one more roll of the dice to come from the national broadcaster—an incident that would see the VFL, and the ABC's Morphett, end up in court.

It was September and I had the job of pulling the winners from a barrel for a big raffle draw being taped for later broadcast on the ABC's Friday night footy show. The prize was worth winning: a family trip to Los Angeles and then on to Vancouver for two international exhibition matches between Sydney and North Melbourne and Sydney and Melbourne.[41] So far, so good. The promotion of these games was notable for a stunt thought up by Jim McKay (by now with Sydney) to build crowds, showing Sydney's John Ironmonger ripping into a raw steak before the game. The things they do …

The raffle promotion had been advertised nationally, but we were doing the draw on a program that broadcast only in Victoria. The ABC should have thought of that beforehand.

I stuck my hand in the barrel and pulled out an envelope: interstate winner. Brilliant.

Drew wasn't impressed and muttered about the need for a local winner for the local audience. Then word came from the control room that the take had been a stuff-up, apparently due to a tape machine on the blink. Or so they said.

I reached in and pulled out another envelope: another winner from interstate.

Weirdly, the tape machine was on the blink again and the control room wanted us to put down another take. At this stage I was getting angry. We couldn't just keep pulling different names out. It didn't matter if the tape machine was playing up—we had to have just one winner. I insisted on getting the next draw right and so I reached in and got another envelope. Thank goodness, it was a Victorian. But they hadn't taped this draw either, so I tucked the envelope into a crevice in the barrel where I could easily reach it again, and the tape rolled for another take. Out came a Victorian winner and everyone was happy. Even Drew.

---

41 In the end the LA match did not go ahead because of slow sales, with the US promoter blaming a minor earthquake that had occurred in LA some weeks before the game.

Well, that wasn't the end of it. Early the next week Lane was at work at the ABC when he got a call from Ron Barassi, who was in those days a part-time columnist for *The Truth* newspaper. Barassi had been tipped off by someone in the studio that there had been a dodgy barrel draw on the previous Friday night's footy show. *Truth* duly ran the yarn and the League was very quickly in deep trouble for breaching the terms and conditions of the raffle. The police called on Morphett and me and really put the heat on. It was all pretty unpleasant.

We had a bit of a wait, but 12 months later the thing had its day in court. Good-behaviour bonds were a nice slap on the wrist, but we'd already done the right thing and paid for all three families pulled out of the barrel—Victorian or not—to take the trip to the US. Fortunately I had put the first two winners into the empty half of a two-sided barrel, so we were able to recover them.

It was a good lesson for me and a rather unusual finale to the ABC's one run at the national rights to our game.

TV wasn't the only thing on a burgeoning agenda for the League, although it was certainly the most public. That Broadcom deal—or, more likely, the break with Seven after such a long relationship—may well have been the foundation on which the current incredible model is founded. Not only did it show that the game could be broadcast via multiple networks, it put a new base under the rights *and*, as far as Seven was concerned, showed how important those rights were to the network as a whole. It had also drawn out interest from other networks, allowing us some strength in negotiations.

I had been in the job for not much more than six months, but already it was clear that this was no walk in the park. On the League's agenda were issues to do with ground rationalisation; club rationalisation and financial woes (never-ending); new clubs; potential relocation of matches outside the published fixture; admission of more teams, including discussions with Tasmania and the ACT; battles with the federal government as we balanced the restrictions of the draft with the Trade Practices Act; our relationship with the MCC; the National Football League of Australia's role in the whole show (see Chapter 20); player contracts; the drifting relationship with the state government; playing more night games and Sunday games, regarding which the City of Melbourne was flexing its muscle; and more deals to be done with TV rights, remembering that the 1987 deals were for one year only. Of course, umpiring matters were a week-by-week item, and it's amusing to reflect on a note in the June minutes of the board about Alan Schwab, in his role as chair of the Laws of the Game Committee, advising directors that "the major matter currently being addressed was the elimination of congestion in play".[42] That, it would seem, is an item that will never leave the League's agenda.

It makes my head spin to even recall all those matters swirling about together, remembering as well that the commission was still beholden to the club directors for anything of substance.

But for all that, TV was (and is) the driver of our key revenues. We even had a nibble (if you call a vague offer of $5 million a "nibble") for a five-year broadcast of matches to the United States, and, bizarre as it seems these days, by July we had not yet gained a broadcaster for the Brownlow Medal.

But interest was hotting up, and on 28 July, a substantial presentation was made by Gary Rice and David Hill (a different person from the ABC's David Hill) of the Nine Network seeking the rights to night games and Sunday matches, working around their existing schedule. Given what was to come with the phenomenon that is *The Footy Show*, it is worth reporting, from the minutes, that "Channel Nine would be prepared to expand its programming on football to include support shows of a panel-show variety etc. In this regard Mr Hill suggested a possible program based around a League teams concept on Thursday evenings, which would include a novelty panel to target younger audiences, and follow the theme of eg. 'Hey, Hey It's League Teams'."[43]

It was not to be, at least in 1988. That home and away season would turn

---

42   VFL Board minutes, June 1987.
43   VFL Board minutes, 28 July 1987.

out to be a big year for the Seven Network, and I'm not just talking about the first series of the enduring soapie *Home and Away*. Mind you, when it comes to soaps Seven was due a break: it will go down in history as the network that palmed off *Neighbours* to its rival Ten. And that has a touch of *déjà vu* about it when you look at the way the Sydney-based Seven bosses under Fairfax discarded football.

One of the first things Skase did when he acquired the network was arrange a trip to Melbourne to check out the lie of the land down at Dorcas Street. He found a station in pretty poor spirits, and didn't mince his words when he met with Gary Fenton.

"This station is ratshit," he told Fenton.

"Yeah, of course it is," Fenton agreed.

"Well, what one thing do I need to do to get Channel Seven back on track?"

Fenton had not doubt in his mind whatsoever: "Get the bloody football back!"

"Right," said Skase.[44]

Remember this was the late 1980s. Skase was close to being at the peak of his powers, as much a national celebrity as he was a successful businessman—or should I say *apparently* successful businessman. This was the time of the razzle 'em and dazzle 'em entrepreneurs, the white-shoe brigade. The country was in love with their fast money and daring deals.

The stories surrounding these deal-makers were abundant and legendary. The 1988 Qintex Christmas party would set the business back a cool $400,000, and then there was the tale of the private jet sent from Cairns to Melbourne and back to fetch a dress for Pixie Skase, Christopher's high-profile wife, who had changed her mind about what to wear for the lavish opening of Skase's Mirage resort at Port Douglas.

I'd seen all this hubris first hand thanks to Skase's involvement with the Brisbane Bears. I was invited to the club's first game, a Skase production at Carrara with fanfare upon fanfare. There was a lunch, of course, and

---

44   Gary Fenton, interview with the author, 2014.

protocol, such as it was, suggested that the chairman of the VFL should sit at the head table with the presidents of the competing clubs, perhaps a major sponsor, the premier and assorted dignitaries. However, I was stuck at a table right over in a corner. Without putting on any airs or graces, I have to say this was not the way things were done. But there wasn't much I could do about it at the time.

Skase didn't even come over with a "Thanks for coming, Ross. Welcome. We're really pleased to be part of this VFL thing." I got nothing. Then again, he probably didn't even recognise me, as I had done pretty much all of my negotiating with him on the phone, with most of my face-to-face negotiations conducted with the club's general manager, Paul Cronin. Of course, Skase and I had form from the Bears' launch in Brisbane when the famous envelope supposedly containing the $4 million licence cheque had been handed to me in front of the media, empty. (The envelope, not the media.)

Even from the back row, I could see this event was magnificent. It was an extraordinary and lavish lunch, truly an extravagant ode to the times. Each table had a spectacular floral centrepiece, which I later discovered had been flown up from Kevin O'Neill in Melbourne, South Yarra's florist to the rich and famous. Piles of seafood were delivered to the tables, with this best-of-Queensland food prepared in Melbourne by celebrated corporate caterer Peter Rowland and flown up with two chefs for the show.

Magnificent in the moment, but not so magnificent when the numbers needed to be accounted for. But then you'd expect that kind of a show in the Queensland of that time. Of course you would. This was Skase exuding success, lording it over rivals and wannabes.

Then there was the raffle. It could hardly be a pre-match lunch without a raffle. Peter Sawyer, Skase's PR man, got up to run the show, saying, "Today's raffle prize is for two people, first class on Qantas, to England. You will stay in the penthouse suite at the Ritz for a week, attend the British Open as our guest, and sit on Greg Norman's table with Christopher at the Open Ball."

A NEW BALL GAME

Everyone went for their wallets, including me. It was too good to be true. But Sawyer hadn't finished: "And the tickets are $5000 each."

That tempered the enthusiasm a little, but Sawyer was having none of it and started nominating people in the room. "Harold Mitchell, you do all of Christopher's media, don't you?"

"Yeah," mumbled Mitchell.

"You'll have a ticket, won't you?"

"Yeah, I'll have a ticket."

"Des Brooks, you're Christopher's architect."

"Yeah," Brooks said, caught in the spotlight.

"You'll have a ticket?"

"Yeah."

On he went around the room, nominating people and twisting their arms to take a ticket. He never mentioned where the proceeds were going, but we all assumed the Brisbane Bears. Most of us were looking to shrink behind others to avoid the public call-out. I was lucky: I was out in the bleachers and Sawyer did not know me from a bar of soap.

He was pugnacious, if nothing else. He forced a guy called Noel Gordon to take a ticket. Gordon was a member of Skase's Chairman's Club, and would find himself Brisbane's chairman down the track, in the heart of the Fitzroy merger. As it happened, he was the lucky winner. He went up to Skase at half-time in the match and said, "I'm Noel Gordon and I won the raffle."

"Oh, good on you, Noel," said Skase. "That's great, yeah."

Gordon was curious as to the next steps in claiming his extraordinary prize. "How do I arrange this? Do you provide me the tickets and all of that sort of thing?"

Skase was pretty offhand: "Oh, look, why don't you organise the flights over so that you place them at the time that you want to go, and book the presidential suite, and I'll make sure the tickets to the golf and ball will be made available to you. No problem at all." Then he added, "And then just send me the bill."

So Gordon booked it all and had a wonderful time, as expected. It cost him around $30,000. You can guess the anything-but-happy ending. Of course he never got paid—not a cent.

Skase was pretty lavish on his own account, though. I remember sitting next to him in the grandstand at a game when I noticed a helicopter landing in the grounds next door. He excused himself, saying, "Yeah, I'll be back shortly, Ross." The game went on. About 40 minutes later he arrived back, beautifully groomed, and I saw the helicopter leave.

He'd flown his barber down from Brisbane and had a haircut during the game. That was Christopher Skase.

At one point during the infamous raffle lunch, I walked out to the gents. It so happened that just as I was walking in, Skase was coming out. He looked at me blankly, so I introduced myself: "Hi Chris, Ross Oakley from the VFL." He said gruffly, "My name is Christopher," and kept walking. I'll remember that, I thought, smarting a little.

The next time we met was in Steve Cosser's office at Broadcom. Skase, then the new owner of the Seven Network, was making a pretty nervous pitch to us for the return of the rights to telecast VFL footy. He needed the rights a bit more than we needed Seven, to be honest, given the interest we were fielding from the other networks.

I stood as he came in. "G'day, Chris, how are you?" I said. This time he copped it sweet.

Skase would go on to pay the right price. It was bad news for the ABC, who, as the national broadcaster and with no advertising revenue to bolster its bid, couldn't come even close in the negotiations. But for football it was the beginning of a new era that would put bigger and bigger dollar values around rights, thereby guaranteeing national coverage and a national audience for sponsors and advertisers.

The Skase deal for 1988 was $5.5 million plus $1 million in contra—a huge lift from the $3.4 million we had been offered by Seven for the 1987 season. These figures would grow to around $7.6 million and $2 million by 1992.

It was the beginning of a whole new paradigm for the League and the game. By 1993 Seven would be paying from $12.5 million in that year to $18.5 million (and $2.9 million contra) in 1997. By 2001, the figures were $33 million and $4.5 million. Then FOX (which introduced pay TV into the equation), Nine and Ten paid $100 million a year for 2002-06. The radio deals for the same period netted $400,000 a year, up from a few pennies in the 1980s.

Our national coverage, coupled with the growing professionalism of the game at all levels, was starting to bear fruit. The current agreement with Seven, Foxtel, FOX Sports and Telstra is worth $1.253 billion for the period 2012-16, which includes $1.118 billion in cash and the balance in contra advertising. The radio agreements for 2012-16 are worth $23.2 million, plus contra support.

Those early heartaches were now firmly tucked away in history. The modern era of communications—and the incredible value of the League brand—had well and truly arrived. There was still much to do, and much ahead of us, but this deal, we all felt, was an indication that the train was on the right track and heading in the right direction, and that all the carriages were being carried along by a pretty powerful engine. The commission was certainly gathering steam.

CHAPTER 14

A new marketing era

It would be fair to say that marketing the game wasn't one of Jack Hamilton's top priorities, or for that matter one of his better developed skills.

But Jack was a man of his times. The idea that football was a business, a product, part of the entertainment industry, and that it might benefit from the sort of marketing attack that could broaden its audience, was barely registering in the late 1970s. This needed to change.

Under Hamilton, VFL "marketing" was the preserve of legendary deal-maker and turner of fast bucks Jim McKay from Active Marketing. Hamilton came to rely on McKay to advise him on these matters. It was all about cash flow—what bucks they could make out of exploiting the developing brand of the VFL—with McKay on rather hefty commissions.

McKay's beginnings were in the humble surrounds of the GTV9 mail room. He'd been one of the brains behind the Sunbury rock festival in 1972 before making the move into advertising. From the J. Walter Thompson agency he handled the VFL account, turning his agile mind to the myriad unexplored possibilities for the brand. VFL Insurance, the first sponsor logos on match-day jumpers—these were the first small steps into a new and potentially lucrative world.

It was when McKay established VFL Travel through a relationship with the travel agency Jetset that things changed for him in a big way. At first the VFL Travel/Jetset relationship was a great fit with one of J. Walter Thompson's big accounts, Ansett Airlines, which was at that time Jetset's preferred carrier. Then Jetset did a deal with TAA (which later became Australian Airlines before being absorbed by Qantas in 1992). Sir Reginald Ansett hit the phone to the agency and the order came down: dump the VFL account.

McKay wasn't copping that. He quickly negotiated his own deal with the then VFL president, Sir Maurice Nathan. McKay had a business, and the VFL had an energetic, albeit outsourced, properties division. This turned out to be a licence to print a fair bit of money. As Garry Linnell tells it in *Football Ltd*: "Within 12 months the Properties Division sat just behind gate receipts and television rights as the game's biggest source of revenue. In 1977, revenue for the division amounted to about $300,000. A year later it was more than $500,000. In 1979, more than $1 million flowed in."[45]

Sponsorship was part of this revenue base.

It was beer that would bring this bullish era undone in the end—the great clash of the beer sponsors that saw Alan Bond's XXXX and John Elliott's Carlton & United Breweries go head-to-head at the beginning of the 1986 pre-season. It would create a nightmare for me in 1987 and months of delicate negotiations to bring a brewery back to the VFL sponsorship table.

Signing two breweries for the one event, the 1986 Foster's Cup, was an almost delusional act of hubris by the League's administration, and it all came unstuck on a rainy Saturday night when the competition kicked off at VFL Park. The Foster's markings were safely daubed on the turf, but there on the goalposts were bright-red and gold rows of XXXX branding! This came as a shock to the CUB marketing executives when they turned up for the pre-match dinner.

It's hard to imagine what the League's deal-makers had been thinking— apart from money, of course. The three-year deal with Bond Brewing was originally worth around $2 million. Then CUB got wind of it and made a

---

45 Garry Linnell, *Football Ltd: The Inside Story of the AFL*, Ironbark, 1995, pp. 47-8.

counter-offer. The League ended up with a pair of 12-month contracts and quite a few unknowns for all concerned. Two beer companies sponsoring one event—it had to end up in a shambles, and it did.

So on that fateful night, CUB was far from happy. Hamilton copped an earful from the angry CUB executives and then had a brainwave. He told Greg Durham, the League's finance manager: "Get down there and wrap the goalposts in tablecloths." Durham stripped the cloths off a number of tables in the corporate dining room and did what he was told. It was never going to please everyone.

Ad man Harold Mitchell tells the story of how he was at home in St Andrews, curled up by the fire in his pyjamas, when coverage of the game began on TV at 8.30pm. Mitchell had done the Bond Brewing deal and couldn't believe his eyes when the first goal of the game revealed goalposts that should have been adorned with the XXXX logo—the deal had cost his client a pretty penny. He rang Hamilton at the football with a fire in his belly and blasted him, insisting, "Jack, where are my signs?" Hamilton just mumbled something.

Mitchell said, "Here's what's happening. I'll meet you and Noel Davey of Bond Brewing outside the ground at half-time and you had better have some answers for us." He then rang Davey (Bond Brewing's general manager) and told him to meet him there. Davey replied, "Why would we do that? I'm not up to facing a former Collingwood full-back in a mood. Let's deal with it on Monday."[46]

The rain was playing its part at the ground. Pretty quickly the tablecloths were soaked through and the XXXXs shone out boldly for all to see. It was a mess. The men from CUB eyed the wet goalposts with dismay and anger.

It did get sorted out, more or less. But at the end of the year, when I was looking for a major sponsor for my first year in the job, both big breweries had walked away, washing their hands of football.

---

46   Harold Mitchell, interview with the author, 2014.

Critical holes in sponsorship were just one of the issues I faced in that first year behind the desk at VFL House. The broader issue of marketing was an area of League operations that I wanted to handle in a different way. It was less about turning a quick buck through licensing deals and the like, and more about building the presence of the game, both by broadening the audience for football in its existing strongholds and by building new audiences of fans in new markets. However, it was also important to make money.

To me, marketing the game was about putting on a show—delivering a game that gave the supporters what they wanted. This wasn't always well understood by the supporters. They liked what they liked, and generally didn't want change. We had to see through that.

The supporters told us they didn't want football on Friday night, let alone Saturday night, but of course we were in the entertainment business and knew that people tend to seek out their entertainment on Friday and Saturday nights. These two nights have now become the most popular times to watch games live or on TV and, of course, the prime-time viewing spaces for the TV networks, despite the fact that for so many years, Friday-night matches were on delay because the League and the MCC were concerned about the impact of live broadcasts on attendances.

Early on the supporters were also not too happy about ground rationalisation—the relocation of their club from playing home games at their traditional suburban grounds, which were full of history and great deeds of the past, to playing them at the MCG and Waverley. But ground rationalisation was not about taking away. It was about giving: improving conditions for supporters, providing seats and cover from the rain, and improving the surfaces upon which players were required to play. This is now seen as a normal part of going to the football.

The views of the fans were understandable. They had great affection for grounds like Windy Hill, Glenferrie Oval, Princes Park, Victoria Park and, back in earlier days, Punt Road, but none of these could provide anything like the facilities at the MCG, Waverley (yes, even Waverley) and, now,

Docklands Stadium, the Adelaide Oval, Gold Coast's Metricon Stadium and Greater Western Sydney's Spotless Stadium.

I came to the League with a marketing background; it had been central to my work at Wynns Winegrowers, AAMI and Royal Insurance. So when our marketing manager, Bruce Walker, retired only six months after my arrival, I didn't believe we needed another marketing manager as such (I wasn't really sure of Walker's role anyway, with McKay in the mix). I assumed the role, but I needed support—a marketing services manager— so we appointed Grant Burgess, a product manager in holiday travel with TAA. In the early days Burgess was my arms and legs as well as taking more control of our merchandising effort, and he did that very well. He later took charge of the whole marketing show.

The priorities were many, but it was clear to me there was a massive immediate need to have a better relationship with our supporters. This was one of the issues identified in the Blue Report of 1985. As it noted:

> The market research commissioned by the VFL in 1983 and 1985 delivers consistent messages on the most important factors:
>
> First, the main factor behind attendance trends is altered lifestyle. As a result, we must now understand that the real battle is 'football versus other interests' not 'Club A versus Club B'. This has profound implications on (e.g.) scheduling of games and other areas where cooperation between clubs is needed.
>
> Second, admission prices and quality of facilities are the uppermost concerns of supporters. Other factors such as the style of game and its excitement are not important issues.
>
> Third, the image of the VFL clubs is low among supporters, who consistently believe that their interests are being neglected.[47]

There was a job to be done on many fronts here. Hamilton's response had been to hire Mike Sheahan as his media director. This was a very good and necessary step that brought in a good operator who not only loved footy and knew how its grassroots worked, but could move easily in the hothouse

---

47   *VFL Football: Establishing the Basis for Future Success*, VFL Commission, 1985.

that was the Melbourne football media to develop a better profile and clearer message for the League. At another level, it was a sign of defensive thinking—securing the League from attack rather than actively projecting an entirely new message to the marketplace.

My thinking was that we had to do both. We had to feed the chooks *and* promote the game. Dare I say it, we also had to provide the best spin on any decision that came out of headquarters. Sheahan, with nigh on 20 years at the coalface of media, was up for the challenge.

Mike Sheahan was uncomplicated; he took a very simplistic view of the world, having been taught always to be black and white, never grey, and never to sit on the fence. Journalists by training are like this, but such an approach was not always appropriate strategically (although no doubt many would bristle at such a view).

Sheahan and I were always on the same page about wanting to take a more positive approach and build a more positive image for the game, even though we had clubs failing all around us. It was a tough gig for him, with change the order of the day and he and Alan Schwab not seeing eye to eye. By his own admission Sheahan was and is rather opinionated and passionate, so he clashed often with Schwab. Indeed, Peter Scanlon, with whom Sheahan had a great rapport, would often use him during commission meetings to force Schwab to open up, which antagonised Schwab considerably. Schwab would talk about something at the table and Scanlon would say, "What do you think, Mike?" Schwab would visibly bristle as Sheahan offered a view that, more often than not, was contrary to Schwab's.

Sheahan made strong stands on some issues that were important to supporters, such as trying to ensure more Grand Final tickets got into the average supporter's hands rather than the clubs profiting by selling them to corporates. If we had changed this balance too much, some clubs would have become financially vulnerable during those years. Sheahan said recently he saw himself as "the voice of the people" at the League, which explains his position on a number of those subjects.

By 1989 I sensed that Mike had become frustrated at not being able to say it the way he saw it to his beloved football public, and I'm sure he missed the daily buzz he got from finding and delivering a story in the media. In July he took up an offer to return to his first love as chief football writer for the new *Sunday Age*. As he reflects: "I didn't realise how privileged journos are until I went to the League and had to face the fact that I couldn't express a view publicly as to how I saw things, which I had been able to do all my working life. Writing an editorial in the *Footy Record* once a week didn't do it for me as I still had a party line to tread."[48]

Sheahan introduced many new ideas during his time at the League, including background briefings with senior journos, which was pretty much unheard of until that time, where we would inform those journos—people who could influence public opinion about our game—off the record. He told me that in the McCutchan era (Eric McCutchan was administrative director of the League from 1966 to 1976) they didn't care about informing the public as they didn't believe anyone had the right to know anything about what was going on. If any journo asked a probing question, it was as if they would be saying, "How imprudent of you! You are not entitled to know that stuff. We are the VFL and we decide what we do and who we tell."[49]

It was Sheahan's insistence that the public had a right to know that led to the changes that opened up the VFL. He says today that he really enjoyed his time at the League, but it was time to move on. I really enjoyed Sheahan's enormous input during those heady days at the VFL, and he certainly played a huge role in the development of the game. Such was his contribution to the media and to football that he was later given the honour of having the AFL Media Centre named after him, and he was granted AFL life membership in 2012.

Out with Sheahan, in with Tony Peek. Peek was a former *Sun* journalist who had worked for some years with Tennis Australia, significantly during the opening years of Melbourne's world-class tennis centre on the banks of the Yarra. Peek immediately went about introducing more media access,

---

48 Mike Sheahan, interview with the author, 2014.
49 Ibid.

including player and coach access; he was particularly keen on putting more structure into this process. Post-match interviews became a mandatory requirement for coaches and players. It was Peek who organised for me to start doing a regular spot on the Neil Mitchell radio show on 3AW. Mitchell had been a severe critic of mine. One day I was speaking at a lunch and a woman in the audience asked if I would be prepared to go on Mitchell's radio show to face the music (or, as I hoped, to celebrate achievements). I said yes and afterwards assured Peek I was serious. He contacted Mitchell and I soon started appearing weekly on Mitchell's show, with the result that he became far more positive towards me and the League. The regular radio spot disciplined me to make myself available every week no matter what issues were out there, so that football supporters could be kept informed. There was no hiding, no preparation, no spin, and it was with the most respected radio talkback host in Melbourne. I am glad that my successors as CEO, Wayne Jackson and Andrew Demetriou, have kept the segment going to this day.

Peek was and is a good strategic thinker and has made an incalculable contribution over 24 years (and counting) with the League; after many years as media and corporate affairs manager, he remains at the AFL as an executive, most recently providing assistance to Demetriou and now to new CEO Gillon McLachlan. By 2014, he was the League's longest-serving staffer.

It sounds at once a bit odd and a bit simple, but I wanted to build more excitement around football. I wanted to encourage a sense that ours was a game going somewhere, a game with a clear sense of purpose and direction, a game you could not ignore.

We had to overcome many strategic problems, but we also had some tremendous natural assets we could use to achieve a more positive image. The hardest part was the simple but awkward fact that saving a game in deep financial strife would require doing many things that traditional supporters would find hard to swallow.

Among a large proportion of Victorian fans there was then a very negative attitude to the idea of spreading the game nationally: it was viewed as losing something rather than gaining. The game of Australian Football would be somehow diminished in many supporters' minds by expanding the competition into new territories—places that had no real connection to the game.

The tough part was that this sort of expansion into unknown and untested territories such as Brisbane was the only thing that might offer the sort of cash flow and new interest necessary to save the game. Sydney had been the starting point, but that had been as much a case of pushing a local problem into Sydney as investing positively in an attack on a new market.

Convincing Victorian fans that growth was fundamental to survival was very difficult. Ironically, the very loyalty of the fan base that created the deep resentment of territorial expansion was also our greatest advantage. But we had to work our expansion, and the changes locally (ground rationalisation, curbing violence, fixture redefinition, night footy), in a way that would attract new supporters but not lose the "rusted-on" supporters in the process.

For the marketer, football was a perfect product because many of its "customers" were emotionally attached to it—every marketer's dream. A solid core of the audience (not enough to make the game pay, but still a solid core) was going to come along week after week pretty much no matter what we did to the game. They were rusted on.

When you think about the pace and significance of the changes we were pushing through the game in that period, it was a good thing that so many of the supporters were so loyal and committed—to their clubs and to the game. No doubt we tested their patience and loyalty, but keeping a tight hold on that group would not be enough. To me, there were in fact three groups of supporters: the rusted-on supporters, the latent supporters, and the less committed supporters—"theatregoers", as we called them.

Football traded on the entrenched tribal loyalty of the hard-core supporters, who would stand chilled and sodden in the uncovered muddy outer and pee in a beer can at Victoria Park rather than miss a moment of the action. They would never desert us—at least, that was our thinking. Not that we wouldn't continue to work hard to look after their interests, but the simple economics of football showed that there were not enough of them to float the game financially through gate receipts and television rights. And, more importantly, there were not enough of them to allow us to spread the base of the sport socially to the point where it became an increasingly attractive proposition for sponsors and advertisers around the country.

However, all clubs had latent supporter bases, some bigger than others. These supporters attended only when they were motivated to do so. We had to start motivating them to attend more regularly and to become members.

The third group, the so-called theatregoers, were those who didn't have the sort of club devotion that meant they would go to the football through thick and thin; they may not even support a team, but they liked to watch a good game. This was where the real opportunity was—the great potential to add substantially to the football audience, whether at games or watching on television. Big games, well promoted into enduring events, at comfortable venues, was the way to go for both the latent supporters and the theatregoers.

We were successful in developing many such events over the years, including Friday night blockbusters, Anzac Day, Queen's Birthday and, later, the Indigenous and Heritage rounds. And then of course there were local derbies in those states with two teams. It came down to numbers. In a big way it came down to getting a greater commitment from these two supporter groups to come to the big games and for us to create more big games at the big venues.

It also came down to gender: we had to attract more interest from women and girls. That was where the real opportunity lay. Jeff Browne, our legal adviser, sums it up: "The new marketing strategy of considering the female position in AFL policy showed a level of respect for women and children not previously seen."[50]

---

50   Jeff Browne, interview with the author, 2014.

Women became more interested in watching AFL because we had an effective drug code, we were taking positive action to reduce violence, we were recognising the important role women played at the grassroots level, and they could buy an inexpensive seat in a grandstand isolated from bad behaviour. These and other strategies put us in a unique position of encouraging a higher percentage of female supporters in our audience—certainly a key growth market.

Engaging women and the two uncommitted groups of supporters had to be the game's significant marketing goal. It was a step beyond the traditional VFL approach of flogging merchandise and simply trading off the name through an ever-increasing range of naming-rights deals.

A key part of the strategy had to be improving our offering and the image of the game—and not just superficially. In significant ways we had to remodel football to produce a game that had a broader and different appeal: get the game right, then promote it right. Of course, we had already taken action to improve the evenness of the game—a vital marketing thrust—by introducing club licence agreements along with the draft and salary cap (see Chapter 6).

Ground rationalisation would take some time to implement effectively, but we had other things we could do in the interim. One of them was putting a curb on on-field violence.

Yes, football is a tough body-contact sport, but there were times—too many times—when that toughness turned to simple, brutal nastiness. Although it had been part of the game for generations, it had also become a significant turn-off for many in our potential audience, particularly the mums; never mind that it was also a blight on the sport. One of the things we had to do was make the game less brutal.

Jack Gaffney, a man known affectionately as 'Jack Let 'Em Off', was head of the VFL Tribunal. His had been a long reign: he had been a valued member of the Tribunal since 1974 and chairman for two years. At every level change was overdue. It wasn't complicated, it wasn't elegant, but it was clear that we had to get Gaffney off a Tribunal that was more sympathetic to the players than was best for the game and its supporters. We needed to establish a new standard of appropriate conduct.

Gaffney had played 80 hard and tough games with Fitzroy between 1949 and 1953. It was clear from his decisions on the Tribunal that he respected that brand of play, and perhaps had a blind spot for the thin line where tough play trips over into the sort of violent conduct that can disfigure the game. The last straw was a decision to fine Carlton tough guy David Rhys-Jones $5000 after a striking incident in place of suspending him. It was a poor signal.

Neil Busse was our choice for new Tribunal chief. A former Richmond and South Melbourne player (1964-69) turned lawyer in post-footy life, it was his brief to tidy the game up. We made the switch in February 1988, in the off-season, and soothed the transition for Gaffney by offering him a new post as VFL Arbitrator, charged with resolving contractual disputes between players and clubs. He was also made a VFL Park life member.

We dumped the old Tribunal pool of 11 and also shelved the idea of letting it meet interstate if that was where an offence had taken place. Instead, we had a panel of six; we had knocked back a suggestion from the Laws of the Game Panel of Review in December 1987 for a one-man panel. The new set-up would prove to be a marked improvement, and it quickly impacted on the nature of the game.

Other moves were already in play.

Up until this stage the VFL had abrogated its responsibility for promoting the image of the game to Channel Seven via its station promos. The view was that the game promoted itself. The problem was that Seven was producing promos that promoted the station. Almost fortuitously, most of the time the goals of the two organisations were aligned. Football was very fortunate that Gary Fenton, the sports director at Channel Seven, had a great affinity with the game and its attributes. Nevertheless, it was time the VFL assumed responsibility for how it was promoted.

Fenton tells the story of how the wonderful football song and promotion

Up There Cazaly was produced as a station promo, not as an advertisement for the VFL. He recalled how, unbeknown to station manager Ron Casey, he called in the advertising agency The Campaign Palace, who, with Des Speakman of Sweeney Research, created a brief for a new station promotion involving the commissioning of three writers to come up with a new song. Fenton requested Mike Brady to be one of the songwriters, as he had spoken to Brady previously about doing some work for the station. His song *Up There Cazaly* was researched by putting it in at the end of several already-paid-for group sessions conducted by Speakman as an afterthought to gain a reaction.

This was about the time of Channel Nine's *Come On Aussie, Come On* campaign and the focus group's reaction was poor, as the research participants believed the VFL was just copying the cricket song! Speakman nevertheless recommended that Channel Seven go with the song, with two provisos: keep the music raw and uncomplicated—i.e. consistent with the game—and make sure the visuals married up with the words.

Fenton worked all night on the edit of the visuals before he showed the package to Casey the next morning. He remembers:

> When I showed it to Casey the next morning he was obviously delighted as he walked across the room and punched me on the shoulder, which was his way of saying, "Well done, well done."
>
> He said, "Just a sec" and went over and rang Jack Hamilton. "Jack, I'm sending Gary over. There is something I want to show you now." As was his way, he didn't tell me why I was rushing over to VFL House. I drove over and stuck the video in their machine.
>
> It played and it finished and there was silence. This was the first time anyone who had seen it had not said, "This is fantastic." I was a bit nonplussed.
>
> Jack explained: "We have also been working on something here for some months." He pulled out a tape and played another themed commercial, produced by Jim McKay of Active Marketing for the VFL. This was clearly not Jim's forte. It was appalling. Rubbish, certainly compared to ours. Absolutely no contest.

> At that point I thought Jack would say, "We will junk ours now and use yours," but no, he said, "Ours is the one we are going with." I was dumbstruck. So I said, "Jack, if you go with that you must understand that I am running my promo on air immediately and it will blow yours off the air."[51]

The rest is history. *Up There Cazaly* became *the* iconic VFL/AFL promotion, and the song, which is much loved by the football public, is still sung today by Brady as football's ultimate anthem. Thank you, Mr Brady!

The other promo never made the light of day, fortunately. We couldn't find a copy of the tape later when we looked, thank God, because Fenton tells me the promo lyrics were sung badly by VFL footballers and went something like: "We play to win / We play well / For the glory of the VFL." Inspirational lyrics, you would have to say.

This never-to-be-seen commercial was the first faltering step into VFL-generated promotions, but things were to improve. We needed to promote the spectacular beauty of the game—obviously not to those who already loved it and followed it blindly, but to those on the edge. I wanted to get the message right, to promote the game nationally and hopefully create a groundswell of interest in territories where we were beginning to have an impression but could do a lot more to spread the VFL word.

The ambition was to create a national game, but to do that we needed to put VFL boots on the ground. We'd done that, but in truth our foothold in the non-traditional states of NSW and Queensland was precarious.

The Sydney project was close to failing. There was more wrong there than advertising could cure, but a solid campaign to raise interest would be a step in the right direction.

It was more complicated than that, of course, because any national campaign by the VFL—and it had to be a national campaign—had to work in all the possible markets. It had to work in the football states and

---

51 Gary Fenton, interview with the author, 2014.

also in the key states of NSW and Queensland, where VFL footy was a foreign concept and a poor relation to the dominant force of rugby league.

We appointed Australia's most creative advertising agency, The Campaign Palace, in 1987 to do our advertising given their past experience with Channel Seven. Due to our lack of funds, we focused on tactical ads early on. The talented Speakman had left Sweeneys and joined The Campaign Palace as MD and the agency was soon winning many awards.

Our controversial tactical newspaper ad, "Black Magic", was confronting but impactful, and expressed the excitement that the indigenous Krakouer brothers could offer supporters of our game through their wizardry on the field for the Kangaroos. We ran the concept past the brothers before we ran the ad, because we knew some people would take the opportunity to make claims of racism against us. They were not only cool with the ad, they were actually chuffed we were using them. It had a real impact, and others followed.

But finding a solution to producing a strategic approach was a seriously complex process, compounded by the fact that we had no budget in the early years to develop a campaign of the scope and coverage required to impact all our target markets, let alone buy the necessary time on air to gain the appropriate effect.

We tried to develop a generic campaign with a unifying theme that appealed not only to our "rusted-on" supporters but our general support base, the theatregoers and those in NSW and Queensland who had little understanding of Australian Football. We also sought to create a campaign that would appeal to other forms of media that would assist wide distribution.

We didn't get it right initially, with an early campaign pitching the idea that VFL football was the best game in the world. Melbourne people already knew that, but Sydney people just didn't believe it. In fact, it wasn't until 1994 that we finally shaped a campaign that truly did the job. That was when The Campaign Palace came up with the "I'd Like to See That" campaign, involving clips of AFL action interspersed with an unlikely set of famous athletes and celebrities from across the world. It was a gutsy call, but we needed to break through in a cluttered sports market, particularly in Sydney and Brisbane. It turned out to be a brilliant campaign and an open-ended one that we could add to over time, with new voices and new vision.

How could you resist super-brat John McEnroe saying, "These guys spit the dummy at the umpire and get away with it? I'd like to see that." It challenged the theatregoers to experience the spectacular elements of our game. In the centenary year, 1996, we added John Lee Hooker, Heather Locklear and Archbishop Desmond Tutu, who said, "I hear you guys worship Aussie Rules. Hey, what sort of religion is that?" Edgy, to say the least.

A highlight was including the famous and enduring George Burns, who was to turn 100 on 20 January 1996, the start of the League's centenary season. Burns was one of those unique artists who was not afraid of poking fun at himself. He was asked if he would do a special additional ad in case he died before the start of the season. He agreed and used an alternative line that said, "A game that lasted longer than me? I'd like to see that."

And he did die before the season began, on 9 March that year. Naturally we used that extra piece of Burns magic.

We weren't alone in trying to build the image of the game: Seven was good at it, too. It would be hard to go past their *Up There Cazaly* station promo as an iconic piece of football marketing. When done well, these things have great power and the capacity to endure. Brady received an AM in the Queen's Birthday honours in 2013 for services to the music industry, and much of his fame surrounds his work with football songs; after *Up There Cazaly* he wrote *One Day in September* and a number of other football songs for Seven's ongoing marketing of the game and its coverage.

There's a feel-good sense from something like *Up There Cazaly*—the same kind of emotional tug that can be formed by a successful advertising campaign. But no matter what strength lies in a campaign and its creativity, the product has to be right. It has to match the appeal of the song or ad. Marketing is about the product being what your customer wants, where they want it delivered, what price they are prepared to pay, and of course how you promote it in the market.

Football needed a bit of fixing up by 1987. As well as curtailing the violence, we needed better playing surfaces with less mud, and the play needed to be more free-flowing and less a series of long kicks between big packs. Things like using the interchange, the speed of the game and bringing in the centre square would be fundamental changes, but in their way they all went towards a broader effort that was about marketing Australian Football—transforming the sport to make it the best, most spectator-friendly spectacle it could possibly be.

Then there was the experience of the day itself: not standing in mud on beer cans to get a view, not queuing for a stinking toilet, not drowning in winter's regular rain.

It could all be filed under marketing, and yet the clubs were only interested in us not spending too much of their money. You could understand that thinking, up to a point, but there's also a point at which if you don't spend—or, better, invest—you'll continue to go broke. A situation, of course, in which half the League had already found itself. There was a very fine balance we needed to be aware of: the tricky line between spending money to secure the game's future and the necessary spending on all the usual, immediate concerns.

Funding governed the speed at which we were able to transform the game.

Our biggest marketing push was the decision to place teams in non-football markets. Sydney was of obvious significance to the League, giving the VFL a toehold—for very many years a precarious one—in the country's biggest market. We *had* to be in Sydney. To some extent the big pushes of 1987—adding the Brisbane Bears and the West Coast Eagles to the competition—were speculative, especially Brisbane, which was a bold venture into foreign territory. But there was no other way of going about it. The future of Australian Football lay in being a nationally marketed sporting product.

National was the key. It was the emerging focus of media and the sponsorship and advertising dollar. National promotion for nationally distributed products: that was what the modern corporate dollar wanted.

It was all part of a big circle of needs. We needed to get our ground attendances up and we needed to get TV audiences up, and not just in Victoria. We had to change with the environmental change going on around us. Football was moving nationally, and we were stealing a march on the other codes in spreading our wings in this way, and also paralleling the national thrust of the media.

The presence of Christopher Skase as an active participant in both VFL football and television was an interesting coincidence; certainly he sensed that the coming future in media lay in national networking and national advertisers. For him football was part indulgence, part canny positioning, part an element in a rather complex and ultimately ill-fated strategic plan. He owned a team in the VFL because many of the people he dealt with in the USA owned an NFL team. AFL legal adviser Jeff Browne, who with me had a lot to do with Skase, recently said, "He was a smooth-talking, pompous, egocentric person involved in football for all the wrong reasons, using football to further his interests and image in USA."[52]

Despite this generally held view, at that time Skase was someone we needed to step up—and he did.

Through all this, all the planning, all the projections and strategy, football's trump card still remained the loyalty and enthusiasm of its core supporter base. We were guilty at times in the early 1980s of not appreciating just how important an asset those true believers were. Early on, some in football tended to treat the supporters as a nuisance standing between the game's past and an exciting future full of possibilities.

Fundamental to understanding our supporters was that they never supported the VFL or its ambitions—they supported their club. (Nothing has changed in that relationship, by the way.) The VFL? Well, we were a nuisance. An irrelevance to some and a necessary evil to others.

Even today people talk about the football of the late 1960s through the 1980s as some kind of golden age, but it was a golden age that could not endure. It had run out of opportunity. It was a time with no tomorrow that had run the clubs and structures of the game into the ground.

---

52   Jeff Browne, interview with the author, 2014.

Back in 1987 at the heart of this so-called "golden era", the easy option would have been to look out from VFL House and see the failing, obstinate clubs and their change-resistant supporter base as nothing but a problem. It would be one of the League's greatest challenges to see how this loyalty could be turned to the game's benefit, how it could become an opportunity fulfilled.

Meanwhile, we spent all of 1987 in desperate search of brewery money. After the double-brewery disaster of the 1986 season (the Foster's Cup presented by XXXX!), no beer maker wanted a bar of the VFL.[53] This meant we were short of the major sponsor dollars that came with them.

I worked at fixing the problem; I worked at it very hard indeed. I kept up a pretty constant dialogue with the major brewers, but it was late 1987 before my discussions with CUB started to feel a little more positive. By that point the company was feeling a little more comfortable with the commission and the League, and the way we were handling our marketing.

But for 1987 it left a massive hole. We just couldn't find a sponsor. We tried a whole host of companies, all of which seemed to be the right fit, and got Sportsplay eventually, who gave us $600,000 at the last minute. There was a fair bit of brinksmanship involved. National Panasonic took the 1987 night series at the very last minute, too—on 19 February.

The fact that the ABC had footy on TV for 1987 didn't help. Their hearts were in the right place, but the on-air product was suffering. Having a broadcaster that could not place advertising and sponsorship inside the broadcast made sponsorship a harder pitch, and also focused our minds on the TV deal that would apply for the next year. The stresses on the team were clearly expressed in the minutes of the board. On 11 March, just weeks before the new season would get under way, I reported to the VFL directors:

---

53   This wasn't the only case of multiple sponsors from one patch. Early in my time, I tried to put an exclusion deal in place to limit the League to one fast-food sponsor, but Brian Cook from West Coast swore he'd done the deal with Hungry Jack's owner Jack Cowin a day before I put the exclusion in place. Sponsors were very sensitive to competition then; this isn't so much the case today, with a maturity of thinking among sponsors and more acceptance of co-presence in the market. For example, in the modern era several individual clubs have car-company sponsors while at the same time Toyota is the Premier Partner of the League.

> [T]he League was still vigorously pursuing a major corporate sponsor for the 1987 season, but continued to experience difficulty given the size of the sponsorship sought, and the fact that the market for such arrangements had been adversely affected by the staging of the America's Cup in Perth, the forthcoming World Expo in Brisbane and the withdrawal from major sponsorship arrangements by the two major breweries.[54]

Sporting sponsorship was still an idea finding its feet at that stage—a slightly difficult sell that hadn't quite hit its straps. This was why the breweries were so much our target: they were low-hanging fruit to some extent. CUB, in particular, had had an association with the sport for close to 100 years and could see the obvious synergies that had existed and would continue to exist.

In late 1987, at last we had strong interest from CUB, a real sign they were keen to come back in for 1988. As if it all hadn't been hard enough, I decided that the deal had to go to tender so there was a hint of competitive tension. I didn't want the deal to be done on some handshake between mates; this was an important moment, and a moment for me to reinforce that things were being done differently under the new administration and would be a little more transparent.

Luckily we convinced CUB that we had strong interest from Tooheys as well. Both breweries were fine with the idea of going to tender, and as it turned out CUB played a very canny hand. On the day the tender closed they came early and parked themselves in one of our offices. They had two documents: one they intended to submit if they had competition, which loaded the upfront payments; and another they would put in our tender box if they had the field to themselves. This meant waiting until the last minute.

On the second floor of VFL House outside my office there was a little letterbox set up specifically for the tender. The guys from CUB were camped on that floor in an office we'd happily made available, with

---

54   VFL Board minutes, 11 March 1987.

an eye on the lift door. The deadline was 5pm. The CUB guys waited; all afternoon they waited and watched. It took the lift maybe half a minute to reach the second floor, and in the end, with no appearance from Tooheys, the clock hit 4.59 and 30 seconds, the CUB guys took one last look at the lifts, and then put in their tender.

We had a brewer as our major sponsor, and a very relieved chairman of the VFL with it.

It was a changing world, though, and football was not the only big organisation looking to refine and tweak its image. CUB was changing, too; its marketing philosophy was evolving quickly. By 1994, as we turned to negotiating a new sweep of sponsorships, the brewer signalled it was looking for a different relationship. CUB no longer just wanted name presence—their name was pretty well established. Their marketing strategy was becoming more product-oriented; they wanted to concentrate on promoting the benefits of their specific products to encourage sales and they wanted to tie sponsorship to the direct sale of product.

It was a different marketing approach. Their major thrust was to get their beer and wine products as part of the pouring rights at various grounds. They wanted to maintain an exclusive beer sponsorship, pay less money but at the same time remain the company of favour as far as the various beer taps and bar fridges of the AFL network were concerned.

In 1994 CUB agreed to stay on, but as a secondary-level sponsor only. Fair enough, but for naming-rights sponsors we were suddenly back to square one. We were scanning the market for an appropriate partner when out of the blue I got a phone call from Lindsay Fox.

It wasn't a long conversation—phone calls with Lindsay are generally short and to the point. He said, "Is the AFL naming-rights sponsorship filled yet?"

"No," I said.

"How much do you want?"

The commission had done some work, attempting to make an estimate of our sponsorship worth, and we reckoned something in the vicinity of

$4 million represented pretty fair market value. Still, the question caught me a bit on the hop.

"We're after $5 million," I told him.

"OK." He hung up.

I thought for a minute. What was all that about? I went back to whatever it was I was doing, and then about an hour later he called back, and said, "Yeah, listen, Coca-Cola will take that up."

"The naming rights? Coke?" I said.

"Yes," came the answer, and he hung up again.

They paid the $5 million—no questions. Lindsay Fox was on my Grand Final ticket list for the rest of my days at the League.

There were light moments in all these negotiations in our efforts to keep the wolves from the door. When the 1987 season was over, it was time for reflection—of some sort. It was also a time when plans were under way for a new season with a new (old) broadcaster, as Seven prepared to return to the fold.

By October, the season had been considered a success. The new clubs were settled (well, as much as they could be under their complicated ownership structures and the difficulties all start-ups face, and we were still fielding new deals with Sydney—notably a proposal from the ACT League seeking a joint-venture arrangement, and then another from New Zealand[55]). An indication of the strength of the game, and its all but national footprint, can be read in a note to the VFL directors on 2 October:

> Chairman made reference to a proposal forwarded to the League by a Western Australian entrepreneur, which called for the re-location of an existing VFL team to Los Angeles and that such team be known as the Los Angeles Crocodiles. It was resolved that no further action be taken ...[56]

---

55 Nothing came of either proposal. Almost every day a new entrepreneur with new ideas would approach the commission, either formally or informally.

56 VFL Board minutes, 2 October 1987.

And none was. I've scoured my brain and my personal records for any further correspondence and/or discussions on that matter but, perhaps not surprisingly, nothing has arisen!

Finally, to round out the year, another bright idea to improve the game. Anybody who has sat in the League CEO's chair, or that of the footy operations manager, would know that not a week goes by when a scheme to "improve" the game is not discussed; many actually reach the League, and many of those are actually considered in some detail. Given the constant debate surrounding congestion, and rules tested regarding kicking backwards and lines across the ground, I refer to a proposal offered by Alan Schwab on behalf of the Laws of the Game Committee at a pre-Christmas meeting of the VFL Board. It suggested that a new rule be trialled in the 1988 pre-season competition:

> That the centre half-forward and centre half-back lines of the centre square be extended directly to the boundary line on each side.
>
> The wing lines of the centre square to be extended to the 50-metre radius at both ends.
>
> At the centre bounce each team must have at least six players beyond the extended centre half-forward and centre half-back lines, of whom at least three must be within the 50-metre goal-line radius, and one within each area bounded by the extended wing line of the centre square, the extended centre half-forward line, the 50-metre radius line and the boundary line.
>
> The penalty for infringement, which would be detected by boundary umpires, to be a free kick to be taken from the centre of the ground by the ruckman of the non-offending team.[57]

There is no reference in the minutes to any debate, nor comments, just the simple line: "Motion lapsed". The concept of a netball-like chequerboard with players locked into zones clearly did not appeal to the directors, nor to the commission, which did not pursue the idea.

The game will always have those who want to make radical changes and

---

57   VFL Board minutes, December 1987.

those who want to retain the status quo. My view has always been towards the radical end of the spectrum, because change is inevitable. As we have seen, the game evolves, creating and re-creating itself year on year—and it gets more and more professional, week on week. May it always be so.

CHAPTER 15

Around the grounds

When it came to marketing the game, there were few elements as important as the places in which it was played.

It would be fair to say the venues for VFL football in the 1980s were a mixed lot. When I began working with the League, games were still being played at Windy Hill, Victoria Park, Princes Park, Moorabbin, Kardinia Park and the Western Oval, as well as at the MCG and the League's nominal headquarters, VFL Park.

To be charitable, the standard of facilities, for players and spectators alike, at the older suburban grounds was variable. To be less charitable, you could make a pretty convincing argument that the quality of the facilities was an actual disincentive for many fans of the game who might otherwise come to matches. The Blue Report had been clear on that point: "the MCG and VFL Park should be the venue for as many games of the top teams as possible".[58] Why? To enhance the experience of both members and "theatregoers".

One little survey result in the report told the tale. Respondents had been given two propositions. The first one was: "The facilities at some grounds, such as the MCG and VFL Park, are excellent." A bit of a leading question, but an emphatic result: 85 per cent agreed. The second proposition was: "The facilities at some grounds are an insult." This time 76 per cent agreed.

---

58 *VFL Football: Establishing the Basis for Future Success*, VFL Commission, 1985.

Not surprising—though this was well before the MCG makeover. By today's standards of amenity, catering and comfort, the MCG was still a pretty basic stadium in 1986, as was Waverley. And that gives a good idea of what you might have found at a suburban ground: standing-room only, cold, wet, stinking congested toilets, stepped standing room to get some sort of view, and very poor catering facilities. You had to be keen—which was entirely the point. The diehards went; many who might have gone, didn't.

The Blue Report carried another very informative table that neatly illustrated the possibilities for the game if only we could stage the big-drawing games at big-capacity venues. It looked at all games in 1984 between the big-drawing clubs of the League: Carlton, Collingwood, Essendon and Richmond. Two of the games had been played at VFL Park and had an average attendance of 65,000. Three had been played at the MCG and had an average crowd of 57,000. Two were played at Princes Park, average crowd 25,000; two at Victoria Park, 28,000; and three at Windy Hill, 24,000. Most encouraging of all, the Blue Report research found that "theatregoers" came in droves to good games at the big venues.[59]

Something had to change. The audiences were there if we could provide the venues to entice and hold them.

It was a key strategic priority to reduce the number of suburban grounds and find ways to increase the number of games played at the MCG and VFL Park. This strategy already had a certain amount of natural momentum, though it's fair to say that early in my term it didn't have the same sense of urgency as others. That said, the nature of the place football found itself in in the late 1980s meant that pretty much all the game's issues and disadvantages needed simultaneous attention. Everything was interlinked, from TV rights to ground rationalisation.

North Melbourne had played its last game at Arden Street in 1985 and the Hawks hadn't played at Glenferrie since 1973 (however, they had moved to another suburban ground, Princes Park). There was a quiet natural

---

59 Ibid.

momentum that was slowly but surely winding back the significance of the suburban home grounds. A crunch time was coming that would force the ultimate suburban confrontations and move Essendon out of Windy Hill, St Kilda out of Moorabbin, Hawthorn out of Princes Park and, finally, like pulling teeth, Collingwood out of Victoria Park.

In fact, Victoria Park would be a task that fell outside my time at the League. Collingwood would play its last game there in 1999[60] but the process of weaning the Magpies from Victoria Park started in the early 1990s. We crept up on their exit, reducing over a few years the number of games scheduled there. Club president Allan McAlister worked against us, thinking that his members were not in favour of moving out of their traditional home—yet the numbers showed that tens of thousands more supporters came to Collingwood games at the MCG!

Poor Allan was caught in a bit of a bind. On one occasion I decided to shift a Collingwood v Carlton game from Victoria Park to the MCG, for the best of all reasons: so that all the clubs' supporters could attend. We occasionally scheduled big games at Victoria Park so that we could reschedule them to the 'G' later, which had the effect of reducing the number of games played at the restricted-crowd ground. This time McAlister dug in his heels and went to the media, saying his team would be turning up at Victoria Park and if the opposition did not front then Collingwood would claim a walkover. I replied by saying that the commission set the schedule of matches and the Collingwood-Carlton game was now scheduled at the G, and if Collingwood did not turn up then they would forfeit the game. It was a classic Collingwood v Commission stand off.

McAlister came to see me and indicated that he had put himself over a barrel; could I get him off the hook with his members? It was obvious to him that the club's best interests would be served by playing at the G and drawing a bigger crowd, but there was a fanatical hard core at Victoria Park who wouldn't have a bar of it.

---

60 This event was, coincidentally, managed by Oakley Enterprises Australia Pty Ltd. It included a lunch in an adjoining warehouse for more than 1000 supporters, managed by Cathy Oswald in her inimitable style. Cathy managed many of these events for the AFL in its centenary year under John Lauritz.

I said, "I'll tell you what I'll do, Allan. You agree to play the game at the G and I'll agree to play five games at Victoria Park next season." Sounded generous, but unknown to McAlister that was precisely the number of games we had intended to schedule.

He thanked me profusely and went back to the media saying that he had extracted a concession for Collingwood to play five games next year at Victoria Park even though the commission was bent on reducing the number of games played there, and therefore he had agreed to play the Carlton game at the MCG.

You could always use McAlister's passion for Collingwood to advantage— because you could always predict his reaction.

Likewise, moving Carlton from Princes Park was a project most appropriately described as long term, particularly after John Elliott spent the best part of $20 million on building the Elliott Stand at the ground against commission advice. At least Princes Park in the pre-Docklands days had the advantage of a reasonable capacity and level of amenity. We were happy enough for Carlton to play there on the basis that its major games were played at the MCG.

All that said, the broad objective as we saw it in 1987 ended up being met. By the time football celebrated its centenary year in 1996, it was firmly headquartered, physically and emotionally, at the MCG. It had taken quite a bit of doing.

For 30 years the VFL had tried to break away from the MCG. In 1959 the clubs had put their heads together and decided that the League should have its own playing headquarters. The land—over 90 hectares of market gardens and dairy pasture in unfashionably remote Mulgrave—was bought in 1962 and the long journey began.

VFL Park was a dream, a representation of football's strength and independence and a bold symbol that the VFL would make its own way, on its own terms, in its own facilities. It was a dream born in many ways in the deep and enduring conflict between the League and the Melbourne

Cricket Club (MCC), which controlled the MCG. And it was very much a dream born of Sir Kenneth Luke, promoted by Eric McCutchan and propelled by Allen Aylett and Jack Hamilton. As Aylett tells it in his memoir:

> In 1959, the VFL embarked on the most ambitious project it had ever undertaken—the establishment of its own football stadium. VFL Park may never have been built (thank heavens it was!) if the VFL president of the 1950s, Sir Kenneth Luke, had not had to fight so many one-sided battles against sturdy MCG Trustees headed by Arthur Calwell and John Cain Senior. John Cain Jnr was to play his own rather disruptive role later.
>
> ... The design of the stadium itself was geared for Australian Rules football. The playing area was specially designed and spectator areas were constructed so there would be no visual interference from pillars or fences.
>
> It was envisaged that the stadium would accommodate 150,000 and that the League's premier event, the Grand Final, would be staged there.[61]

Over decades the VFL's dream of a Waverley headquarters and, most importantly, a Waverley Grand Final would be a wedge that would divide three great institutions: the state government, the MCC and the VFL. It was a bitter and, by the time I took over, quite dysfunctional relationship.

Matters that had festered for 20 years had come to a head over the VFL's determination to hold the 1984 Grand Final at VFL Park. The government of John Cain junior wasn't having a bar of it, and the MCG trustees and the MCC were digging in on a VFL claim for a better financial deal on the use of the MCG by football. Dr John Lill, former secretary of the MCC, told me that at one stage Aylett—who was quite correctly pushing for a reduction in the percentage of gate receipts paid to the Trust, from 17.5 to 15 per cent—had been confronted with a "dead bat" from Trust chair and former premier Sir Henry Bolte. Aylett stated that if the Trust would not

---

61 Allen Aylett with Greg Hobbs, *My Game: A Life in Football*, Macmillan, 1986, pp. 201-2.

move, then the next game between Collingwood and Melbourne would not be played at the MCG. Bolte, in typical style, said, "That's a chance I'm prepared to take."[62]

But the Grand Final discussion was at a stalemate, as Aylett recalls, and the VFL offered a "compromise": "Late in 1983, when the matter was deadlocked, the League said we would consider the MCG as the 1984 Grand Final venue if we could lease the entire ground (including the MCC Members' section) for the Grand Final day ... VFL Park members would have had exclusive use of the MCC Members' reserve."[63]

You get a sense from the proposal of the distance between the MCC and the VFL at the time. How the VFL could have imagined that the Cricket Club would allow its holy of holies, the MCG pavilion, Long Room and all, to be overrun on Grand Final day by the members from VFL Park because they'd rented the place is ... Well, it's a stunning proposal and one they could not have seriously expected would be agreed to.

In the end Cain drew a line in the sand and threatened to prevent the Grand Final moving through legislation if he had to. The thing was a mess, but in many ways summed up the state of play and the strange, obstinate alternative realities inhabited by the MCC and the VFL. In truth, each needed the other and both could claim, with good reason, strong bonds to the MCG turf.

In the end, the failed bid to stage the 1984 Grand Final at Waverley was something of a death knell for the ground. But its fundamental problem was access: you could get there only by road, and it was quite a trek from much of Melbourne. The argument in the early 1960s had been that the ground in Mulgrave would eventually, given the growth patterns of the city, be located handily in Melbourne's demographic heart. That may have been the case, but the public transport network said otherwise. In Melbourne

---

62 John Lill, interview with the author, 2014. The Trust later agreed to the reduced fee and, while it was considered a temporary measure, it still stands today, with the great proportion of rental at 15 per cent of the general admission price, and reserved seat premiums. Match-day costs, met by the clubs from admission charges, are more than $100,000 per match and account for the cost of police, security, cleaning, gate attendants, ushers and umpires.

63 Allen Aylett, *My Game*, 1986, p. 270.

the trams and trains radiate from the city like spokes in a bicycle wheel and pretty much exclude the wedge of the eastern suburbs that includes VFL Park. If you wanted to go to Waverley from the northeastern suburbs you had to get a bus or train into the city and then come back to Waverley by another train and bus (or bus all the way if you really wanted to suffer). The total hike would take easily over an hour and a half. Or you could drive and spend the same amount of time in traffic.

Quite simply, the VFL's flagship ground was a pain to get to, a pain to park at, and an even greater pain to drive away from—and it was windy, wet and cold. But for the League, it was a huge dream to walk away from, and that happened only slowly. So much of the VFL's vision of itself was tied up in Waverley. That great pan of a ground had been designed to take another level of seating through most of the circumference and raise the capacity to well beyond the 145,000 mark—though the 10,000 spectators at the back of the stands would be sitting in the next suburb.

The ambition for it had always been huge, but it was wrong-headed in so many ways. The clearer solution for football was to step up our use of the MCG, heal the rift with Victorian cricket and the MCC, and slowly pull the pin on the underperforming suburban grounds. These were sensible but hard choices.

It's not that I didn't see what could be done. Very early in my term I had serious conversations with the state government; I needed to know if there was even the slightest possibility that major capital works might save us, that perhaps a rail link might be built along the Monash Freeway to VFL Park.

It was some years before we received the final word: "It won't happen, Ross. It will never happen." That was the considered view in 1992 of the Kennett Government's transport minister, Alan Brown, who met me in his office on his knees, saying, "All hail the AFL, all hail the AFL," and then gave me the bad news. By then VFL Park was a lost cause. In five years work would begin on Docklands Stadium, and VFL Park (then called Waverley Park) would be history.

Even back in 1987, it was pretty clear to me that if we could get an MCC deal done, VFL Park would never be more than a second ground where we played the occasional match of the day, and perhaps a shared home ground for a number of clubs. I realised that it was not appropriate: it was never going to be allowed to host a Grand Final, was never going to have the transport infrastructure that would make either its existing or potential capacity a logistic possibility, was never going to be expanded to give it a capacity that might make it more viable as a big-game venue (never mind that an ultimate 145,000-capacity crowd might mean it would take the better part of a week to get out of the car park).

Of course, VFL Park did come into its own when the MCG's Great Southern Stand was being built through 1991, and the memorable Grand Final between Hawthorn and West Coast was played before a capacity crowd of 75,230. I am sure Sir Kenneth Luke would have been watching from above, a very proud man. Unfortunately the match was not to be remembered for West Coast confirming the strength of the national competition, or Jason Dunstall's six goals, or Paul Dear's Norm Smith Medal, but for Angry Anderson's rendition of *Bound for Glory* next to what has been immortalised as a Batmobile! Champion marathon runner Robert de Castella sat perched in the back of the vehicle, watching on with a sense of the occasion on his face.

What was not obvious was the comedy going on behind the scenes. On that day we were also honouring boxers Jeff Fenech, Fighting Harada and Lionel Rose, but Lionel was having a little trouble with a middle-ear problem. He was perched on top of the back seat of a convertible waiting to go out on to the ground, and as it took off he rolled off the back of the car into the dirt! Lionel picked himself up, dusted himself off with a little help from staff and was put back in the car with a staff member crouching on the floor holding on to his legs to avoid a further excursion off the back of the car.

In many ways, it was a special day for football; in others, it was a day that will remain part of footy's inestimable log of larger-than-life tales.

For all those fond memories, once it was clear in the mid-1980s that there was no going ahead with the grand plans for VFL Park, the necessity of a restored conversation between the VFL and the MCC became obvious.

As League chairman I was automatically on the MCG Trust, and my seat had been filled less than joyfully by the previous couple of incumbents. The relationship between VFL and the MCC had become poisonous. It was absurdly dysfunctional for two bodies that held so much of Melbourne's sporting life in their hands.

Not that I approached the MCC in a craven way. When I was on the Trust I'd put it to the trustees bluntly: "Where would you be without the football audience? The crowds, the catering rights, the straight-out gate monies?" I even suggested at one Trust meeting, tongue in cheek, that we should rename the ground the "Melbourne Football Ground", to make my point.

Our estimate was that football accounted for more than 70 per cent of revenues at the MCG, and yet the calendar of usage of the ground was split 50-50 between cricket and football and we had to put up with a wicket in the middle of the ground that routinely reduced the place to a mud heap in a wet winter. As we saw it, most cricket matches other than Tests and international one-day games could be played at smaller venues (John Lill told me money was spent on Punt Road Oval for this purpose[64]).

The odds and the Melbourne establishment were stacked against football, and it's not hard to understand why the Ayletts and the Hamiltons were not too happy, and why Sir Kenneth Luke and the VFL's administrative director, Eric McCutchan, had invested so heavily in VFL Park and tried to get some independence for the VFL. Jack Hamilton had found the commission view hard to swallow and this was a significant reason I was in the job. I think the VFL Commission saw my arrival as an opportunity to rebuild the relationship, to rectify a relationship between football and cricket that had become destructive.

As it happened, I wasn't a complete unknown to the MCC or the cricket establishment. My father, Hector, was a champion Victorian cricketer and

---

64   John Lill, interview with the author, 2014.

later became president of the St Kilda Cricket Club and a Victorian Cricket Association (VCA) delegate. I'll let legendary sportswriter Ken Piesse tell the tale as it appeared in the biography of my father he wrote for the St Kilda Cricket Club:

> Hec Oakley was an outstanding all-round sportsman—a first-class cricketer—an attacking right-hand batsman with a wide array of strokes, an accomplished amateur footballer, a national table-tennis champion and state tennis player, as well as a single-handicap golfer. As a young boy, Oakley had fallen from his bicycle and impaled his right knee on the stump of a bamboo tree. When it became seriously infected, a specialist planned to amputate below the knee. But the family's doctor recommended it be put into plaster for six months, the only long-term effect being that Oakley swapped to kicking the football with his left foot, rather than his right!
>
> In 1929-30 he was invited to play cricket for St Kilda and by the end of the season he was in the state team after starting with innings of 11, 98, 100, 102, 90 and 67. One writer was moved to describe him as "another Don Bradman". A predominantly off-side player, he played for St Kilda for more than a decade and a half with great success.
>
> For Victoria in the Sheffield Shield, Oakley made four centuries, his most memorable being his 108 in three and a half hours against South Australia during his second season in 1930-31. His highest first-class score was 162 against Tasmania in 1938-39. He made 83 not out and 50 while wickets fell around him against the MCC Bodyliners Bill Voce and Bill Bowes in 1932-33.[65]

So I was part of a sporting family from birth. My brother Denis was also a champion goalkicker with Sandringham in the VFA (I watched him kick 16 goals in one game against Dandenong) and a more brutal player than I ever was, despite his calling as a man of the cloth. A Uniting Church minister, he was known as "the pugilistic parson" and served a number of

---

65 Ken Piesse, *Down at the Junction There's a Cricket Ground: St Kilda Cricket Club, the First 150 Years*, St Kilda Cricket Club, 2005.

suspensions in his time. I played cricket in a premiership team at school and later for the St Kilda twos until I decided to concentrate on football full time. Bill Johnson, the son of MCC secretary and Australian captain Ian Johnson, was a fellow Wesley College student and one of my best mates at school, though a better cricketer; he was captain of the school firsts.

This heritage inserted me into the cricket network without question. It might sound a bit silly, and all very "old Melbourne", but the truth is there was a rapport, and that meant I was halfway to healing the MCC relationship. That's Melbourne: it's an "old school tie" city—or it certainly was back then.

The MCC's John Lill and Don Cordner and I hit it off and started to talk like reasonable people about the importance of football to the ground and the importance of the ground to football. It went both ways.

It wasn't all down to me, of course. A lot of pre-conditioning had already been done by Peter Scanlon. He met first with Lill and Cordner to talk about how the VFL could work more closely with the MCC—which came as a complete surprise to both men, given the stance of the VFL previously. Indeed, Cordner was shocked that someone from the VFL was even talking to them. They were as anti the VFL as the VFL was anti the MCC, but between them and at Scanlon's urging, they set up a subcommittee to look at the issues. Scanlon's job was to get them to agree that bringing our two bodies together made sense. Hamilton knew Scanlon was going to see them: he supported him going, but his heart wasn't in it. He saw it as selling out to the enemy.

Scanlon tells the story of inviting Cordner to a match at Waverley, including a dinner that ended, as they always did, with Scanlon inviting everyone on the table to toss in $5 and pick the game's winner, the winning margin, and who would kick the first goal. (It's a Scanlon thing—still is.) He remembers Cordner saying, "Oh no, Peter, it is proper to only put in 20 cents each."[66]

Jeff Browne, our legal adviser, who came to know Cordner through this

---

66   Peter Scanlon, interview with the author, 2014.

process, said, "He was an old-fashioned bloke, very well respected, very MCC-centric, but on the ball and he knew what the end game was for the MCC. He was actually prepared to give ground that no one had been prepared to do previously to get the end result. He saw this as the big moment to actually get something done at the G, but was not quite sure how to go about it."[67]

Colin Carter (later to become a commissioner) from Pappas Carter Evans and Koop was employed as a mediator on 9 December 1986 by both parties to continue the process to a reunion.

In all the research it was very clear that the majority of our supporters saw the MCG as the home of football. They weren't too keen on Waverley. So it was clear that if we pushed on with Waverley we were making a rod for our backs. It would have been a total disaster. Waverley had a great surface and good corporate facilities, but it was in the wrong location for transport, and wasn't a pleasant place to visit as it was in Melbourne's rain belt.

Two things dominated our focus. First, we needed to lock in the Grand Final at the MCG on favourable terms, and we might need to sign a very long-term deal in order to do that. Second, we needed to gain rights for our VFL members and provide them with appropriate facilities at the G.

In early April 1987, Browne and I met with Cordner and Lill with the specific intention of getting the sticking-point issues formally on the table. Browne was a great sounding board in all the negotiations; he played a big part in what was eventually achieved. I reported back to the commission at the meeting of 7 April. As recorded in the minutes, "Chairman advised that the purpose of the meeting was to determine the areas of common interest between the MCC and the VFL ... it was agreed this objective was now more approachable after the meeting."[68]

There were seven key points to the discussion:

1. The general accommodation of 32,000 VFL Park full members at the MCG and the availability of acceptable seating and dining facilities

---

67   Jeff Browne, interview with the author, 2014.
68   VFL Board minutes, 7 April 1987.

2. Future development plans for the Melbourne Cricket Ground and their impact on VFL involvement/tenancy

3. The issue of splitting the available accommodation for members between VFL Park and MCC members, i.e. MCC Members–traditional area, VFL Park Members–Northern Stand

4. Available advertising exposure for the VFL on fences and matrix screen

5. Season starting time, noting present occupancy arrangements in favour of cricket in February, and the availability of the ground for pre-season night series to be conducted by the League

6. Reciprocal membership arrangements between VFL Park and the MCC and the availability of rights during cricket season to VFL Park members

7. Length of tenure of any agreement to be entered into between the two parties.[69]

There was a lot of to-ing and fro-ing. Accommodating the VFL Park members was a critical issue for the League, one of both finance and good faith. It all came down to which stand, and that came down to a narrow choice from the poor options available. We were offered the Olympic Stand. Nope, it was a hideous concrete wasteland. The Ponsford Stand? No, it was behind the goals and had no dining facilities. All that was left was the old Southern Stand, that long sweeping shed that filled half the ground. It wasn't acceptable, either. It had no facilities of any sort—well, none that would be worth paying a membership to enjoy—and that was a deficiency that went further than simply satisfying the needs of the VFL.

This was a turning point. What emerged through our negotiations with the MCC was the pressing need for a refurbishment of the ground. It wasn't spoken about at first but soon became increasingly apparent, in large part through one of those strange mergings of fate and common interest that played such a big part in the story of football through these tricky and eventful years.

---

69   Ibid.

In 1988, with negotiations between the League and the MCC progressing but really no closer to a firm and mutually agreeable conclusion—an impasse caused by the ground's physical limitations as much as anything—a routine inspection of the structure of the 50-year-old Southern Stand found "concrete cancer".

A disaster? No, a blessing. The balance between the MCC and the VFL shifted subtly. They had a major $150 million project to undertake, and to get it done they needed our help.

An offer came from the MCC (how things had changed!): if we rebuild it, will you be involved? The conversation started along those lines. A letter from me to Cordner dated 8 June 1988 set out the deal. The League agreed to pay $1 million a year during the building process, and a section of the new Daryl Jackson-designed stand would be set aside for our members.

The state government was happy with the way things were going—though Premier Cain couldn't help himself, and insisted that he have a representative at all negotiations even though the government wasn't putting any money in (they were just providing a government guarantee in order for the Trust to get a lower interest rate on the substantial loan required to build the facility).

As Browne recalls it, "There were many forces working against this deal, so the VFL had to drive the negotiations and make all the running, with the government, represented by Rowen Craigie (now of Crown Casino fame), putting many stumbling blocks in our way—although they were not of Rowen's making."[70]

Cain was a very political animal who never missed an opportunity to have a shot at the VFL when he needed a diversion. He knew there were political points to be scored in siding with a basically conservative sporting constituency and taking on the organisation that was doing so much to change the nature of football. Cain had a big hand in the MCG redevelopment too, of course, a role he outlined in great detail in an essay he wrote for *The Age* in March 1992, on the eve of the opening of the

---

70 Jeff Browne, interview with the author, 2014.

Great Southern Stand. His article described the long battle between the League and the MCC, a battle well represented by Cain's opening sentences: "The VFL had, for many years, resented being a 'prisoner' of the MCC trustees. Those who ran football believed it was their game and they should be able to conduct it—especially the finals—on a ground they controlled on terms and conditions that suited them."[71]

Cain had made it very clear from the time he took office in 1982 that the government supported the MCG as Melbourne's major stadium and that the Grand Final should remain at the G, and he did work in the background to find a solution. But I was grateful, in that same essay, that he acknowledged the rapprochement had come when I wrote to the MCC chairman, Don Cordner, proposing a long-term agreement between the MCC and the League for the G to become the "home of football". Cain wrote: "I know Dr Cordner regards this initiative by Ross Oakley as the catalyst of the Great Southern Stand. He says it required great imagination and courage. I agree …"[72]

But as with all things, there were tensions to be resolved. The government took the view that the public should always have access to prime viewing space—a point nobody disagreed with, but there were also commercial imperatives to be resolved. It was important not just to the financial viability of the development, but also to the ongoing viability of both the League and the MCC, that the new stand have attractive corporate facilities. Cain acknowledged this point but insisted that the general public must not be disadvantaged in any way by the inclusion of corporate boxes and dining facilities and all the rest. There must have been quite a bit of backroom muttering in the Labor Party about the big end of town taking over the people's ground.

What it came down to was a set of stifling restrictions on the design process. Lill remembers a meeting he went to with Premier Cain, ministers Rob Jolly and Tony Sheehan, and architect Daryl Jackson. Cain insisted that the superboxes be at the back of the stand, which Lill objected to on

---

71 John Cain, "Centrepiece for the people", *The Age*, 29 March 1992.
72 Ibid.

the grounds that corporates would not pay the amount of money needed to cover the cost of construction if the boxes were in the worst location. Jackson came up with an acceptable compromise: putting seating in front of the boxes on the third level, which would mean that new spectator access had to be designed into the third level of the stand at great cost.

He must have been pulling his hair out. It's hard to imagine anyone of his reputation copping such a level of design interference and having to compromise the services being offered within the new building. It was a similar story at the National Tennis Centre (now Melbourne Park), which was built at around the same time. There, the superboxes were consigned to the very back of the seating. Top dollar for the worst view in the house.

At the MCG the inclusion of public seating in front of the superboxes guaranteed that superbox patrons could cop quite a bit of lip through the open glass from the general public seated in front of them. It rather diminished the superbox experience, shall we say.

But that wasn't the end of it. It seems "someone" also decreed that there would be no toilets in either the superboxes or the corporate dining rooms, despite the original drawings clearly showing them in place. Never mind how much you were spending to have your corporate day or night at the football—when it came to using the toilet you could go to the same facilities as the general public. What if the Queen were to visit the ground as an AFL guest? Where would she, er, be able to make herself comfortable? Well, she could go over to the MCC committee room, where they had toilets!

An email from the architects to Lill points out that dedicated toilets were not required by regulation as there were sufficient public toilets outside the boxes and dining rooms. It was a cost- and space-saving decision that "seemed reasonable". This decision wasn't communicated to the League at the time.

The government would argue that the MCC needed to watch costs. The government had budgeted the project at $210 million against the MCC's $150 million, allowing for concern that the project would go the way of many others in the government's portfolio. The eventual cost of the stand came in at $147 million.

The toilet ban didn't last. A year or so into the life of the new stand, and after a change of government, the boxes were retrofitted—at great cost.

The eventual deal on the construction of the Great Southern Stand between the League and the MCC was for 30 years, and saw us in the new stand and pretty much looking at a new future for the game in 1992. Indeed, the capital payback had been budgeted at 27 years—which, with the increased crowds and more games at the ground, was achieved in about 17 years.

We'd come a long way from the anger and abuse that had summed up the relationship in the early 1980s. Browne reflects: "I got to know [you] best in this process and believe that if the MCG agreement—which the football world has to date underrated as far as its importance in the game's history—had not been achieved, we would not have seen the development of the MCG as it is today and would certainly not have been able to achieve the level of ground rationalisation that has been possible."[73] Scanlon's, Carter's and Browne's roles in achieving the historic agreement were pivotal, as were those of Cordner and Lill.

Of course, once the deal was done the stand had to be built. We must all recognise a job well done by Lill and the rest of the MCC committee—we now have a world-class ground in which to watch our football. And, although there were times when Cain's involvement was less than helpful, there is one point in which his intransigence was a clear positive: the government's assistance was also dependent on the MCC making membership available to women.

To achieve everything the League needed, we had to remove the limit on games played on the MCG and get the restriction on Sunday football lifted. It was nonsensical that every other sport was able to operate on Sunday but not football. We had to get approval from the government.

I spoke with Minister for Sport Tom Reynolds when the Kennett Government was elected and he agreed with me on the Sunday football issue. He raised it with the premier, who agreed, and we worked out a plan

---

73   Ibid.

to make the change slowly, without too much ballyhoo. Reynolds had a plan: "What we will do is gradually change the number of games you play on Sunday without announcing it to the media, and eventually it will be considered standard practice."[74]

We did just that without any blowback, and when journalist Mike Sheahan asked Reynolds a couple of years later about the increase in Sunday games, Tom simply said, "Oh, that's been going on for years." Sheahan accepted this and did not run a story.

The Trust also had to do a major upgrade on the surface of the ground, tearing up the grass and installing a modern drainage system to ensure the surface could cope with more games. This was all done in the spring of 1992.

We were a bit annoyed that we were the only tenant of the MCG that had to get its prices agreed on by both the government and the Trust before we could make any changes; a change of government also fixed this.

The MCG, and the League with it, have never looked back. All the marquee games are played there, and drop-in pitches have turned the surface into a year-round sward of smooth green.

There was still a lot of shuffling to be done, with the arrangements of teams and grounds only really being settled after the opening of Docklands Stadium in 2000. Essendon, Carlton, Western Bulldogs, St Kilda and North Melbourne now call Docklands home and Collingwood, Melbourne, Richmond and Hawthorn call the G home, but in essence all the clubs play their big-crowd-drawing games at the G and their lesser-crowd-drawing games at Docklands.

At these two grounds with their superb facilities and ability to cater for varying crowd sizes, football can now accommodate the needs of both the spectators and the teams—something that might never have been achieved had the League not given up on the Waverley dream and made peace with the MCC.

---

74   Hon. Tom Reynolds, interview with the author, 2014.

CHAPTER 16

State of the clubs

The historic deals to bring in the new clubs had been done; the price had been agreed. Now what?

Well, that was up to me. With only a little over three months to go, it was my job to get the Brisbane Bears and the West Coast Eagles on to the field for the 1987 season. And that was a job and a half.

None of the contractual detail had been negotiated, let alone agreed. This put the League in an awkward position. Quite simply, the new clubs had us over a barrel—the League had committed to a 1987 competition that included a team from Brisbane and a team from Perth, and there was no going back on that. All we had to do was negotiate every last condition around those fundamentally in-principle arrangements, from home grounds to team lists and air travel.

So the new clubs had a fair bit of bargaining power. After all, each had paid the League a $4 million licence fee for the privilege of joining; the other clubs wouldn't have let them in otherwise. And having received their lifesaving injection of cash, the other clubs had a pretty narrow interest in how the new arrangements for the Bears and Eagles worked out. They were so focused on immediate issues of cost and benefit, of quick dollars in the here and now, that they didn't look ahead 10 years to the possibilities of a national game. The club presidents just wanted cash in hand so they could balance their books.

The commission had to devise ways for the ailing competition to grow its revenue base in the future. It was a fundamental and lasting tension between clubs with interests on a narrow horizon and a League that realised the only true way to fulfil those narrow interests was by growing the competition for the benefit of all. Not always an easy balance.

In those early weeks of 1987 the VFL had to sort its own mind out, too. What were we doing with the airline agreement, with corporate sponsorship, accommodation deals in Melbourne and interstate? Then we had to take those elements and build them into a negotiation process with the Bears and the Eagles.

We put our best team together: it was me with lots of help from Jeff Browne; Graeme Samuel and Peter Scanlon had done some early work on getting the new licensees' minds in the right space, and without that work we wouldn't have had the deals done before the beginning of the pre-season competition. I needed the support, as I was also sorting out the general state of play in the League.

There was, however, a will to do the deal. The new teams wanted to come into the competition and had already made a significant financial commitment—that was the bottom line.

There was a fair bit of guesswork involved. The costs of running a non-Victorian club were much higher than for the other clubs. Travel was a major part of that, but only a part. A factor in our negotiations had to be understanding that the entire interstate operation was an ambitious undertaking that would be hard to sustain, at least for a period. The costs were a mystery, and so was the revenue potential. We had no real sense of what it might be.

In a lot of ways, establishing the Eagles was the easier of the two tasks. Unlike the Brisbane Bears, the Eagles would begin their playing days in a familiar Australian Rules territory—a huge plus. But still mistakes were made. From the outset the club was run by Richard Colless as chairman and John Walker as CEO, with other notables Neil Hamilton and Murray

McHenry. The CEO and chairman were not able to spend as much time together personally supporting each other as they should: unbeknown to all in football except those close to the Eagles, Colless was domiciled in Sydney during the seven months of his 1987 presidency of the West Coast Eagles.

While it was very much in keeping with the high-flying corporate mood of the times, the Eagles made a huge miscalculation by issuing debentures in the corporation rather than simply offering memberships. The supporters were there, but they had no idea what a debenture was and avoided the idea in droves. The low number of memberships meant that in the 1987 season Eagles supporters would pay at the gate and that money would be split three ways, between the home club, the League and the visiting club. Without effective ticketed memberships, the Eagles were robbing themselves of valuable revenue.

The club had some pretty smart business minds involved, but the debenture idea was never discussed with the League. On reflection we'd probably have advised against it, but things were moving too quickly.

Anthony Barker details the debenture disaster in his remarkable account of the history of West Australian football, *Behind the Play*. The West Coast Eagles were originally owned by a firm called Indian Pacific Limited. The football club was the linchpin of a broader, ambitious (and ultimately unfulfilled) business model, and the float of IPL was a drive for football membership—a very West Australian idea. Very much of the times, too. As Barker writes, though:

> They were running ahead of contemporary trends in the assumptions they made in aiming at affluent investors when they floated IPL.
> And in the process they made a damaging business decision.
> … the key to football revenue was club memberships. Money taken at the gate was divided between the competing clubs, whereas season ticket revenue was retained by the host club. It would have been difficult for the Eagles immediately to build a large membership and take advantage of this system.
> But in aiming the float at the top end of the market and focusing a

> membership drive on the Eagles Supporters Club, the IPL directors made the task much harder. Supporters Club membership did not bring with it a season ticket. Such a ticket was available to those who bought an IPL investment package, ranging from $1500 to $2000, containing a bundle of 50 cent shares and a $500 debenture.
>
> People in Victoria, where a simple club membership bought a season ticket, looked on in amazement at this arrangement.[1]

Indeed they did. But even in the wild west of WA the concept was a flop. My meetings with CEO Walker were few and far between, but I had a memorable one in Melbourne shortly after his appointment when I visited him in his hotel penthouse suite and found it strewn with ice buckets of French champagne. I was staggered at such excesses in a football environment that was struggling to stabilise its finances. It was explained that it was necessary because IPL was a public company and had to entertain and behave like one. Walker clearly hadn't been involved in the public companies I had run or worked for!

Colless said of the time: "Of the money we raised, somewhere between two and three million dollars just disappeared for unbudgeted items. It was actually quite shambolic."[2]

Walker left the position of CEO during the year and Bill Kerr took charge—literally. When Kerr took over he said that the nearest thing to an accounting system he found was "a suitcase full of cheque butts", a claim described as "bullshit" by Walker.[3] (Kerr was later to gain a moment of fame, at least in footy circles, for a timely and impassioned speech he delivered at the League's Hobart conference in July 1989, in which he spoke of the need for mergers in Victoria. He was so convincing that he had clubs talking about the prospect with some intent and we were left thinking there was a real chance of a merger occurring. However, by the time we got back to Melbourne and representatives talked to their boards, the impetus

---

[1] Anthony J. Barker, *Behind the Play: A History of Football in Western Australia from 1868*, West Australian Football Commission, 2004..

[2] Richard Colless, interview with the author, 2014.

[3] Anthony J. Barker, *Behind the Play*, 2004, p. 215.

had dissipated. Samuel was a little more cynical, saying, "The chance of achieving a merger had disappeared by the time the delegates got on the bus to come home."[4])

Nevertheless, IPL was in trouble. A rescue package of $5 million was hastily organised, with five people putting in $1 million each: Neil Hamilton, Colless, McHenry, Mark Hohnen and Robert Armstrong. This started a period of bitter dispute and resulted in Hamilton requesting that his business partner Colless remove himself from the chairmanship in July 1987 to concentrate on their business in Sydney, several months earlier than Colless had planned.

IPL failed as a business, and eventually its holding in the West Coast Eagles was taken over by the WAFL—but we had a little way to travel before that happened. It was just as well the team started brightly on the field: they made the finals in 1988, a great achievement.

And Brisbane? Well, Brisbane was a whole other kettle of very complicated fish.

The key question, and it became increasingly pressing as the months marched on and the pre-season competition approached, was where would the Bears play? This issue confounded the commission from as early as August 1986, when the minutes of a meeting chaired by Jack Hamilton recorded a presentation made by an eventually unsuccessful consortium led by sports promoter John Brown. The Brown bid would firstly be recommended and then defeated by the combination of the QAFL, actor Paul Cronin as front man and Christopher Skase as backer—but in the Brown consortium's favour, it did at least suggest a reasonably coherent proposal for the redevelopment of the QEII stadium in suburban Brisbane as part of its pitch for the licence.

It would have cost many millions to upgrade the home of the 1982 Commonwealth Games. Brown itemised it for the benefit of the commission: $1.25 million for developing a suitable playing arena (work that would

---

4   Graeme Samuel, interview with the author, 2014.

involve removal of the existing running track), a $1.1 million contingency for any possible future restoration of that athletics track, $250,000 for the relocation of the Brisbane Athletics Association, and a future contingency of $4.8 million for the provision of lights.

The Cronin-Skase bid was eventually successful, but it was unclear on precisely where the team would play, with the initially floated proposition being a development that would be an adjunct to the Brisbane Entertainment Centre at Boondall.

We didn't know it then, but neither Boondall nor QEII—nor various ill-fated attempts to gain access for football to Brisbane's home of cricket and greyhound racing, the Gabba—was ever a serious part of the Skase strategy for the Brisbane Bears.

The minutes of the commission meeting of 30 October 1986 contained the first fateful (and misspelt) reference to a location that would dog the conversation with the Brisbane consortium for the duration of the Skase involvement:

> In respect of the playing venue of the Brisbane Bears Football Club, chairman advised that the licensee's present strategy appeared to be to find a temporary venue for 12 months and that a permanent location be established on freehold land for use from 1988 onward. Concern was expressed by the commission in respect of the location presently proposed as a temporary venue, noting that present indications were that a ground at Karara (sic) on the Gold Coast appeared to be the objective of the licensee. It was noted that whilst the commission was prepared in principle to support the idea of a temporary venue, given the club's name, Brisbane, it was felt that for identity purposes such temporary venue should be located closer to Brisbane.[5]

Carrara (we'd learn that spelling soon enough) might have been nigh on an hour's drive from Brisbane, but it was far, far closer to the Gold Coast business interests of one Christopher Skase. We weren't happy about it, but there wasn't much we could do in the short time before play began in

---

5   VFL Commission minutes, 30 October 1986.

1987. The deals had been done, the licence approved, monies (eventually) exchanged—in the end there was no option but to go with Carrara. That said, the commission made it plain, again and again, that it viewed the Gold Coast base as a temporary arrangement to see us through the Bears' first season. Little did we know.

It wasn't over by a long chalk, of course, and Skase employed his favoured techniques of delay and obfuscation. In January 1987 the commission gave in:

> Chairman advised that the Brisbane licensee had requested approval of the commission to its choice of venue for the 1987 season, noting that a permanent home for the club was still being sought. It was noted that the licensee had chosen the Carrara ground located approximately 12 kilometres from Surfers Paradise and 75 kilometres from Brisbane on the main Nerang/Broadbeach road.[6]

I'd been up there and had a good look around, and hadn't really liked what I found. The ground was below par in terms of both facilities and access, but the biggest issue, as I told that commission meeting, was a simpler one. Carrara was not Brisbane:

> Chairman tabled report resultant from his visit to the site which described the physical characteristics of the ground and the improvements that would be necessary to bring it up to standard as a VFL venue. Chairman advised that there were two shortcomings in respect of the venue that were of major concern, those being the accessibility of traffic to the site and the fact that the "Brisbane" team would be well removed from the Brisbane metropolitan area.[7]

From Skase and the Bears the argument kept coming back: sponsors wouldn't support the team unless it was at Carrara. Pretty hard to swallow, but true, too, that the commission and the VFL had pushed at this too hard and fast. It was—and I say this with the luxury of hindsight—far too big a task to expect the team to get up and running in a traditional rugby league state in the timeframe the League had pursued. Most of the grounds that

---

6   VFL Commission minutes, January 1987.
7   Ibid.

might have suited were rectangular, and the playing pool offered pretty slim pickings.

Eventually we ran out of options and time. Carrara it had to be, an hour from Brisbane with hastily erected stands and facilities. Very much sub par.

We couldn't have been clearer with Skase and Cronin: Carrara was a one-year proposal, no more.

Our anxieties were borne out in that 1987 season. The best that can be said is that the Bears took the field. Coach Peter Knights was a good signing, Mark Williams, Brad Hardie … But the list by and large was always going to struggle. Again, we at the League hadn't really done as much as we might have to help.

Alan Schwab had put together a deal that forced each VFL club to donate players from its list to the new team—two players from each of the top eight teams and one player from each of the bottom four. The result was predictable, with clubs sending the halt and the lame up to Carrara. Carlton gave the Bears one guy who had by that point moved overseas, and another with a career-ending injury.

It was a rotten deal. Few of the clubs were prepared to be generous in those days, but they had to agree, however grudgingly, to the rules: give us your four million bucks, and here's a couple of old hacks.

The commission relied very heavily on Schwab to construct an arrangement to build two teams that could be reasonably competitive, and it wasn't at all easy. He was trying to put together something the clubs would accept. He was the club man in the administration and had all sorts of networks, linkages and favours to call upon within the boys' club. The awkward truth is that his loyalties were divided. He would have been as much worried about what the existing clubs would make of him as getting a good result for the new teams. But that was football in 1987—a bit "between two worlds".

As it was, things went well enough for the West Coast team. It had the rich traditions of a football state to draw on, not to mention the playing cream of the WAFL crop. The Eagles made the finals series in 1988, well on the way to that celebrated 1992 premiership.

The road was somewhat stonier for the Bears. They opened the 1987 season with two wins—including kicking 23 goals in round two to beat Geelong at Kardinia Park—and had six wins for the year (not bad on today's expectations), but, more significantly, their games had small crowds and equivalently poor revenue flows. Carrara was to blame as much as anything: it was simply too much to expect a new fan base to drive an hour from Brisbane to watch a match in pretty shoddy facilities that the locals were more than likely going to lose.

The Bears pulled 98,616 fans to the 11 matches at Carrara in that first year, an average of 8965 per game—a disappointing outcome by any standards. As a point of comparison, the struggling Fitzroy's lowest average per game during my time was 13,562 (in 1991).

Through the year we kept banging away at attempting to arrange a new headquarters for the Bears. I had talks with Brisbane's mayor, Sallyanne Atkinson, but Town Hall was against using the Gabba, perhaps in part because of a negotiating position put by the club, against our better judgment at the League, that the Bears wanted management rights at the home of Queensland cricket. Not much chance under those terms.

We took things to a pretty advanced stage, though. As I reported to the commission in June 1987:

> Discussions had been held between members of the League administration and the firm Leighton Contractors regarding a major feasibility study being undertaken by the company on behalf of the Trustees of the Woolloongabba Cricket Ground. It was noted that further discussions would be held with the company this week, prior to calling an informal discussion with the chairman of the Brisbane Bears, Mr P. Cronin, to provide information in regard to the redevelopment of the venue to provide a forum for discussion of the future playing venue of the Brisbane Bears.[8]

---

8   VFL Commission minutes, June 1987.

There was some kind of hope: the Gabba trustees were keen to redevelop the ground and needed a winter tenant to make the figures work. For its part, the commission was keen to close the door on Carrara, and the club was broke and desperate. The August meeting noted a last-roll-of-the-dice request from the Bears: "Chairman made separate reference to a request of the club to conduct a 'free' or discounted admission price day for its last home game against Footscray to determine whether there was any dormant support for the Bears playing at that venue."[9]

There wasn't, as it turned out.

Paul Cronin was called in to front the next commission meeting in September. He made no bones about what a poor year it had been at Carrara, and proposed three alternatives for a home ground in the coming 1988 season: the QEII stadium at Chandler, the Gabba and, yes, Carrara.

The mood in the room was tense. There were time lags on even the early negotiation process for both Chandler and the Gabba that would see nothing substantial emerge in either case before at least October, and even then it would be nothing more than discussion. In the meantime, Cronin told the commission of roadworks that would improve access to Carrara, and the club's unshaken belief after the disaster of 1987 that the ground could be made to work. As he said—and much of this has turned out to be true—the Gold Coast was an expanding area that over the coming decade would reach a population of more than a million people. The effective border of Brisbane would be elongated to the south.

None of that would do much for the fortunes of the Bears in 1988, and after the poor attendances and performances of 1987, the club was already heavily in debt. Cronin left the meeting with a flea in his ear. As the minutes recorded:

> Chairman reiterated the commission's view that Carrara was not considered to be a suitable venue for the future conduct of VFL football in Queensland and that it was the strong view of the commission that the club should secure an appropriate venue in metropolitan Brisbane ... it was resolved that correspondence be directed urgently to

---

9   Ibid.

> Mr Cronin advising that the commission was of the view that Carrara was an unacceptable venue for 1988 and that should the Brisbane Australian Football Club be unsuccessful in securing an acceptable venue in metropolitan Brisbane by 3 October 1987 then the commission would advise the club of its intention to participate in negotiations necessary to reach that objective.[10]

The Bears stalled. We tried to get Christopher Skase to front the commission meeting of 2 November, but he was "not available". We wrote to him, stating again that Carrara would not be an acceptable venue for the coming year's football. He came to Jolimont for a meeting in late November and, with Cronin, made a presentation that in a nutshell argued that "the Gold Coast was Brisbane and Australia's playground" and that "a home ground at Carrara complements the Bears' Brisbane base". The population was growing, and the Bears' Carrara strategy would "create a football ground integral to Australia's holiday playground, the Gold Coast. Chandler (the QEII option) will be a peripheral suburb and just one of many other sporting facilities." Last but not least, in the Skase mind Carrara was a money magnet: "The operating economics of corporate sponsorship and individual attendance is better at Carrara. High personal expenditure in a holiday atmosphere is a magnet to sponsors."[11]

We were on the losing side of this fight, if only because time and circumstances were so much against us. Skase was utterly determined. Carrara was part of his vision for the Gold Coast region, a vision that had his other interests squarely in the frame.

The process staggered onwards. I had last-minute talks with the Queensland government, hoping for some kind of breakthrough. Mike Ahern was premier, and his minister for small business, communications and technology, Rob Borbidge, seemed keen on finding a way of getting the Bears to the Brisbane area.

After a series of encouraging conversations through 1987, everything

---

10   VFL Commission minutes, September 1987.
11   VFL Commission minutes, November 1987.

turned on a dime. Borbidge had changed his mind. "Ross, I'm a great believer that if someone is putting money into something, they have a right to determine where that activity is located," he told me. I guess Skase had been having the odd word as well.

In the last days of 1987, Skase played his ultimate trump: he threatened to pull the Qintex money out of the Bears unless the commission agreed to let the team play 1988 at Carrara. That would have been a disaster for the Bears, who were then in debt to Qintex for many millions of dollars. Removing the Qintex guarantee would almost certainly bring the club down; there was no one else to pick up the pieces.

The commission waved the white flag in February 1988:

> Chairman confirmed that all parties had accepted the reality that the Bears would have no alternative but to use Carrara as their home venue in season 1988, but that in respect of subsequent years a dispute existed between the QAFL and the proprietors of the Brisbane Bears over whether the club would remain at Carrara or should transfer to metropolitan Brisbane as was required in the original licence and participation agreement with the QAFL.[12]

We learned many lessons from this sorry sequence of events, not the least of which was that the VFL needed to be very wary of the power conferred by private ownership. Beyond that, it would be fair to say that at the end of 1987 I was knackered.

There were still plenty of loose ends.

Richmond was in deep financial trouble—on the brink, it turned out, of being unable to continue trading as a viable entity. The club had reported an operating loss of $1.025 million, leading to a total loss of $1.422 million. It was utterly broke and needed help from the League to pay its cash bills over the Christmas period in 1987. There was a question regarding whether loan monies the club had received from the Bond Corporation were convertible to share capital or redeemable.

---

12   VFL Commission minutes, February 1988.

We needed some quick answers. At its December meeting the commission seriously considered appointing an administrator at Richmond, but decided a better option was to send in the League's financial supervisor, Jim Poulton, to try to get a grip on the Tigers' finances and work out a way forward. That way, at least some of the club's issues could be kept in house for the moment.

It was that serious. And we were none too happy with the way Richmond had conducted itself. As the commission minutes reveal: "It was noted that the club had not submitted McKinsey-format financial information by due dates and ... had subsequently indicated a deliberate policy of withholding such information."[13]

The League's finance manager, Greg Durham, wrote to the club offering an advance on the Tigers' 1988 revenue of $300,000 to tide over its cash-flow issues, and demanding that Richmond show in writing from Bond Corporation "that $600,000 detailed in the 1987 financial accounts as a convertible loan is non-refundable under any circumstances". The letter concluded with a stern warning: "The directors of the Richmond Football Club [must] provide a written undertaking that the club will comply with all future VFL financial reporting requirements, noting that failure to do so will provide the commission with grounds for immediate appointment of an 'administrator' as detailed in your licence agreement."[14]

The Tigers weren't alone: St Kilda and North Melbourne were also chasing advances on their 1988 disbursements, Fitzroy was chasing corporate support from Hecron, and St Kilda was flirting with some form of share ownership. North Melbourne was also actively scouting for interest among potential private owners.

It was the spirit of the times. Skase would be broke and on the run in just over two years, but at the end of 1987 bold entrepreneurs seemed to offer a bottomless money pit. Despite the clear issues in Sydney and Brisbane, the Victorian clubs were looking at the Brisbane and West Coast examples and flirting with the concept of private ownership.

---

13   VFL Commission minutes, December 1987.
14   Letter by Greg Durham attached to VFL Commission minutes, December 1987.

The commission had to hose that down. We drew a line in the sand and said, "If you want a private owner who's going to take more than a 10 per cent interest in the club, they will need to pay a licence fee, and the fee stands at $4 million."

That calmed things down.

In the end, again with the benefit of long hindsight, in one sense private ownership failed. There would be new owners in Brisbane by the end of the year, and the ownership travails of Sydney continued despite the club's on-field brilliance. But private cash had its moment. Without Skase's cheques and guarantees the game would have been dead in the water. Without Skase and Bond, Edelsten, Reuben Pelerman, Basil Sellers, John Geraghty, Craig Kimberley, Mike Willesee and, indeed, Colless, McHenry, Neil Hamilton, Hohnen and Armstrong ... Without all the individuals and corporates who put their money in, much of it—no, probably all of it—never to be seen again, football would have struggled to survive its financial crisis point of the mid-1980s.

We needed the money then. Private ownership was a stage in the game, a flirtation that helped us through a financially difficult period. I'm forever grateful that it happened and I thank those who contributed—but likewise I am grateful that it was just a moment in history and not something that forever changed the fundamental nature of the game and its membership and fan-based structure.

CHAPTER 17

Up yours Oakley

Reducing the number of Melbourne teams in the VFL was not just some idle fancy. It was part of the agreed strategic direction of the commission.

Back in 1986 the League would have given its right arm for a merger of clubs in Melbourne. Indeed, many discussions were held: between Melbourne and North Melbourne, St Kilda and Melbourne, Fitzroy and North Melbourne, Fitzroy and anybody—no doubt there were others that never made the main table.

The Blue Report and subsequent commission papers made a pretty clear case: 11 Melbourne teams was not a viable proposition. And they were right: the structure of the competition remained much as it had been as an amateur—or quasi-professional—competition with modest costs and sustainable revenues. As the commission had reported to the clubs in July 1986, those days had passed, and football at the elite level was now an increasingly professional sport with increasing costs to match. Not only that, but there were also great threats to revenue for all but the most successful clubs. As the Blue Report had put it:

> The costs of maintaining 11 near-professional teams in Melbourne

are huge on a per-capita basis. It would be astonishing to find that a competition structure appropriate to an amateur game proved to be viable for a more professional competition.[1]

The commission was more pointed: "The change to a professional game has been rapid and while the commission has shown some progress with the salary cap, there are no precedents in the real world which suggest that the clock can be turned back to an amateur game."[2]

Managing this was easily the toughest of my challenges. The intent of the commission was clear, but we were not yet in a position to force the issue. There had been many discussions—some serious, some feeling the water—between clubs, and it seemed at least one merger might be inevitable. But it had to be done with a soft touch, as we would see.

The problem was obvious enough: the League and its clubs were simply trying to extract too much money from a single sporting market. The fact that 11 teams more or less grubbed a living from the Melbourne (and Geelong) market in the late 1980s was utterly remarkable, and evidence of the sporting fervour of Melburnians. Think of any other world city that could pour supporters and their dollars into that number of local professional clubs in a League that could each pull an average weekly attendance of more than 25,000 supporters per game and annual attendances of over three million. London? Not even close. New York? Nope.

Melbourne was unique, but the strains were showing. As things stood, moving the competition to a national one was little more than an exercise in refinancing Victorian football. The Victorian clubs had been bailed out, at least in the short term, by the Perth and Brisbane licence fees, but that was entirely the wrong basis on which to build a national competition. We were fortunate that a strong survival instinct existed, or the grand plan may never have happened.

The national competition had to stand on its own feet as a national entity, and it had to do it for the sake of sustaining a national game, with

---

1   *VFL Football: Establishing the Basis For Future Success*, VFL Commission, 1985.
2   Discussion paper for VFL directors and club presidents from VFL Commission, 30 July 1986.

all the promise and potential that held. It wasn't just a scheme to allow underperforming Victorian football clubs to come that little bit closer to breaking even, although the national growth would further assist them in achieving that over time. It had to not only *be* national—it had to *act* national and *think* national. It could not be a bandage; it had to be a cure.

The League was being squeezed by multiple opposites: diminishing revenue, an unyielding push for professionalism and all its costs, and a broadening entertainment market. And those pressures were building: clubs continuing to pay players more and more, and increasing entertainment options tempting crowds away from a good old game of football.

It was a pretty simple equation given the competition's financial situation, and one backed by the experience in other sporting markets around the world: it would not be possible to modernise and nationalise the game and at the same time keep 11 teams in Victoria. Indeed, in one scenario the commission had floated for discussion (private and/or corporate ownership), there was potential for just five Victorian clubs by 1995, with two each in Sydney, Adelaide and Perth and one in Brisbane. Whichever way you stirred the pot, it would seem there was no way the bulk of the competition could survive unless we rationalised the Victorian numbers. It would have been nice to have had the cash to subsidise the weaker teams more, but that was going to take some time to generate and most likely would be a band-aid solution.

It's not as if the League didn't canvass the options. We looked, reluctantly, at corporate or cooperative ownership, and we looked at loaded drafts to give the lower-ranked clubs some hope. We looked at the idea of putting a levy on the bigger-drawing clubs to siphon off some of the gate monies from the big games (today's analysts are facing the same issues)—that didn't end well.

It would be fair to say that in the late 1980s, though the clubs had been dragged to the idea of a commission and an expanded competition, they were still a pretty self-absorbed bunch who put their own interests before the game. The game was still tribal, so the idea of dipping into club money to help a rival was virtually unheard of.

Things have changed, of course—up to a point. Today there's a better understanding of the interdependencies, a sense that in the modern competition, in which the sum is greater than the parts, everyone needs everyone else. We even have a Collingwood president who not only understands this concept but supports it!

We shouldn't kid ourselves. The bulk of the changes to the League that had brought us to a budding national competition administered by an increasingly powerful commission and executive had only been possible because the clubs had little or no choice. On the brink of insolvency they did what they had to do to save themselves and, by extension, the League.

Left to their own devices, and in better financial (that is, amateur) times, they would have continued to follow the paths of self-interest and the status quo. Every time.

Better financial times, that was the key to it—and for some clubs, a pretty remote hope. Money kept the pressure on. Money kept football changing. In a funny way, insolvency kept the entire game moving through the water.

As I have mentioned, a lot of clubs were desperate for a dollar, and suddenly, with Skase in Brisbane, Edelsten in Sydney and Indian Pacific in Perth, the debt-freeing possibilities of private ownership caught everybody's attention. Although the commission tolerated private ownership in order to float the two new clubs and keep Sydney alive, it was not eager to broaden that net. Its preference, as stated many times, was to rationalise the numbers in the Victorian market.

Private ownership of a Melbourne club was just a bridge too far for the commission, a move that threatened a real fragmentation of the League into disparate commercial entities—selling off the firm, as Peter Scanlon would say. There were good reasons for it in foreign territories, where that sort of commercial commitment made sense in order to gain the new ground we needed to grow the national competition—or at least it did for the moment.

And so clubs like Fitzroy, North Melbourne, St Kilda, Richmond, Footscray and others stumbled on, scraping funds together as was their long habit and somehow making ends meet with the assistance of the commission, which on many occasions provided them with advances against annual dividends, and even office space for a period of time. Tin-rattling was the *modus operandi* of many.

Fitzroy was doing well enough by 1989 that it emerged as the senior partner in the failed merger deal that would be the next twist in the club's long series of tales, all seeking a certain and productive future. "Well enough" is a relative concept, and the comparison in this case was with Footscray.

By late 1989 the Bulldogs were insolvent and on the verge of being placed in administration. That didn't happen, but what was about to unfold was a sequence of events that would be the most dramatic and challenging of my time at the League, that tested the relationship between the League and its public, that would paint me as the villain in a drama driven by financial pain and a simple desire to protect the future integrity of the League.

On the bright side, they were events that would show that the great strength of football lay well beyond any balance sheet. It lay in the heartfelt commitment and passion of the fans, if you could find a way to extract those things. And one man did: a local solicitor and passionate Bulldogs fan called Peter Gordon. Passion and commitment and hard work would ultimately save the Footscray Football Club, along with support from local business houses, particularly the chemical giant ICI.

All that was ahead of me when the commission met on the morning of Tuesday 3 October 1989—a fateful meeting. Discussions between the commission and the presidents of Fitzroy and Footscray had been progressing well, with the final dealings on the merger being done the Sunday before with just two members of each board present. "Amalgamation of Clubs" was the first item at the 3 October meeting, and the minutes reported the outcome of negotiations and the processes leading to the day's agenda:

> Chairman advised that agreement in principle had been reached between the two club presidents and that the Fitzroy Board of Directors was supportive to the proposal and that members of the Footscray

Football Club board had been briefed by the club's president pending a confidential meeting with the commission at 12 noon.[3]

The situation out west was more than dire. It was presented to the commission that in the previous decade, Footscray had lost "a total of $3.9m", and had made a minor profit in just one of those years; that "guarantors to the club's overdraft of $400,000 desired to withdraw from such arrangements alleging condition to the guarantees had been breached by the club".[4] There were clear grounds for an administrator to be appointed. The relatively smooth path to a merger, with each club in agreement and the League supportive, was an obvious way forward.[5]

Things might have been cool, calm and collected around that decision at League headquarters that morning, but the horse had already bolted. The merger push was to be won and lost on the uncertain battlefield of public relations. We knew PR would be part of the story, but we never guessed just how big a part. When the commission met that day to set the merger ball rolling, we were already on the losing side.

Despite the support of president Nick Columb, many on the Footscray board were not pleased, in particular chief executive Dennis Galimberti. On the evening of 2 October, Galimberti had got wind that negotiations for a merger were entering their final stages, and had run straight to the media. The morning that the two clubs would meet with the commission to confirm arrangements, Melbourne had awoken to a screamer headline in *The Sun*:

> VFL CLUBS "TO MERGE"
>
> VFL club Footscray is set to merge with Fitzroy, Bulldog chief executive Dennis Galimberti said last night.
>
> He said the new team would be known as the Fitzroy Bulldogs, with their home ground at Princes Park.

---

3   VFL Commission minutes, 3 October 1989.
4   Ibid.
5   Also on the agenda that day was a note that correspondence had been received from the St Kilda Football Club indicating its "willingness to be involved in merger discussions and/or a relocation to VFL Park". St Kilda would not end up being a merger candidate, but it would move from Moorabbin to Waverley in 1993.

> As the first step in the merger, Footscray's licence to play in the re-named VFL, the Australian Football League, is expected to be terminated today.
>
> An emotional Galimberti, 33, said: "The deal has been done for two weeks and will be announced tomorrow."[6]

In terms of supporter reaction, Galimberti's evident displeasure was just the beginning. From a League point of view there seemed no option but a merger, and this view was shared by Fitzroy and Footscray presidents Leon Wiegard and Columb. Things for both clubs were grim, but at Footscray the club was on the verge of irreversible crisis. That was very much the point of the merger exercise: something had to change. It might not be popular, but the alternative would be dire: letting a club simply go to the wall. Footscray had been attempting to raise funds as part of a "Bulldogs Connection" group but had raised little more than $30,000, which was not going to save it.

As the commission meeting started, I gave a quick report on the state of play with the merger, presenting a document called "Background to the Fitzroy Bulldogs" that, among other things, laid out the commercial position for both clubs but focused pretty squarely on the toxic debt position at Footscray. Galimberti was clearly aware of the situation the club he led was in, but chose to go the PR route.

The stage was set for a meeting with Footscray directors at 1pm. It didn't promise to be easy, but the commission was of one mind on the issue. A merger was the best resolution to a situation that, if left to run, could result in prosecution of the club and the sheeting home of financial responsibility to individual club directors.

The room was tense, it would be fair to say. There were seven Footscray directors—Messrs Columb, Beattie, Gibson, Dudley, Moody, McDonald and Adsett—and close to the full commission (Peter Nixon was unavailable but had been fully briefed). I began by expressing my concern at the morning's negative publicity courtesy of Galimberti's briefing. He had quit

---

6   Tony De Bolfo and Michael Stevens, "VFL clubs 'to merge'", *The Sun*, 3 October 1989.

the club overnight, but as everyone in the room knew, the publicity had not helped the merger cause.

This was not a situation, or so we saw it at the time, in which emotion could play a constructive part. A supporter's deep love for the Footscray club wouldn't bail out the club's finances: it had not during the past 18 months—indeed, in the past decade—and we believed it would not now.

I walked the Footscray board through the financial position and its likely consequences. They had an $800,000 shortfall in the current financial year, an accumulated trading loss over the previous decade of $3.8 million ($3.9 million when non-trading matters were considered), debt on the books of $2 million, and no prospect of any financial reversal. Then I made my clinching point to the directors of the failing club. The minutes set it down:

> Mr Oakley expressed the commission's view that the Footscray Football Club Limited was currently insolvent and by continuing to trade and incur debt, the directors were, in the commission's view, in breach of Section 556 of the Companies Code and if this situation was allowed to continue, then directors could be exposed to convictions, resulting in personal fines and/or jail sentences as well as ultimately becoming responsible on a personal basis for the club's liabilities.[7]

I think that pretty much described the state of play. But there was more:

> Mr Oakley made further reference to recent correspondence forwarded to the current directors, a copy of which had been forwarded to the League commission from one of the guarantors of the club's present overdraft facility with Westpac Banking Corporation.
>
> Mr Oakley noted that a number of serious allegations had been made by the loan guarantor and should such allegations be substantiated, dire legal consequences could flow.
>
> Mr Oakley indicated that … the commission's view was that the club's position was non-recoverable.[8]

I had one last point to make to a Footscray board sitting in rather grim

---

7   VFL Commission minutes, 3 October 1989.
8   Ibid.

and stony contemplation: "Mr Oakley ... contended that the only option available to the directors of the club was to consider merging with another League club and that if the board of the Footscray Football Club was prepared to consider such a possibility, it would have to be consummated this afternoon as, if agreement could not be reached, the League proposed to immediately move towards the appointment of an administrator and/or liquidator."[9]

There's no denying this was a tough, heartbreaking moment for the Footscray directors. Columb made one last plea for salvation, asking whether the club could sell its present players to other clubs to erase its debt, but under League rules this was not possible. I wanted a quick response—we had to act quickly before regulatory authorities became curious as a result of the overnight press.

The commissioners left the Footscray board to it and moved into an adjacent room to await the decision. The tension was too much for Albert Mantello, who had his ear to the wall trying to hear what was going on next door. He drew a graph on the whiteboard with a line going up and down according to the tone of the conversation—quite the comedian was Albert. We weren't encouraging him in any way, but it did rather ease the tension. Unfortunately the indelible pen he used left a lasting impression for all to see, much to his embarrassment.

The discussion didn't take too long. After about 30 minutes, Columb sent word that the commission should arrange for representatives of the Fitzroy Football Club to attend and start talks around a merger. Once Columb had announced the club's willingness to meet with Fitzroy to complete the deal, three Footscray directors—Gibson, Moody and McDonald—resigned on the spot, and at 3.06pm we adjourned the meeting.

Wiegard and a Fitzroy delegation were there in quick time and the deal was promptly done. It was late afternoon and already VFL House had a decent gaggle of media waiting. And in a taste of what was to come, an angry group of demonstrators decked out in Footscray colours, and

---

9   Ibid.

prompted by the day's news, chanted defiantly outside. We called a press conference for 5pm, arranged for Footscray legend Charlie Sutton to be there and prepared to face the music.

I spoke on behalf of the commission, Wiegard and Columb on behalf of their clubs. Charlie, one of the true gentlemen I met in my time in the game (and one of the toughest players), gave his reluctant blessing and we were done.

It had been a hard day at the office, but I never doubted that we had done the right thing. It was the only thing we could do given the responsibilities of the League to the rest of the competition and the game generally. And, given the perilous financial state of the club and the stress on its directors, it seemed the only thing they could do as well.

All hell, however, was about to break loose.

The next day, the *Sun*'s banner headline was *DEATH OF THE BULLDOGS* and the main story read:

> Footscray Football Club yesterday ceased to exist.
>
> And last night the western suburbs were boiling over the move, which VFL executive commissioner Ross Oakley said was approved by the Footscray board yesterday.
>
> The 65-year-old club faced two choices, Mr Oakley said—merge or become extinct.
>
> And with that he announced the formation of a "new force in VFL football"—the Fitzroy Bulldogs.[10]

Given Footscray's parlous situation, we believed the deal was a good one. The new club would be debt free, with the accumulated deficits of both Fitzroy and Footscray paid out by redeploying the allocations from the League that would otherwise have gone to Footscray. The Bulldogs would play in Fitzroy's colours with a Bulldog symbol. The new team would be allowed to exceed the salary cap for two years until a new playing list bedded down that would be drawn from the 125 players at both clubs.

---

10   David Fisher, "Hurt fans fight, but it's done", *The Sun*, 4 October 1989.

The team would train at the Western Oval and play its home games at Princes Park, and the new coach would be Rod Austin.[11]

The supporters of Fitzroy, led by an optimistic Wiegard (who even scented the possibility of a flag, with Fitzroy finishing just a game outside the finals that season), seemed to endorse the deal, perhaps because their name and most of their colours had been retained—not to mention that years of tin-rattling and facing down debt were behind them. Footscray fans were another matter entirely. The front of *The Sun* said it clearly. All the words were one thing, but the photograph told the unfolding story. Its caption read: "It's too much … Sandra James, 19, weeps outside VFL House after learning of Footscray's demise."[12]

The club's legends fuelled the fire. Doug Hawkins, who had at the time played 222 stellar games for the Bulldogs, told the paper he wanted his name pulled from his eponymous wing at the Western Oval: "I'm going to make sure that I can take it and put it on my back fence up in Bacchus Marsh. When the kids get older they can have a look at that."[13]

Down in the ranks at Fitzroy there was displeasure, too. Fitzroy captain Paul Roos was nonplussed: "How can clubs expect player loyalty when things like this happen?" Star utility Richard Osborne was likewise put off by the secrecy that had necessarily surrounded the negotiations: "It would be nice if we had a say in what goes on."[14]

Maybe. The fact was that, yes, the clubs and the League were engaged in running a sport, but they were also running a series of businesses that provided the corporate basis for the competition. In theory you would want everyone on the same page and involved in every stage of the process. But with this merger—a merger forced by calamitous financial circumstances—the emotional response simply could not be brought into the calculations.

By week's end the League had an interim administration in place for the new club. League financial supervisor Peter Ballantyne was acting as

---

11 Rod Austin, a Carlton premiership player, would coach Fitzroy in 1989 and 1990. He later worked in the AFL's football operations department until his retirement in 2012.
12 *The Sun*, 4 October 1989, p. 1.
13 Ibid.
14 Ibid.

chief executive, aided by VFL finance manager Greg Durham and Barry Capuano, who was consulting to the League on planning and interstate management—a much better team than either club had previously boasted.

The supporter anger bubbled under all week, and by Friday 6 October we were in the Supreme Court with a group called "Save the Dogs" who were seeking a stay in proceedings to prevent the merger.

That was the day I first came across a name that would shape my immediate future: Irene Chatfield.

The Save the Dogs group was led by Peter Gordon, a 31-year-old western suburbs lawyer. His first memory of the Bulldogs' plight was sitting at his mother-in-law's home a year earlier, in 1988, when the club was facing relocation from its traditional Western Oval home. He told me for this book that his mother-in-law thought that it was "terrible" that the Bulldogs were leaving the Western Oval to play at Princes Park. She said, "The problem with this is that everyone complains, but no one does anything about it." Gordon thought about that and said, "That's right. I should do something." He formed the Save the Dogs group.

Initially the aim of the group was to keep the Dogs at the Western Oval. They didn't understand that behind the relocation talk was a serious threat to the life of the Footscray Football Club. As Gordon recalls:

> I called a meeting at the Footscray Town Hall and 2000 people turned up. I found out that I had a bit of a bent for public speaking and was able to engage the passion of the supporters. This surprised me as I was a junior lawyer who had never even appeared in court much and I had been raised in a family who shunned publicity. My big sell at the meeting was "The Ross Oakleys and John Elliotts of this world do not own this game—they run it for the time being. And they have no right to run it against the wishes of the supporters." After a nervous start I really warmed to the experience.[15]

When the battle to keep the Bulldogs playing at the Western Oval had

---

15   Peter Gordon, interview with the author, 2014.

been won, Gordon was asked by club president Columb to change the name of his group to "Bulldog Connection" (Columb saw this name as less confrontational to his board) and suggested that it assist in raising funds for the club.

Columb and Galimberti were troubled by the emergence of the Save the Dogs group and had publicly criticised both it and Gordon. So it was a surprise to Gordon when midway into the 1989 season, he took a call in his Footscray legal office from Galimberti. Gordon continues:

> Galimberti said, "I'm really worried about how the club's going and I believe that the only guy who can save it is you." I agreed to stay in touch with him. I kept the Save the Dogs group together, even under Columb's more innocuous name suggestion, mainly to have a group ready to move if political issues hotted up again.[16]

That August, as I have outlined, Galimberti had good reason to be worried about the Dogs' circumstances, but once the merger had been announced, Gordon began to be much more involved. He goes on:

> When the merger was announced, our group met as soon as we could at the old social club. We were confused and desperate but we wanted to do something. Dennis [Galimberti], who was also trained as a lawyer, had had discussions with some other lawyers who were Bulldog diehards and they thought there might be some legal avenues.
>
> We were looking for a plaintiff to front a legal challenge. We were aware that the League may come after them and bankrupt whoever fronted the action if it failed. We asked one of our group, Carol Liddell, who said no when she learned of the bankruptcy risk. Just as we were beginning to despair, Irene Chatfield came forward and said, "What about me? They can come after me—I have no assets." Everyone laughed for the first time in a few days. We agreed to go with Irene.[17]

Irene, a wonderful, long-time, fierce, heart-and-soul, badged-duffle-coat supporter of the club—and, I might add, a charming woman—made the

---

16 Ibid.
17 Ibid.

court application, arguing that the League had acted irregularly in the merger process. The action was brought on the basis that the company was not insolvent and the directors had acted outside their powers as they did not have member support.

Tony Nolan QC, acting for the League, was convinced that Footscray was not solvent, but said, "If you can prove to us in 21 days that you are solvent then you will get the licence back." His last words to Irene's barrister, Tim Ginnane, were "We want to give you just enough rope to hang yourselves"—a piece of hubris I would personally have preferred he had not engaged in. The court agreed to the deal. The club's debt position was then $2 million and they had three weeks to raise it. This horseplay gave *The Sun* its Saturday headline:

> **BITE-BACK**
>
> Footscray Football Club rose from the dead yesterday—and supporters have three weeks to save it.
>
> "This is the chance we've been looking for," said lawyer and "Save the Bulldogs" co-chief Peter Gordon.[18]

That Friday night Gordon took a call from the powerful Collingwood president, Allan McAlister. It was his first real taste of VFL club politics. McAlister invited Gordon to his Ivanhoe home for a drink, and after a few pleasantries and a cup of tea, McAlister said, "Almost no one thinks you can do this, but I'm not like everyone else. I think you can. And I want you to know that if it gets close, if you're only one or two hundred thousand dollars away at the end of three weeks, Collingwood will tip in the rest. All we ask in return is that you transfer [your star player] Tony McGuinness to us."[19] An amazing suggestion!

Gordon says he made a mental note of this lateral opportunity: "If it turned out we were one or two hundred thousand away, I wasn't going to be too proud or too precious not to do a deal to save the club."

Immediately the Save the Dogs group knuckled down and went into

---

18   Michael Stevens, "Bite-back", *The Sun*, 7 October 1989.
19   Peter Gordon, interview with the author, 2014.

planning mode—a 21-day military operation to save the club. Gordon remembers:

> Our first action was to organise a public rally for supporters at the Western Oval. With 30 minutes to go before the announced starting time, almost no one had turned up in the drizzling rain. This prompted Bill Jacobs from 3AW, who was covering the rally and had forecast it would not be a success, to say, "I told you so." But then almost 20,000 people appeared, seemingly from nowhere.
>
> I had spent the day before getting people to agree to serve on the board and convincing and organising the Footscray players and [former player] Terry Wheeler to attend the rally. In my mind I had to use this opportunity to create an atmosphere of hope, of rising like a phoenix from the ashes—it was the only hope left at the club. I had receipts printed and got the local council to guarantee that contributors would get their money back if we were not successful.
>
> In my speech I painted a very bleak picture of our future at first, then said, "We have a chance TODAY to stop these 'men' in their tracks. I am announcing today that I have formed a board." I named and introduced them and then said, "And the first decision we have made is to appoint Terry Wheeler as the coach." I proceeded to introduce him to the crowd, who were now getting excited. "Would you now please welcome the team," I said, and out from the race they walked. This was one of the great moments. A wall of sound hit me on stage, very inspiring. I had an adrenaline rush, but it was somewhat frightening at the same time.
>
> And then I introduced Irene Chatfield, the woman who was risking everything for her club. That wall of sound hit me again—I've never heard a footy crowd roar like that. I said, "You have our commitment to re-establish your club, but it is only going to work if you give till it hurts."[20]

And they gave, these mostly working-class people, till it hurt. They gave an astonishing $700,000 at the rally, a great deal of that money from purchases of a bumper sticker that would end up being a memorable part

---

20 Ibid.

of my reflections on life in the League spotlight. "Up yours Oakley" was a real money-spinner for the bite-back team.

The publicity the rally received was amazing and created great momentum. It got the front page of *The Sun* the next morning, with a photo showing Gordon's son Sean looking mournful and offering his money box as his contribution. The emotional wave was growing.

Gordon continues the story:

> The next phase we had planned was a tin rattle and doorknock on the next weekend. We raised close to $500,000 from that following weekend, then we held a concert and a Legends match. A small group of us organised things on the run with willing support from an increasingly large group of people who were gaining hope day by day.
>
> I called a meeting at my office for 6.30am the day after the rally to plan western-suburbs-wide coverage of the tin rattle for the next weekend. At the rally, Ian Baker, the local member for Williamstown, had publicly pledged the support of his office. But when he wasn't at my office by 6.35am, I rang him and woke him up. "Where are you?" I said. "You're late."
>
> He said, "Ah ... mate ... err ... it's 6am—can't you fill me in later?"
>
> To which I said, "Let me make this very clear to you. You promised publicly, and got political kudos by doing so, that you would work in this campaign around your area. So if you are not organised to do so by this weekend, my next press conference will be to inform everyone how you don't keep your word."
>
> "I'll be there shortly," was the curt reply.
>
> The full resources of his local Labor Party branch were duly rolled out in his neighbourhood the following weekend.[21]

Gordon said to me recently, "Looking back, I'm sure there must have been a nicer way to do that. I actually amazed myself in that period because day after day I acted as a completely ruthless prick and I had not previously seen myself that way." He got that right—at the time I saw him that way too.

---

21 Ibid.

But in hindsight, what a marvellous campaign he put together. I count Peter as a friend today and still marvel at how he was able to save what we all thought was unsavable.

The real success of the campaign was generated at the public rally at the Western Oval that Sunday, the day Peter Gordon came of age and commenced a wonderful stewardship of his club that continues today.

It was also a day on which even I made a significant contribution to the fundraising effort, thanks to that bumper sticker carrying my name. Pretty soon the stickers were everywhere. They were eventually joined by another: "Merge Oakley into outer space".

Being the villain of the piece didn't bother me too much. I knew passions would be stirred, and to be honest the commission had no thought that we would win the inevitable PR war. We weren't doing this to make friends. The merger was not so much what we wanted—it was what we considered to be the only path possible.

We had anticipated the possibility of legal action, and through the entire process took pains to keep all the detail as tidy as possible. We were keen that the League should be beyond reproach.

Someone had to be the focus of the anger, and I understood that. I'm not sure my family did, but I did. I was always going to wear this. It was a very tough time, particularly for the family. I had guards on my home at Wheelers Hill for nigh on three months, and there were death threats. One night the guards removed a guy who was trying to climb over the fence. My children were escorted to school and my daughter, Melanie, was chastised by her headmaster for removing an "Up yours Oakley" sticker from a worker's car in the school car park—much to his embarrassment when he became aware of who Melanie was.

It was a highly charged environment, a really big concern. I tried to keep things calm for the family, but it had an impact. My wife, Christine, was stoic, but as she says, "Reading the papers, watching the TV … I guess I was upset, but I was never furious. If it were to have affected us personally it might have been different. To me it was just part of a pretty big company negotiation, but one with a lot of passion and prejudice involved."

She was not told at the time about the death threats or the guy who jumped the fence. If she had, she may have had a different slant on things.

A short time after the court decision I had sent a letter to Gordon clarifying the commission's position. I said that we not only required the club to cover the $2 million debt it carried, but it had to demonstrate to us that it could trade on profitably. In response he was now looking at locking in new ongoing revenue streams for the club.

None of the heat was going out of the public campaign. The government was dragged in, with western-suburbs MPs getting organised and demanding action from the Labor premier, John Cain, and Trades Hall. The premier played it cautiously, but he was agitating behind the scenes. If this club was anything, it was a club of Melbourne's working class. How could a Labor government let them fall over?

Joan Kirner, a local member of parliament at the time and a wonderful football supporter, summoned the heads of all the big petrochemical companies on Altona's Kororoit Creek Road to Spring Street and put it on them, saying, "You people get away with a lot in terms of the environment and you need to do something for the community. I expect you to put $250,000 into the Footscray Football Club." It ended up being $200,000, but it wasn't a bad get.

Michael Feehan, then a young executive at ICI (later to be called Orica), convinced his company to come good as a major sponsor. ICI had had some bad publicity in the local area due to chemical leaks. Gordon said:

> Mike realised that good corporate citizenship went beyond dishing out hamburgers at the local park: it was about positive engagement with the wider community on a larger scale. He made that case compellingly to ICI. Mike may not have been so open with his employer that he and his family were also lifelong Bulldog supporters.[22]

---

22   Ibid.

Had there been some further political pressure applied? Who knows, but in those crazy days anything seemed half-possible. All sorts of rumours flew.

Under great backroom pressure to do something, Premier Cain took on Columb, who was a wealthy man in his own right, saying Columb should pitch in racehorse winnings to help the Footscray coffers. "That's the least he could do, I would have thought," said Cain.[23] Columb's filly Courtza had won the 1989 Golden Slipper, the world's richest race for two-year-olds.

Gordon wanted more than gestures. The "Up yours Oakley" sticker was engendering great small-business support, but the Transport Accident Commission (TAC), a major sponsor of the Bulldogs, had looked at pulling out because of the smell surrounding the club. They were a critical partner and Gordon needed a bit more government help to keep them on board. He put it on Cain and his right-hand man at Spring Street, David White, saying, "We are in your heartland and this area has always delivered safe seats for the Labor Party, but if you mess us around now you will have a level of trouble you have never experienced before."[24]

Responding on behalf of the government, White said to Gordon, "Calm down, calm down. We want to do a deal with you and will direct the TAC to continue their sponsorship for the next three years, but there is one condition: we insist that you stay on as president."

Until then, Gordon had had no intention of doing that and had actually spent time in the previous week trying to convince Deputy Premier Robert Fordham to be the new president. Gordon's memory of White's parting words is: "If we are to commit government funds to this, we need someone to blame if it goes wrong. And let's make this clear: if it goes wrong, the person we are going to blame is you."

Great way to start a new position with such responsibility. But Gordon left Spring Street that day contemplating for the first time that this would be a much longer commitment than the three-week guerrilla campaign he had committed to.

He was elected unopposed as the Footscray president 10 days later. As for

---

23   Quoted in *The Sun*, 14 October 1989.
24   Peter Gordon, interview with the author, 2014.

Tony McGuinness, fortunately he never had to wear the black-and-white jumper under McAlister's secret deal.[25]

Footscray Football Club had not only covered its debt, but managed to get a head start on much of the following year's revenue as well.

I was overseas at the end of the battle, on duty at the end-of-season London game. The commission met and waved the white flag. I was on the phone with Peter Nixon and Graeme Samuel from London when Scanlon, in Melbourne with Mantello, spelt it out for us: "Ross, guys, they've raised the money. We're over a barrel here. We've got to give them their licence back."

And so it was. The night the licence was handed back, Eddie McGuire asked Gordon to go to the Channel 10 studio, then at Nunawading, at 5 o'clock to do an interview. Gordon said it was too far away from Footscray at peak hour, but McGuire was not to be beaten and said, "I'll send our helicopter for you. We will land on the Western Oval, then fly you to the studio."

Gordon, who was still reeling from the tumultuous events of the past three weeks, was a bit overwhelmed. Here he was flying across Melbourne to Nunawading to participate in an interview with Eddie McGuire, with the chairman of the AFL Commission taking part from London by satellite linkage.

The newsreader commenced the interview by asking me for a comment. I said, "Congratulations, Peter, on getting your licence back—but you know it took something like this to get your supporters off their butts."

Peter said, "Yes, that's right, but now that we have this impetus we want to cement our future."

The newsreader said, "Peter, what will be your demands of the League going forward?"

Gordon replied, "We want 11 home games at Western Oval, none at Waverley Park, and we want a five-goal start every time we play Hawthorn."

---

25 Irene Chatfield, the Bulldogs fan who was the plaintiff in the legal challenge, was named the League's inaugural Football Woman of the Year in 1998 and was awarded Life Membership of the Footscray (Western Bulldogs) Football Club in 2008.

Unfortunately, for some reason I could not hear this answer. But I could hear Eddie, who chipped in and said, with a smirk I couldn't see, "What do you think about those demands, Ross?"

In innocence I answered, "We will seriously consider all those requests."

Footscray entered the 1990 season in a much stronger position than any other club, and traded at a profit of $553,000 that year while introducing a skinny kid from Daylesford into its line-up: Chris Grant played the first of 341 games in round one. The team won 12 matches for the year and finish seventh; Fitzroy, coached by Austin, struggled and finished 12th, ahead of Sydney and Brisbane.

None of the solutions gained during those days of passion were long term, of course. Nothing that happened in this welter of well-intentioned fundraising did anything to shift the fundamental financial position of either Footscray or Fitzroy—but that would play out over time.

The one thing we did learn, the big and positive message from the whole affair, was that we should never underestimate the passion and loyalty of ordinary fans. That passion could be a curse, but it was a force beyond the calculated reasoning of business and finance. It was the glue that held football together. We the commission, and all in the League administration, had a better sense of that now, and it was a very important lesson.

The deal was done on 24 October and announced on a *Sun* front page that told a bigger story for football. "Bulldogs saved" was the slim strip on the bottom of page one, which was dominated by a much bigger headline and full-face portrait: *SKASE ON THE ROPES*.

My world was about to be rocked again.

CHAPTER 18

Mergers and acquisitions

Believe it or not, but Christopher Skase never got in touch.

In late 1989 his business affairs were in ruins and the long arm of the law was reaching for him. The creditors were anxious and his fortune was being stashed away. Shortly he would follow his remaining money to a villa and yachting paradise in Majorca.

Not that we knew that then. The hunt for the suddenly vanished Skase would take until 1991—and that was hardly the end of the story, either. Skase left a lot of people in the lurch, and it would be fair to say that, massively inconvenient as it was, his sudden departure from the financial helm of the Brisbane Bears did not rate all that highly in the litter of missing millions he left in his wake.

As I say, he didn't contact me. He left whatever excuses might have been made to his faithful and long-suffering front man and club servant, Paul Cronin. Poor Paul was left holding the baby and grappling with a fairly complex web of financial detail.

In November, with Skase a fading shadow and his Qintex empire in receivership, Cronin made a presentation to the commission and laid the parlous situation of the Bears on the table. The club was broke. As the minutes note:

> Mr Cronin had indicated that the companies involved in the Brisbane

Bears structure could survive providing a capital injection of $3 million prior to Christmas and a further $3 million by February 1990 was provided.

Mr Cronin further advised that none of the club's existing creditors were likely to make a move against the club prior to Christmas, however they needed the League's co-operation to bring forward its December distribution entitlement of $100,000 in order that staff salaries could be met.[1]

The $6 million was just the beginning of it. The club was hoping to pin down total new equity of $12 million to secure its debts and guarantee its program of capital works, much of that around necessary improvements to the Skase-favoured home ground at Carrara.

The impact of the Skase departure went beyond the club. The same commission meeting heard a report from the Queensland Australian Football League, "which detailed that league's precarious financial position due to outstanding debts from the Brisbane Bears and unfunded promotion and development commitments due to the financial position of the Brisbane Bears".[2]

We even wondered whether we'd be able to keep the players. Several of their contracts had options clauses that needed to be exercised by 31 December, or the players would be keen to place themselves in the pre-season draft.

The commission resolved on the spot to bring forward the $100,000 payment. The rest of it was more complicated.

The ANZ McCaughan bank would turn out to be of great assistance: it held a mortgage over the Bears' VFL licence. We were all chasing the same man and the same money. Taking a considerable and praiseworthy initiative, the bankers went out and found a man who would see the Bears through this period and would put his millions behind the fledgling club for precious little return.

---

[1] VFL Commission minutes, November 1989.
[2] Ibid.

Enter Reuben Pelerman, Queensland multimillionaire developer of hotels and hospitals, philanthropist, and soon-to-be owner and saviour of the Brisbane Bears.

So there we were in the early summer of 1990, Jeff Browne and I, in talks with ANZ McCaughan and Pelerman's two representatives, Judah and Gerald Moses, trying to nut out the final details of the deal. We were sitting in a builder's hut at the Carrara ground, which as it happened was the club boardroom—a builder's hut with a table in it. It was stinking hot and we were trying to get the deal done quickly—but apparently not quickly enough for Reuben. The door flew open and there he was in his King Gees and gumboots. "Is the deal done yet? The toilets have arrived. I want to install the toilets," he said.

Even Judah and Gerald cracked up. I don't think the ANZ guys were too impressed, but soon enough the deal was done and the toilets were duly installed under the close supervision of the boss, Pelerman. It was rumoured that he had bought the Bears because his wife, Ann, really liked the boys in their short shorts, but I never confirmed this with him—or with her.

Pelerman would remain hands on, albeit in a slightly idiosyncratic way. Robert Walls was coach in the Pelerman years and recalled the period with something close to fondness:

> In the early '90s, everything at Carrara was easily dismantable [sic]. Portables were used as admin offices, change rooms and gyms. It didn't instil confidence ... A couple of times a week, Reuben ... would swing off the Nerang-Broadbeach Road to check things out. Depending on the weather, his Jaguar would slip and slide or create billows of dust as he drove into the car park. On match day, Reuben would entertain his guests in the room next to my coach's box. The crayfish and champers would be in full swing as the ball was bounced. By half-time, however, Reuben and his guests would often be gone. That also didn't instil confidence.[3]

---

3   Robert Walls, "Treasured memories of Bear years", *The Age*, 13 July 2012.

It seemed we were fated to have private owners who might give their all financially but whose relationship with their new club was often … well, unique.

Yes indeed, Pelerman had his little quirks. He saved the club, but was slow to pick up on some of the nuances of League football, particularly player movement. Every time I went up there, he'd ask: "Did you bring Tony Lockett with you?"

The club staggered on, seeing off a threatened players' strike in the 1990 pre-season and Cronin's resignation. Pelerman asked the club's football manager, Shane O'Sullivan, who he would recommend as the new CEO and O'Sullivan said, "Get Andrew Ireland."

Ireland was summoned to Pelerman's home. He relates the story: "I was 'interviewed' by Reuben at his home and he was just wearing Speedos, a slightly off-putting sight for a prospective new employee. He didn't talk salary or terms of any sort, just what should we do with the club."[4] Indeed, he left salary negotiations to O'Sullivan, who told me recently: "Andrew and I got together and worked out what he (Ireland) should be paid relative to me, as football manager. Whatever we decided was OK with Reuben."[5]

After Ireland joined as CEO in 1990, the club certainly had a better management structure. A member of Collingwood's 1980 Grand Final team, Ireland had gone to Queensland, joined the QAFL and became its CEO in 1987, marking the start of an illustratious career in football administration. Financially it was still struggling to make ends meet, but under Ireland it committed to getting the Bears from Carrara to Brisbane, which was a cause of some tension internally for the club.

Pelerman may have been the last word in generosity, but he was also a volatile character. There are multiple stories of him throwing up his hands and wanting to close the club down or sack half the list. Ireland told me, "I always knew when Reuben had been in my office, because when I returned the light had been turned off."[6]

---

4   Andrew Ireland, interview with the author, 2014.
5   Shane O'Sullivan, interview with the author, 2014.
6   Andrew Ireland, interview with the author, 2014.

Pelerman had reached the stage where basically he was saying enough was enough, and in 1992, after losing several million dollars on the venture, he voluntarily relinquished his ownership of the licence and the club reverted to a member-run structure. The following year, the commission got its wish for the club to play in Brisbane at the Gabba.

Like the makeover at the MCG, transforming the Gabba involved rebuilding the ground in a way that would benefit Queensland cricket as well as football. Unlike the transformation of the MCG, it involved the removal of a greyhound track.

Pelerman needed a sweetener to ease the transition, but the only thing we gave in return for his cooperation was the catering rights at the Gabba for three years. This was his consideration for moving on and allowing the team to relocate to Brisbane. It didn't last long—he wasn't making much out of it and it was difficult to manage from his headquarters on the Gold Coast.

When Pelerman died in 2004, the club issued a short statement:

> The Brisbane Lions lost one of the most important people in the club's history this morning with the passing of former Brisbane Bears owner Reuben Pelerman.
>
> Pelerman rescued the club in early 1990 following the collapse of inaugural owner Christopher Skase's Qintex empire. Pelerman propped up the battling Bears for two seasons until handing the club over to a membership-based structure in February, 1992.
>
> When the well-known Gold Coast businessman inherited the Bears, all marketing options for the 1990 season had been sold, and the money [was] gone. But Pelerman honoured his commitment and kept the club alive on virtually no revenue.
>
> "All involved with the Brisbane Lions, and particularly those who knew him, have been saddened to learn today of Reuben's passing," said Lions chairman Graeme Downie.
>
> "Reuben took over the ownership of the Brisbane Bears at a most difficult time and kept the club afloat.
>
> "He lost a considerable amount of his own money for the cause, and

transferred ownership of the Bears' licence for little consideration, to help it transform into the successful membership-based merged club we have now.

"Without his contribution, the Bears may well have ceased to exist, so we have a lot to thank him for. Reuben Pelerman holds a special place in the history of the Brisbane Bears and Lions.

"He was a self-made man and a true philanthropist."[7]

With the team in Brisbane, it began to attract more interest, and people like Alan Piper and Noel Gordon—both future club presidents who had been on Pelerman's advisory board—wanted to stay involved. A group of high-profile supporters agreed to loan the club about $400,000, which helped it financially while it settled in Brisbane. The Bears were moving along nicely enough, and they were fundamental to the evolving history of our new national competition.

If I had a misgiving, it lay with the club's recruitment and performance. Success had not been quick for the Bears, hamstrung as they had been from the beginning with a dreadful allocation of players in their inaugural season, courtesy of the "old school" VFL; a wooden spoon in 1990 under former QAFL coach (and former Fitzroy player) Norm Dare told the story. Then Walls signed up in 1991 and gradually the list was transformed, and with it the club's fortunes.

We'd done our bit as a League with priority draft picks, but by the time Walls arrived, the Bears had the oldest playing list in the competition. I was running out of patience with that. The plan had to be to build for the future, not go for the sugar hit of seasoned players past their zenith and problematic short-term success. Building for the future was Walls' approach, too. I informed the Brisbane board that if they continued with their current recruitment strategy I would withdraw their priority draft picks. Slowly but surely change came. In 1991 Michael Voss was picked up from Brisbane's local zone, and then came Justin Leppitsch (1992), Nigel

---

7   Brisbane Lions media release, 21 January 2004.

Lappin and Chris Scott (1993) and Jason Akermanis (1994).

There were finals appearances ahead for the Bears, and the transformation into the Lions and the dynastic success that would follow with Leigh Matthews as coach, Ireland as entrenched CEO, and Piper and Graeme Downie as chairmen. But that was down the track a bit.

Back in Melbourne the foundation teams of the competition continued to grapple with money and the treacherous verges of insolvency. Peter Scanlon was working quietly and secretly on a super merger, a deal that would create 'Melbourne United'. That was his dream: a meld of North Melbourne, Fitzroy and Richmond into the Manchester United of Australian Football. But in true form the deal could not be made because the respective parties could not decide on colours, a jumper design and who would be president.

"Because they were all inner-city clubs, they were all to be equal partners, and no one was taking anyone over. I nearly got it there," Scanlon recalled. "They were all here in my office talking about jumpers and other very important matters.[8]

We were to "acquire" three new teams between 1991 and 1996 and achieve one merger. The Adelaide Crows were the first acquisition. They were a composite team that first played in the 1991 season, blessed by the full might and parochial fervour of the South Australian National Football League (SANFL) and the passion of Adelaide's football supporters.

Not that the South Australian league had always been enthusiastic about joining the AFL, let alone the VFL. Certainly not after SANFL president Max Basheer had come to Melbourne in 1982 to make a compelling submission to the VFL Board regarding the entry of a composite team to the VFL competition. Yes, they'd wanted in, back then. Basheer had received an ovation from the board when he finished, which left him feeling very positive about his prospects. However, he received a call from Jack Hamilton the next day in which Hamilton told him that the VFL directors had rejected his proposal because they thought the SA team would be too

---

8   Peter Scanlon, interview with the author, 2014.

strong in the Victorian competition. (Left unsaid was "... and we would not be able to pinch all your best players".)

The two states shared a long and bitter rivalry, and jealousies ran deep; the vehemence of a generation of state-of-origin clashes is evidence of that. Ted Whitten versus 'Knuckles' Kerley—legendary stuff. And then there was the long-running bitterness across South Australia that the Melbourne-based competition always poached the brightest and best from the Adelaide teams because they could. It was a lot to overcome, but having at least one Adelaide-based team was essential for a League that, after four seasons, no longer saw itself as an expanded VFL competition but a fully-fledged AFL national competition, performing since 1990 not as the VFL but the Australian Football League (AFL), complete with new badge and colours.

South Australia was a true-blue football state. How could we have a national league that was scrambling for footholds in enemy territory like Queensland and New South Wales but had failed to take a foothold in home territory?

Serious negotiations through the late 1980s had come to nothing even after our name change, with the SANFL resolving to stay out until at least 1993. The SANFL Board had advised the commission in May 1990 that it would "consider" entering a team in the AFL competition in 1993, "subject to there not being more than 14 clubs—nor would it pay a licence fee".[9] Jeff Browne said, "The SANFL did not want to be part of the AFL in 1990 unless it was entirely on their terms, and they felt safe in this belief until they were eventually coerced into joining some time later."[10]

In desperation and to force their hand, we began dealing directly with two powerhouse clubs of the SANFL, Norwood[11] and Port Adelaide, but most directly with Port Adelaide through its general manager, Ian McKenzie, and president, Bruce Weber. SANFL general manager Leigh Whicker tells the story:

> We invited Alan Schwab to a luncheon in Adelaide and asked him to

---

9   *AFL Annual Report 1990*, Australian Football League, Jolimont, Vic.
10 Jeff Browne, interview with the author, 2014.
11 Norwood had expressed interest as early as 1986.

stay for a drink afterwards. He said, "No, I have a meeting to go to." Max Basheer smelt a rat, and we found out later he was on his way to meet Ian McKenzie, the general manager of Port Adelaide Football Club. The next day Max received a call from Scotty Palmer, Schwabby's mouth in the press, who said, "Max, Port are about to be granted a licence by the VFL directors to field a team in the AFL," to which Max said, "That's rubbish." But on Monday the whole story unfolded and we were asked to meet Bruce Weber, president of Port, who had a heads of agreement from the AFL.[12]

Alan Schwab described the full sequence of events in the 1990 AFL annual report. He wrote:

> [S]erious discussions began between Port Adelaide and the AFL Commission and its executives, and on Monday 30 July 1990, a heads of agreement was signed which sparked off one of the most publicised and debated happenings ever.
>
> Eventually the brave bid by Port Adelaide ... did not eventuate, as an injunction prevented them from negotiating with the AFL, and history now records that the Adelaide Football Club was established after a dramatic turnaround in thinking by the SANFL.[13]

Adelaide's entry came after weeks of bitter wrangling, with many friendships shattered. The remaining nine SANFL clubs took out the injunction, attempting to block the Port deal. There's a forlorn film of me on YouTube being interviewed as events unfolded: "If the [SANFL] clubs for one reason or the other knock it back ... you know, you win some and you lose some."[14]

A deal was done in chambers after Basheer said he would not back away from the SANFL clubs' stated position but would agree to talk to the AFL while the injunction was in place. This gave the SANFL clubs a window of opportunity to come to Melbourne and lobby the AFL clubs

---

12 Leigh Whicker, interview with the author, 2014.
13 *AFL Annual Report 1990.*
14 "PTV: SA Footy History—part I" [online video], 2012, http://youtu.be/36PZ4zTDBd0 (accessed 22 May 2014).

to support their revised position that they would put a composite team in our competition. It had been revealed through all the kerfuffle that the SANFL had registered the name of "Adelaide Football Club" some four years earlier.

Basheer and Whicker headed to Melbourne to talk to Schwab and me in the Southern Cross Hotel about a deal. I arrived to see a trolley of grog from I know not where being wheeled into the meeting room. We sat down in the "old VFL" way of doing a deal, being fortunate to conclude the discussions before we were rendered unable to speak. The SANFL duo left us with the words, "We will give this a real good go."

The clubs accepted the deal and a board was formed in October 1990, with Basheer and Whicker the interim administrators of the new club; soon after, Graham Cornes was appointed coach. We signed the paperwork in February 1991 in Adelaide. Welcome, Adelaide Crows.

Importantly, one of the AFL's non-negotiables was that the SANFL had to establish an independent board of a similar nature to that of the AFL Commission to conduct its affairs in future. Whicker says, "That turned out to be the best thing that happened to South Australian football."[15]

The model for South Australia was similar to the one used for the formation of the Eagles: secure the composite team first because they had to develop a new supporter base, and admit a local team or teams with an established supporter base second. We reasoned that this was the best way to ensure support for both teams and build a strong rivalry.

A second team out of Perth was always in the commission's plans—it was just a case of when. While the concept of a Fremantle team in the League had been talked about by the East Fremantle and South Fremantle clubs as far back as 1987, courting entry in 1990, this prospect had ignored the existence of a five-year exclusive rights clause in the West Coast agreement with the League and the strong rivalry between the two traditional Fremantle clubs. To overcome this problem, the two clubs

---

15   Leigh Whicker, interview with the author, 2014.

initially looked at the possibility of relocating a Melbourne club, but that was never going to happen.

To the AFL, Fremantle was the obvious home for a second team as it had always been the strongest centre for football outside of Perth and had the potential of a pooled supporter base that had shown allegiance to both the East Fremantle and South Fremantle clubs in the WAFL. While the move by the two Fremantle clubs to apply independently for a licence had been a daring one, the commission would never have done something that was not supported by the West Australian Football Commission (WAFC)—and the Fremantle clubs' move was not.

In 1990, WAFC chairman Dr Peter Tannock presented a "vision for the future" document to the WAFC. It included a second team out of Perth, but stressed that the viability of the Eagles was a major consideration in the timing of the second team's introduction. The Eagles had not yet become a powerhouse in the competition, so the hesitancy was understandable. Ross Kelly, the first president of the Dockers, always felt that the WAFC did not want a second team but was pressured by the AFL Commission to take action. The Eagles were certainly against the move at that time. Tannock denies this, saying, "While the WAFL clubs were very negative about the move, 80 per cent of the initiative for a second team came from the WAFC."[16]

In June 1993 Graeme Samuel and Alan Schwab joined Ron Alexander and Jeff Ovens from the WAFC to examine the issues involved in a second WA team joining the AFL competition. The result was positive. Both commissions accepted the task force recommendation that a new team commence operations in 1995. A "port club" was the favoured home and, as reported by Anthony Barker, "even though Tannock denied any AFL pressure he acknowledged that commissioners Oakley and Schwab were strongly supportive of a second team, from Fremantle. Schwab, in particular, believed that a Fremantle club was very important in developing and sustaining a long-term traditional football culture in WA."[17]

---

16 Anthony J. Barker, *Behind the Play: A History of Football in Western Australia from 1868*, West Australian Football Commission, 2004, p. 284.

17 Ibid.

It was vital to build genuine rivalry between the Perth and Fremantle football communities. Both traditional Fremantle clubs were genuinely hostile as a result of not being involved and did everything in their power to upset the apple cart, and their entrenched rivalry eventually denied them involvement in the new club. Tannock later conceded that not including them in the mix was probably a mistake. Richard Colless, previously West Coast's inaugural chair and soon to become Sydney Swans chairman, was also not impressed as he could not understand how the AFL could ignore the existing traditions of East Fremantle and South Fremantle in developing a new Fremantle brand.

As a result the new club had a lot of work to do, particularly considering Eagles CEO Brian Cook's remarks that "the Eagles had more people in the Fremantle postcode area as members than the Dockers did".[18] Dealing with rival member numbers is always going to be the legacy of a second team coming into a marketplace and why it is important that the second team already has a strong supporter base. There were the usual concerns about recruiting restrictions; Tannock felt the Dockers had a good go with draft picks but wasted them on poor choices. Kelly, considered an outsider by many Fremantle residents, was the first president and proved to be an inspired choice as he soon made a positive mark on the club.

And so the Fremantle Dockers joined the competition in 1995 and on 14 May that year the first Western Derby was played in front of 40,356 fans. Although the Eagles won that match convincingly, it was the forerunner of many great derbies in years to come.

Port Adelaide's journey to join the AFL was a tortuous one with several false starts. The club's early efforts to join the competition by bypassing the SANFL system infuriated the other SANFL clubs, who perceived this behaviour as treacherous. The fallout from Port Adelaide's failed bid was disastrous, with some even calling for the state's most famous and most decorated club to be expelled from the SANFL.[19] As mentioned, after

---

18 Ibid.
19 Port Adelaide continued to compete and to dominate the SANFL competition, however, winning nine premierships in 11 years between 1988 and 1999.

legal action to thwart Port's efforts the SANFL had agreed to establish the Adelaide Crows.

The League had previously indicated that it did not initially want an established team from South Australia but a composite side, and that's what we got. We told the SANFL at the time the Crows deal was done that a second team would be contemplated in due course and we favoured Port Adelaide to be that team. Many in Adelaide felt that Port was the "fall guy" that forced the SANFL to field a team earlier than it had intended to. Maybe so!

The anger from Port's failed AFL bid continued to simmer below the surface. In 1994, the League announced it would award a second AFL licence to a South Australian club for entry potentially in 1996. Port Adelaide was our choice, but we faced some opposition from other SANFL clubs. You must remember that Port Adelaide in the Adelaide competition is akin to Collingwood in Melbourne—lots of love, and just as much hate. Basheer and Whicker were aware that the commission would not compromise on this selection but said they would assist us to find a way to achieve the outcome we wanted. I was invited by them to come over and put the case for Port Adelaide. In front of a rather hostile meeting of the SANFL clubs, I explained that a "traditional" club with an established supporter base had to be the second club as it would be too hard to build support for another composite club.

There is no doubt Basheer and Whicker played their cards well, and they won the day after I left the meeting. In May 1995 and again in October, the commission confirmed that we would have a 16-team competition in 1996 and Port Adelaide would be admitted in 1997.

In August 1995, then-commissioner Wayne Jackson (a South Australian true-blood who was later to take over from me as AFL CEO) and I attended the launch of the new club in Adelaide. Port Adelaide, whose nickname was the Magpies and whose traditional colours were black and white, had been required as a condition of its entry to find new colours and a new nickname to avoid clashing with the Collingwood Football Club. A new guernsey had been created and it was unveiled at the launch. The new club's colours were black, white, silver and teal, and its nickname was 'The Power'.

Although the AFL insisted that the new licence was to be given to a "traditional" club with an established supporter base, the AFL team, called "Port Power", was not to account for its history. Port Adelaide had been in existence since 1870, but the club history was to be split, with the Power's to date from its inclusion in the AFL competition and the Magpies' to be retained and then start again. This was a condition imposed by the SANFL—who were concerned that a combined club would become a superpower in the domestic competition—but supported by the AFL. It went so far as to not allow the administration and training facilities of the Port Magpies to be removed from their base at Alberton Oval.

Happily, the majority of Port Magpie fans saw no distinction between the old and the new, and over time the lines have become so blurred as to not exist. The SANFL approved the "merger" of the Power and the Magpies in November 2010, at which time the club's history officially became the Power's property, and Port Power players not playing senior AFL footy were again wearing the prison-bar guernsey of the Port Magpies.

During this time there was plenty on the commission's agenda back in Victoria. The failed Footscray merger of 1989 had been a disaster for the Fitzroy Football Club. For Footscray it was something from which the club could build, with new finances and a revitalised supporter base. For the Lions, the promise of the merger—a deal that would have placed Fitzroy on top of the new combine had it gone ahead—came to nothing.

Fitzroy lost sponsors in the aftermath, and while Footscray emerged debt free, thanks to the community tin-rattling, Fitzroy retired to lick its wounds, still $700,000 in debt.

The Lions would try everything over the next couple of seasons to find a way to underwrite their future. There were home games in Tasmania in the 1990 and 1991 seasons, a move to the Western Oval in 1994, a game in Canberra in 1995. A merger, which had been part of many discussions surrounding Fitzroy for most of the previous decade, was back on the table—not surprising given the financial noose tightening around the club. On-field things were just as dire, with the Lions finishing 12th in 1990, 14th in 1991, 10th in 1992, 11th in 1993 and 14th in 1994, a period in which they won just 35 of 110 matches.

In August 1994, Dyson Hore-Lacy, who had taken over the presidency of Fitzroy from Leon Wiegard in 1992, and Ian Ridley of Melbourne fronted the commission with a proposal for a Fitzroy-Melbourne merger given Fitzroy's debt, which was then revealed to the commission as $2 million but later that month became $2.6 million. The Melbourne-Fitzroy Football Club or Melbourne Lions was the goal. The pair were hoping the AFL would take on Fitzroy's debt and retain all its players for the new club, which could then make its selection from a combined list of 84.

It *seemed* there was agreement on the terms put before the commission—of name and board structure, with David Crawford mooted as the possible chairman. However, that was hardly the case, as the commission heard Fitzroy's tales of woe, including a request that a debt on their hotel "asset" of $650,000 be cleared by the League, and Melbourne's list of needs, which were yet to be resolved in discussions between the two clubs, as noted by the minutes as "players, national draft, salary cap, membership guarantees, promotional assistance and an establishment grant for the new entity".[20]

It all fell apart by early September, with the final stumbling block being not debt or administrative arrangements but, as was so often the case, the club's name and colours. Some things in football run deeper than money.

This had been close to a last roll of the dice for Fitzroy. At the commission meeting after the one that had seen the death of the Melbourne Lions, the commission authorised me to apply greater stringency to Fitzroy's finances and apply the League's financial solvency rule. What this meant in practice was an assurance from the club that it could pay its debts as and when they became due, and that it would be able to do likewise over the year to come.

---

20 AFL Commission minutes, 5 August 1994.

We were asking the same questions of St Kilda at the time, so Fitzroy was no Robinson Crusoe.

The club struggled on, but by 1996 it was clear it was being strangled, with debts beyond $2 million and no major sponsor (and little hope of securing one). Auditors were sent in and a process of negotiation began with Fitzroy, which by March 1996 had failed to reassure the commission (and the Australian Securities Commission) that its finances could be stabilised, and was seeking loan funds from the League to keep the club afloat, a request rejected by the commission. So serious was the situation that a contingency plan had been put before the commission should the club be unable to field a team.

At Fitzroy's annual meeting on 29 April, the members were briefed on the options of taking the AFL's offer of paying $6 million to any club that would facilitate an approved merger, or fighting on. As with all such meetings, the outcome was unclear, with some wanting to take the money and live a new life, and others wanting to continue to fight the fight they had been engaged in for a generation. The club was receiving no support in the media, with senior reporters in all outlets clear in their view that Fitzroy would fail, and sooner rather than later.

In the meantime, Brisbane, who had been talking to Fitzroy for some years about the prospect of joining the two clubs, entered the fray. The commission met on 3 May with Brisbane president Noel Gordon and CEO Andrew Ireland to discuss their position on a merger.[21] Gordon, who could see the sparkle the League's funding would provide the Bears *and* the extra value coming from first pick of the Fitzroy list, was very keen but initially had only moderate support from his board. Graeme Downie, a board member who later became president in their premiership years, said, "Noel was the driver of the deal. The rest of us were ambivalent, including Alan Piper, our major financial contributor and director. Noel pursued it

---

21   In 1986, before the Brisbane licence had been won by the QAFL/Cronin consortium, Allen Aylett, then a director of Sydney, had put a motion that the licence discussion be varied to transfer all the Fitzroy players and coaches to the new licensee. The motion was defeated, but it showed clearly that a switch north was a serious discussion point. A decade earlier, it had even been mooted by some in the Fitzroy administration to take the club to Sydney.

with some fervour using David Dunn from Blake's as legal adviser. The discussions progressed well for a period, then died."[22] Andrew Ireland said, "We found out that Fitzroy had started to talk to North."[23] Not long after that meeting with the commission, the Brisbane merger offer was formally rejected by the Fitzroy board.

Greg Miller, North Melbourne's CEO, recalls the period as tumultuous, and one in which North was seduced by the AFL into believing it had all the cards. By early May, it seemed a deal had been done, with the *Herald Sun* reporting on 15 May that an "in principle" agreement between North and Fitzroy had been reached.[24] But nothing was certain in these uncertain times.

Meanwhile, the media were turning a little nasty, and a lot personal. In the *Herald Sun* of 17 May, Tony De Bolfo wrote: "I hope that Fitzroy's tongue-tied mouthpiece Dyson Hore-Lacy has the guts to tell his members what really *is* happening to their club."[25] Trevor Grant, never one to take a backward step (as I had found out on my first day in the job all those years earlier), wrote that while clubs and the game had made great steps towards professionalism, when it came to mergers they had "the unbelievable capacity to revert to their old amateur status".[26] The reality was that each party to the discussions was fighting to the death for the best outcome for its interests, and clarity with the media was not on anyone's agenda.

Through June, all parties were of the view that a North-Fitzroy merger would win out, but by month's end the tide turned in yet another direction, as the Nauru Insurance Company (NIC), Fitzroy's only secured creditor, stepped in and appointed an administrator — Mike Brennan of the accounting firm Ernst & Young—to recover a debt of $1 million plus. This was indicative not just of the misgivings the company had as to Fitzroy's capacity to pay, enhanced by the masses of media covering the story, but also of the difficulties Nauru itself was facing. Fitzroy had offered part payments—42 cents in the

---

22 Graeme Downie, interview with the author, 2014.
23 Andrew Ireland, interview with the author, 2014.
24 Philip Cullen, "We're gone", *Herald Sun*, 15 May 1996.
25 Tony De Bolfo, "Who's kidding whom?", *Herald Sun*, 17 May 1996.
26 Trevor Grant, "Clubs own worst enemy", *Herald Sun*, 17 May 1996.

dollar—to the NIC, but this had been rejected, and the company decided it had no other recourse than to put the club into administration.

Brennan, who seemed to revel in media attention, revealed that the club's future was entirely dependent on AFL support: without that support, it could not continue. With the clear merger options—North Melbourne and Brisbane—before the commission, and the $6 million offer to include payment of debt, the League had no issue in allowing the club to continue, and put up an indemnity to the administrator to ensure Fitzroy's next match, against Geelong at Whitten Oval on 29 June, would go ahead. Indeed, any other option would have been a real slap in the face for the competition as a whole. Not surprisingly, the Fitzroy players were more than restless; their unrest was mollified, to some extent, when the League's football operations manager, Ian Collins, met them and assured them that the AFL would guarantee their payments, whatever happened through the merger discussions and beyond.

With Brennan appointed, the Fitzroy board had little or no capacity to control the agenda. This was really the end game for the club, but as with everything at Fitzroy, there were one or two twists to come. Much had gone on between North and Fitzroy through June—the name of the new club, the colours (blue and white with a Fitzroy emblem), and the likely set-up of the merged board had been decided. However, on Tuesday 2 July, Miller informed Hore-Lacy that North Melbourne now wanted only four Fitzroy members on the board of the merged club and that he, Hore-Lacy, wasn't one of the chosen ones. Hore-Lacy, somewhat fed up with the constant amendments to the deal, asked North to give an undertaking to Fitzroy that there would be no more changes to the agreement struck between them on 25 June, before Brennan's appointment. No such undertaking was given. In his book *Fitzroy*, recalling the moment, Hore-Lacy wrote: "I ... asked Greg, 'Can you give me an undertaking that the agreed position between North Melbourne and Fitzroy would not be changed?' Greg said he could not give that undertaking."[27]

---

27   Dyson Hore-Lacy, *Fitzroy*, Lion Publications, 2000.

There was a touch of hubris about North Melbourne's approach, with the club recognising that it was well and truly in the driver's seat and that, with Port Adelaide to join the competition the following year, the commission was more than likely in favour of one fewer club in Melbourne. Miller told the media that North's request for an extended playing list was an important part of the deal, and that without 54 players on North's 1997 list there would be no merger with Fitzroy. Calling on the best of Fitzroy's list was a red rag to the other clubs, as North already had a very strong list; the Kangaroos had finished sixth in 1995 with Fitzroy a distant last, but had asked for a list of 54 against Brisbane's offer of 45, or eight from Fitzroy's list. This was despite a commission paper of June 1995 outlining in some detail the likely list composition following a merger: it showed that North and Fitzroy combined would not be allowed more than 50 players on their list.

On Wednesday, Brisbane was told by Fitzroy to get to Melbourne immediately if they still wanted to be involved in the merger discussions. The Brisbane crew arrived that afternoon and indicated their position. Two deals were on Fitzroy's table now: a proposal to merge with Brisbane and a proposal to merge with North.

It was strange to me—the Fitzroy board making all sorts of demands—because as I had to point out to Hore-Lacy, who was a QC himself, that the club was in administration and had lost the right to fully determine its own future. The club clearly preferred that future to rest in the North Melbourne deal, whatever shape it may end up taking. Admittedly, Fitzroy still had some negotiating strength, particularly in relation to its tabled deal with North Melbourne, but the ultimate strength lay with the commission, the clubs and the administrator. All Fitzroy could do was hope for the best.

Both Brisbane and North were then summoned to a meeting of the AFL clubs at the Punt Road Oval on the Thursday (4 July), chaired by Leon Daphne, president of Richmond. Downie recalls:

> We went to the meeting at Richmond where both clubs were to make their pitch to the other clubs as they were still involved in making the decision on entry and exit from the competition. Brisbane put the same

> deal to the clubs they had been discussing with Fitzroy previously, but North wanted a dramatically better deal involving more players and offering less retention of Fitzroy intellectual property.[28]

Ireland goes on: "The clubs favoured Brisbane because North had got a bit greedy by asking for about 20 players whereas we only asked for six to eight players."[29]

As much as Fitzroy was backing the North Melbourne deal, the other clubs were wary and voted 14-1 against the idea. North then did an about-face and said it would accept the same deal as Brisbane, but it was too late. The presidents would not have it. North had had its chance. Things were slowly changing in the way deals were done in the League, although there was certainly some self-interest shown by the clubs in rejecting what would have been a potentially unbeatable North over the next five or six years. Even without the playing benefits that would have come with the merger, that was pretty much the case anyway, with the Kangaroos winning flags in 1996 and 1998 during a golden era for the club.

Slowly but surely, through a process of attrition, the idea of a Brisbane-Fitzroy merger was about to have its day.

At 4pm on Thursday 4 July, in a week in which we'd had to call in security in the face of all sorts of anonymous threats (something I had got used to), the commission met to resolve the future of the Fitzroy Football Club. The long saga was coming to an end, in my view in a way that provided the best possible outcome for a club that could no longer stand on its own two feet—and not just in 1996, but for so long into the past. I addressed the meeting. According to the minutes:

> Mr Oakley advised the meeting that he had addressed a meeting of clubs held at the Richmond Football Club which had been called to discuss the proposed merger with Fitzroy and the following matters were then noted:

---

28 Graeme Downie, interview with the author, 2014.
29 Andrew Ireland, interview with the author, 2014.

> A proposal had been submitted by Brisbane and it seemed likely that North Melbourne would withdraw its proposal and submit a revised proposal including changes to the size of the player list of the merged club. On the basis that two proposals were now available for consideration by the commission, both proposals would need to be evaluated and a further decision made by the commission as to which proposal would be placed before the clubs.[30]

The Fitzroy administrator joined the meeting, "and advised that at the club meeting at Richmond, 13 or 14 clubs had voted in favour of endorsing a merger, but 14 clubs had voted against the terms of the proposed merger with North Melbourne".[31] The size of the combined player list was the fundamental issue.

And of course that, in the end, was the issue for the clubs: on-field competitiveness. It was ever thus. Self-interest would again rule the day, although in this case there was some justification for their concern. The clubs saw the Brisbane-Fitzroy merger as a lesser threat and so endorsed it. Perhaps if they could have seen into the future, they would not been so supportive of the venture. The League had put $6 million on the table to see a merger done, money that was on offer for whatever good deal could be arrived at. All we wanted at the AFL was for it to be successful. We wanted the deal to land on its feet. And with the Brisbane Lions it did just that.

Brennan (whose fee of between $200,000 and $300,000 was to be paid from the AFL handout) indicated that, while the Brisbane deal was "a better deal for the creditors of Fitzroy and was more likely to be approved by the clubs",[32] he would accept either deal on the basis that a collapsed club would reap him no return.

On that lengthy July day the commission, after receiving final bids from each club (including a revised bid from North Melbourne), withdrew its support for North Melbourne and endorsed Brisbane's offer. Once that

---

30 AFL Commission minutes, 4 July 1996.
31 Ibid.
32 Ibid.

view was put to North, the club immediately "withdrew from any further discussion on the merger proposals".[33]

The long, emotional and draining process had, we believed, delivered a good deal for Brisbane and for Fitzroy, and our view was that North Melbourne's bid had cost it the box seat it had held for much of the previous weeks. The key features of the deal were noted in the minutes, led by the club's new name: "The merged club will (subject to Brisbane Bears member approval) be known as the Brisbane Bears-Fitzroy Football Club Limited and will trade as Brisbane Lions Australian Football Club."[34]

The details followed. For seven years the merged club would wear an away strip in Fitzroy colours, albeit one with a Lions emblem rather than that of the Fitzroy Football Club, and after that time it could change to a strip based predominantly on the Fitzroy colours. The logo would be the Fitzroy lion "in perpetuity", with three Fitzroy nominees to be appointed to the board of the merged club. The merged club would have an initial list of 44 players for 1997 (with at least eight from Fitzroy's list as priority picks), reducing to 42 in 1998, and there would be a lift in the salary cap. It would be $300,000 higher than the Bears' cap for 1997, $200,000 higher in 1998 and $100,000 higher in 1999. The club would play 11 games at the Gabba and as many Victoria-based away games as possible, but no fewer than six to be played at the MCG or Princes Park (then called Optus Oval).

And then came an important detail: "After the merger an appropriate entity will act as trustee of the Fitzroy memorabilia, which will be utilised in the football operations of the merged club. This entity will also represent the interests of the Fitzroy members."[35] The Brisbane Lions would be a respecter of the traditions of the older club—so important and, as it turned out, so true (although we weren't all that happy with the way Noel Gordon lorded it over proceedings in his appearance on TV's *The Footy Show* that evening).

A reconvened meeting of the AFL club presidents endorsed our recommendation of a Brisbane Bears-Fitzroy Lions merger. The fine

---

33   Ibid.
34   Ibid.
35   Ibid.

details of the deal were wrangled over the next couple of weeks, and by the commission meeting of Sunday 21 July, ironically held in Perth, there were papers on the table to be noted and ratified, and it was "resolved to recognise, accept, adopt and implement the Brisbane/Fitzroy merger".[36] Obviously, with all those active verbs in the minutes, we did not want to leave any doubt as to the path ahead.

There was a mixed response publicly, but that was to be expected. Some hours after the commission had ratified the deal, the Fitzroy cheer squad showed their contempt for all it stood for, proclaiming on its banner (developed without the approval of the club) before the match against Collingwood at Victoria Park: "Seduced by North, raped by Brisbane, and f—d by the AFL". There was always going to be the hard core who said, "It's not our club any more"—my wife's sister-in-law, for one, who hated the deal and sounded off at me in the media.

Sadly, there were many who discarded the new club, and some swore off the game altogether. Others were more conciliatory: Fitzroy legend Kevin Murray thought it was "fantastic", and Minister for Sport Tom Reynolds, a Fitzroy fan, was onside and went on the new club board.

In the end it was the dull impartiality of the AFL draw that had the last word, consigning Fitzroy to a final match away in Perth, against Fremantle— a club in just its second season. We probably could have handled that a little better, but a draw is a tough thing to unpick, and Fremantle did give the Lions a respectful farewell despite the 86-point thrashing it handed out on the field.

The proof of the pudding was the triple-premiership dynasty that was just around the corner for the Brisbane Lions, with Chris Johnson and Martin Pike from that last Fitzroy team taking part. Each of those premierships was marked by a morning-after public reception at the old Brunswick Street home of the Fitzroy Football Club, in front of four to five thousand supporters.

---

36   AFL Commission minutes, 21 July 1996.

Were we done with mergers? Not quite. At the same commission meeting that signed off on the Fitzroy-Brisbane deal, "Mr Oakley tables a further draft of a letter detailing the package of arrangements to be provided by the AFL for a potential Hawthorn-Melbourne merger."[37]

We weren't out of the woods yet. There was still a sense that the Victorian clubs were still too many in simple numbers if we were to grow the competition nationally in the way we wanted.

The Melbourne-Hawthorn deal would stir extraordinary passions and great theatrics. The AFL still had $6 million on the table for a successful merger, and for a then down-at-heel club like Hawthorn, it seemed a path to salvation. Well, that was the official rationale. Hawks supporters saw matters differently and, led by club legend Don Scott, launched "Operation Payback".

The crunch came at the end of the final home and away game of the 1996 season, when Melbourne and Hawthorn, by a bizarre twist of fate, played each other. The "merger game" was a full-on contest in front of 63,196 at the MCG in which Jason Dunstall kicked 10 goals and the Hawks won by a point. After the siren, Hawthorn's Chris Langford, later to become an AFL commissioner, ripped off his jumper and waved it defiantly above his head.

Jumper waving had been a theme that week. Scott had addressed an anti-merger rally at the Camberwell Civic Centre. At one point he'd held an example of the merged club jumper above his head, ripping and tearing at it to pull off strips that eventually revealed, guess what, a Melbourne jumper. His words were those of a great statesman: "A Velcro Hawk on a Melbourne guernsey!" At this meeting commission chairman John Kennedy, a Hawthorn legend, was disgracefully abused by Walter Jona, a Hawk supporter and former politician, in front of the Hawthorn faithful, causing Kennedy to walk out of the meeting.

The Hawthorn meeting voted no to a merger. A simultaneous meeting of the Melbourne membership, led by president Ian Ridley, voted yes. There would be no merger and, on reflection, the game is better for it. Melbourne would go on to play for the premiership in 2000, and Hawthorn, revitalised,

---

37   Ibid.

and driven by one of the game's most passionate presidents, Ian Dicker, would win the flag in 2008 (under the direction of an equally passionate but perhaps more expressive president, former state premier Jeff Kennett) and become, again, a power club on and off the field.

The merger period was another lesson—as if we needed any—about the power that lies in passionate club support. Money was one thing, common sense was another, but the true determining factor of so much in football is the passion of supporters who wear their birthright on their sleeves and will fight to the death to hold on to what has always been theirs.

It's what makes the game great. It's also what makes the game a bugger to manage.

CHAPTER 19

From sadness to glory

As I have noted, there was hardly a day in those early years of the commission when Sydney's troubles were not on the agenda. After Geoffrey Edelsten resigned as chairman of the Swans in July 1986 not much changed, even though the club had some on-field success under coach Tom Hafey.

By 1988 we had to put in an administrator, and in May of that year the League acted decisively, buying back the controlling shares held by Powerplay for the princely sum of $10, while seeking a new owner. The ownership went to a group including Michael Willesee and Peter Weinert, but for all their best efforts the spiral continued. In Jim Main's story of the rise, fall and rise of the Swans, in *Shake Down the Thunder*, Weinert describes the moment:

> A number of members of the interim board formed part of the new private ownership group at the end of 1988, along with others who had been invited to join. We agreed to pay $5 million over five years, plus a number of other payments towards some of the club's assets ... There were 14 owners of varying degrees of shareholding ... The new ownership group was formed early in 1988, but didn't take control until December that year.[1]

---

1 Jim Main, *Shake Down the Thunder: From Ugly Duckling to AFL Premiers—The Story of the Sydney Swans*, Geoff Slattery Publishing, 2006, p. 124.

Geoff Slade, one of those shareholders, told Main of the slide: "[W]e lost money hand over fist—$12.5 million to be exact. I think we were sold a pup, or to be fair, I don't think we did our due diligence properly. We went into it with passion and excitement when there were so many pitfalls."[2]

By 1992 it was clear that, unless the League was prepared to offer the Swans a new deal, the club was finished, crippled by debt. Weinert wrote to the League outlining the club's issues: "We basically said, 'Unless the AFL gets behind the club, we can't see how it can survive'."[3]

In the end it was the football world's collective loathing of Carlton that helped save the Sydney Swans—and the Swans needed saving. Collingwood, Carlton's most vehement enemy, was at the centre of it. Where did Carlton come into it? Let me explain.

By the early 1990s the Sydney experiment, the most crucial of the League's interstate adventures, was at rock bottom. Match attendances hovered around the 10,000 mark and in 1990 the team made a $1 million loss. Ownership had been reorganised, but by the end of 1992, with another wooden spoon in the trophy cabinet, the Swans were at breaking point.

The importance of the League's Sydney team cannot be overstated. Without a presence in the country's biggest market, the entire notion of a national competition would be set on its backside.

The commission was considering options. Failure of the Swans was a real possibility, but leaving the Sydney market without a football presence was not. Plan A was to throw the Swans a $2.7 million lifeline and some draft and salary concessions. This was not the deal the Swans ownership group was looking for: they favoured a redirection of their licence fees back to the club, something the commission had already decided was not acceptable. And if the board knocked Plan A back, Plan B was to do a deal with Carlton that would see the Blues play away games at the SCG. As the minutes of the 6 October 1992 meeting record:

---

2   Ibid., p. 131.
3   Ibid., p. 140.

> Mr Scanlon suggested that, pending a decision from the Swans and with the consent of the Melbourne-based clubs, a meeting be held with certain club officials to gauge their reaction to the alternatives of financial and player support to the Swans, or a Melbourne-based team playing in Sydney.[4]

We decided to test the waters with a small group of the opinion-makers of the League, and called together Melbourne's Ian Ridley, Hawthorn's John Lauritz, St Kilda's Stuart Trott, Essendon's David Shaw and Collingwood's Errol Hutchesson, on the understanding that the meeting was strictly confidential and must not be discussed outside the meeting.

The reaction was not that positive. We'd had discussions with Carlton, meeting with both Ian Collins and John Elliott, and it would be fair to say they were keen about the prospect of playing "away" games at the SCG. It would have been a good earner for the Blues, up to $2 million a year potentially, but Elliott wanted it to be more than a simple option before he would entertain the idea seriously.

We couldn't really push forward ahead of public opinion here—which is to say we had to sell it to the other clubs first, and at this point they weren't buying. North had offered itself as a club to play away games in Sydney, but this was not favoured by the commission because we needed to lead from a position of strength and needed Carlton's connections in Sydney for the option to work.

There was one other possibility we put on the table at that meeting of club officials: a merger between the Brisbane Bears and the Swans, an east-coast combine team. It was our least-preferred option, but something for the mix that would at least keep the notion of a national competition alive. Keeping Sydney afloat was our absolute preference.

Sending Carlton north, well, that drew gasps from the complete board meeting at which the commission finally floated the idea. At the meeting, on 22 October, to which I had invited as observers the club presidents who were not already directors of the League, I broached the concept

---

4   VFL Commission minutes, 6 October 1992.

of financially backing Sydney. Weinert, chairman of the Swans, spoke eloquently and passionately on behalf of his club with little reaction from those present. I then introduced the Carlton option of playing away games in Sydney, and Collingwood president Allan McAlister jumped to his feet in horror.

McAlister had come to the meeting already outraged. The politics here were being played with a will, and Weinert had got wind of the Carlton plan and was determined to see it sunk. As he told Main in *Shake Down the Thunder*:

> One of the proposed options was that Carlton would use Sydney as a second home base, play its home games in Melbourne and all its away games in Sydney. A couple of us at the Swans got wind of that proposal and decided to play the political game to ensure the club survived as the Swans. The rivalry between Collingwood and Carlton at that time was extreme, so we fed Collingwood information about the Carlton plan. We soon got the Magpies onside to the point where they were very upset that their great rivals might secure the extraordinary advantage of effectively having two home bases.[5]

"Over my bloody dead body!" That was McAlister at the meeting, suitably primed but attempting to give an impression of shock and outrage.

I said, "Allan, you are not a director of the League—you're here by invitation. Please sit down."

And he said, "Well, we can fix that." He walked over, grabbed Collingwood's director Hutchesson, pulled him out of his chair and sat down in his place. "OK, so now I am the director."

McAlister went on to make his argument with passion. Quite simply, the Carlton idea would turn the Blues into an unstoppable powerhouse team. Better to come to a financial deal to save the Swans. McAlister recalled the meeting for Main:

> I just had to say something at that AFL meeting, as I did not want to see Carlton being gifted an enormous advantage over the other clubs. Apart

---

5   Jim Main, *Shake Down the Thunder*, 2006, p. 140.

> from anything else the Blues would have access to all the sponsorship possibilities in Sydney. I therefore argued that up to $2 million was not an excessive figure and, in fact, represented little more than $100,000 per club. I also argued that the Swans were an original VFL club and it would be sad if they were wiped out.[6]

Slowly the conversation turned to accepting the proposed Sydney deal—all on the back of the collective hatred of Carlton. Weinert's impassioned plea for support on behalf of his group of owners had its impact, but it was the idea of basing another club—a hated club—in Sydney that got the deal over the line. As Weinert recalls:

> Ross Oakley eventually called for a vote and asked all those in favour of the proposal to allow the Swans to survive to raise their hands. We needed a simple majority, at least eight of the 15 there, and as I saw the eight hands go up I realised that we'd done it, we'd saved the club.[7]

The deal eventually went to the commission on 13 November, when the details of the proposed agreement between the AFL and Sydney Swans FC were tabled and approved. We had managed to emerge with our preferred option. The Swans (and the Bears) were given draft concessions, and the $1.95 million in licence fees paid by the Swans would be directed back to the club.

The next step, as the money ran out again, would be Sydney's gradual transition away from private ownership to a membership-based operation, and the national competition would move on to another chapter.

Tribalism had saved the day again.

Shifting the Swans from private ownership to a team dependent on membership meant a shuffling of the personnel and formulating an entirely new structure—one that would have public rather than simply corporate appeal. It was clear that supporters who had previously had no feeling of ownership of the club were happy to allow the private owners to

---

6   Ibid.
7   Ibid., p. 144.

dip into their deep pockets to run the club. But now it was theirs. Now they were motivated to stump up and support their membership-based club.

In season 1993, after Gary Buckenara was sacked and Brett Scott took over as caretaker, Ron Barassi would be appointed coach after round six, Ron Joseph would be chief executive, Richard Colless would begin his long and productive association as a director and, briefly and tragically, Alan Schwab would be seconded to Sydney from the League to get things in order as acting chair.

Sounds easy when you say it like that, but Barassi needed more than a little convincing. He hadn't coached a senior League team since his unsuccessful return bout at Melbourne ended in 1985.

About 10.30 one night the doorbell rang at my home in Erin Street, Richmond. We were just a street away from Barassi's pub, the Mountain View in Bridge Road. I went to the door and Joseph and Barassi were there. "Ah, the two Ronnies," I said, and had them come in.

Joseph had propositioned Barassi to come and coach the Swans, but Barassi was looking for reassurance that the commission would back him if he took the job. He wanted to make sure he would have a club that was able to survive in a decent state, a better state of corporate and financial stability than there had been previously. Quite simply, he wanted to know that the commission was behind the Swans.

I reassured him, telling him that nothing was of higher importance to the League than the success of the Sydney Swans.

The next night the doorbell rang again at about 10.30, just minutes after closing time. It was Barassi again, on his own this time.

"You are going to financially support the club?" he asked.

"Yes, we are."

"And the commission is of the same view? That this is vital to the competition?"

"Yes, they are."

"And you will personally see that this happens?"

"Yes, I will."

"OK, then I'm in."

Barassi had probably reached his peak as a coach, but his reputation, aura and status as an AFL legend were supreme. His appointment as coach was a vital sign—to the players, the supporters and all the sponsors and media—that Sydney could now be taken seriously. It was a critical move.

And Barassi was as good a marketing asset as he was a coach: he could drive corporate support and he could drive membership. I wonder how much the AFL was thinking of Barassi's importance to Sydney when they announced Kevin Sheedy as coach of Greater Western Sydney in 2009.

Like everything else in football, completing the Swans package was complicated. At the same time as the commission was wrangling with Sydney's debt and poor performance, other clubs were looking at the commission with concern that too much power had drifted towards AFL headquarters.

From the inside we had pretty much the opposite concern, but both points of view drew to a single conclusion: the commissioning of a report from David Crawford, who at the time was one of the country's best-credentialed receivers and managers (see next chapter for more on the Crawford report). He would go on not only to have a significant corporate career, but also to make other forays into the analysis of sporting competitions.

Early 1993 was a time of some tension between the clubs and the League. In a way, the relationships that had been sketchily defined with the foundation of the VFL Commission in 1985 needed to take another step. We could either go back to an arrangement that vested control of the code in the clubs, or more formally place that trust in the hands of the commission as the game's duly constituted, exclusive administrating body. As things stood we were in a halfway house, with the board of directors—the club-based body that had run the game for a century—still having a good share of the power balance.

There were other issues, too, such as the strange relationship that had existed since those early days of compromise and strategy that saw me given the dual roles of chairmanship of the commission and chief executive officer of the League, with Schwab as executive commissioner.

In March 1993 Crawford delivered his report. It was a logical bookend to the Blue Report of 1985, and brought a sense of clarity to relationships that had grown without structure since that time as the League shifted and evolved. Much had been done. As Crawford himself pointed out:

> It is important to understand the need for the current review is a result of many factors, not the least of which is that the commission has been successful in the implementation of most of the recommendations contained in the 1985 [Blue] report and there have been significant achievements over the past seven years.[8]

He told the media when presenting the report: "What I have proposed in this report is for an independent, unbiased commission which must be capable of taking objective, logical decisions in the best interests of administering AFL football in the future."[9] My role would be more clearly defined: under Crawford's recommendations I would no longer wear two hats as commission chairman and chief executive of the League—in retrospect, an untenable situation. I would have the single role of chief executive officer, which did not change what I had been doing for seven years but relieved me of the dual role, with the chair of the commission becoming a separate part-time role. I was asked who I would prefer as chair and without hesitation I nominated Hawthorn legend John Kennedy.

The commission would be expanded to eight, and the relationship between the clubs and the commission would be redefined. The clubs would retain powers to appoint part-time commissioners at the annual meeting of the AFL and have the ultimate rights to admit, expel, relocate or require a merger of a club by a two-thirds majority of the clubs voting to reverse a decision of the commission. (Such was and remains unlikely, as the League will always seek feedback from the clubs before making any key decisions, as we saw in the inclusion of the Gold Coast Suns and Greater

---

8 David Crawford, *AFL administrative structure review - findings, March 1993*. Peat Marwick, 1993.
9 Stephen Linnell, "Clubs give up their control", *The Age*, 2 March 1993.

Western Sydney in recent years.) The board of directors, the body that had directed football since its foundation and had done so unfettered before the creation of the commission, would be abolished.[10]

Football would change from this point, and the role the commission had played since 1985 of steering the development of the competition and the code would be formally acknowledged.

Crawford also recommended that Schwab's voting role on the commission was an unnecessary duplication. He would no longer have a vote at the commission table. That was tough on Alan, but it also resolved a tricky division of responsibility that had been established in 1985 when keeping him on side, with his club support, had been an essential political ploy in the establishment of the commission. That moment had passed, and to be perfectly honest Schwab's influence with the clubs, his political clout, had also faded. There were other issues affecting his performance, drink and women prominent among them, so the Crawford recommendation was a circuit-breaker.

Schwab's change of circumstances coincided with the growing need for a strong presence in Sydney to take the reins temporarily at the Swans and steer the club back on to the rails while it re-established itself financially and as an on-field force. I decided to send Alan north as interim chairman of the Swans—a fateful decision, as it turned out.

Alan Schwab's body was found on the afternoon of Friday 18 June 1993 in his room on the 24th floor of the Boulevard Hotel in Kings Cross. He'd been due at a number of club-related appointments and had been a no-show. Barry Capuano, who had been working in Sydney with Alan, rang me and I then rang the hotel management to ask them to check his room.

The manager found Alan dead in his bed.

This was the second death that had rocked the football family in my seven years at the helm. Jack Hamilton had been killed in a car accident in 1988, driving back to Melbourne from a break in the country. His lovely

---

10   The VFL board of directors sat for its last meeting on 19 July 1993, presenting the commission with all but total management rights.

wife, Joan, had survived the crash and I can remember only just managing to make it through an interview before having to excuse myself to avoid weeping on air. There was a massive funeral for the man who had devoted his life to football and didn't get the chance to enjoy his well-earned retirement.

Alan's death was also huge news. He had last been seen in typical style, enjoying a long liquid lunch with his rugby league mates. The media and police scrambled for detail. A few days later, *The Age* was reporting the bare bones of a scandal:

> A homicide investigation is under way into the death of the AFL administrator Alan Schwab, whose body was found in a hotel room in Kings Cross on Friday.
>
> NSW homicide squad detectives are awaiting the results of a toxicology test, which may determine whether Mr Schwab, one of Australian football's most influential figures, had traces of heroin or methadone, the heroin substitute, in his blood when he died.
>
> It is believed that traces of a drug were found in a cup in his hotel room. It is believed the drug may have been added to the drink by someone other than Mr Schwab, and without his knowledge. Detectives are also trying to determine whether he was alone when he died.
>
> A spokesman for Glebe Coroner's Court said an autopsy on the body had failed to determine a cause of death and that the results of a toxicology test would be known by Friday at the earliest.[11]

The drama dragged on. The coronial inquest was two years away and rumours swirled. There was talk of a prostitute, a missing mobile phone, a missing wallet. "I've lost a great friend and football's lost one its best men," Barassi told the media, and that was the truth of the thing.

Alan's death was a tremendous tragedy and a huge loss to football. The flags over Waverley Park flew at half-mast that Saturday and teams lined up for a minute's silence. He was eventually laid to rest after a service that filled St Paul's Cathedral to capacity and had all the trappings of a state funeral.

---

11   Gerard Ryle, "Schwab murder probe", *The Age*, 23 June 1993.

About six months later the Boulevard Hotel manager rang me, asking for contact details for Alan's wife, Lynne. While renovating the room, workers had pulled the bedhead off the wall in the Schwab penthouse suite and there, plopping on to the carpet, was Alan's missing wallet. That was one mystery solved, at least. For months the police had fingered his death as possibly murder or misadventure, with the missing wallet as evidence of theft. But no.

Several months later, a coroner's inquest found that Alan died from the combined effects of methadone and alcohol, and that a prostitute named Nicki Stimpson had been in his room on the night he died and had probably supplied the methadone that helped kill him. Stimpson herself died of a drug overdose in Queensland in 1996.

Back in Melbourne we adjusted slowly to life after Alan. Whatever his and my difficulties, in the end we'd had a productive, friendly and positive relationship. He was always fun to be around, always had a story to tell of past exploits. His departure left two gaping holes in the administration of football: a knowledgeable and canny club man at the commission table, and a wise head on the board of the Sydney Swans.

The replacement at AFL headquarters? Well, the commission dillydallied for nearly six months thinking about future succession until I said at a meeting, "I'm going out to find someone myself within our club ranks." There was pretty much only one man in football administration who fitted the bill: Ian Collins, CEO at Carlton.

'Collo' and I had had our differences over the years, but he was a clever and intelligent club administrator and knew more than most about the game. Poacher turned gamekeeper, he was the best football operations man in the business. He knew where all the loopholes were in the rules, and I wanted him on my team.

Sydney was trickier. After Schwab's death, we sent Ken Gannon north as interim chairman, and pursued and finally secured a man who would in the end make all the difference: Richard Colless. Appointed West Coast's inaugural chair in 1987, he handled that role from Sydney, somehow managing to keep the Eagles ship in reasonable order from the other side of the country. A remarkable performer.

I spoke to him soon after Schwab's death and said I wanted him to step up as Swans president. He rang Terry O'Connor, who had been West Coast's chair and now sat on the commission, and was a great mate from Colless's WA stint. Don't forget just how dark these days were for the Swans—we may have stitched an arrangement just months earlier to see them move forward from the brink of financial disaster, but onfield they were still a marginal proposition, albeit a marginal proposition coached by the great Barassi. Colless was right to wonder at the depth of support for the side around the commission table, but O'Connor had no doubts. Yes, he told Colless, the commission would be very supportive. You should do it.

Even so, Colless approached the move cautiously, ringing me many times for reassurance, particularly financial reassurance. But eventually he said, "Yes, I'm in."

That was one of the biggest days for the national competition. Colless stayed in the job for 20 years, until the end of 2013. During that time the club won two flags and got close to more. Even more significantly, Sydney is now a club with a robust corporate and football culture that is envied and admired around the League. A club that once had to tempt players north now stands on its own feet and attracts star players entirely on its own merits.

I was there that night in 1996 when Sydney beat Essendon to make it through to the one day that really matters in any season of football. The Swans, that transplanted embodiment of hopes and dreams going back to a twinkle in the eye of Allen Aylett, had made a Grand Final for the first time in 51 years.

That preliminary final ended in high drama, with Tony Lockett leading strongly to take the grab then going back to kick after the siren, directly in front but 50 metres out with the scores level. The resulting dipping, fading punt drew a behind and unleashed mayhem.

I have never seen a stadium erupt the way it did that night. They went off—invaded the ground, dancing, yelling. They pulled a point post out of the turf and paraded it triumphantly, head high, around the ground. The Sydney Swans were off to a Grand Final.

It was the turning point we had been waiting for. In a handful of turbulent and testing years the club had lifted itself to win a place in Sydney's heart and get into an AFL Grand Final.

Sydney was the linchpin of the success of the national competition—there is no doubt about that. Without a team that was properly structured, had the right people in charge and had success on the ground, the Sydney market would have been lost to us. In almost every respect it was important to get that right.

So many people, over such a long period, played a role in the Sydney Swans saga, but the one thing that pulled it all together in the end was the appointment of Richard Colless as chair. He was no doubt the making of the club, and from that, he was critical to the success of the entire AFL national competition.

CHAPTER 20

Coming of age

Slowly but surely the national competition was coming of age.

In 1990, with teams in Victoria, WA, Queensland and NSW and a new one about to join from South Australia, the thoughts of the commission inevitably turned to our name. The Victorian Football League no longer rang true, and with the talks in progress that would eventually lead to the entry of the Adelaide Crows, the VFL brand was actually starting to have nuisance value. The Crows were not thrilled about entering a Victorian competition or even, for that matter, a national competition with a Victorian name. Fair enough.

It went deeper than that, of course. There was now a sense that the VFL Commission was becoming truly independent after years of tough decision-making, restructuring and reform. The commission was now clearly the single body in control of the destiny of Australian football and its present conduct. Decisions were being made for the good of game, by a body that held the game's future success as its first priority.

It was time the League had a name that recognised the national nature of both the competition and the League's authority in the code. The big question was, which name? The League owned the rights to "National Football League", but we weren't all that thrilled with its echoes of American football. There was a time before 1985 when the "National

Football League of Australia" had actually been the controlling body of the game, responsible for setting the rules. It was represented by delegates from each state and territory and the VFL was a constituent, with two very powerful members in Alan Schwab as a delegate and Allen Aylett as president of the organisation.

In 1985 Melbourne lawyer John Adams, who had strong North Melbourne connections, was commissioned by the NFL to investigate and report on the game going national, but times were changing with the appointment of the independent VFL Commission in January 1985. The VFL's Blue Report discussed the state of the competition and how the League was to expand nationally off the back of the Elliott report and other VFL reports that had been produced through 1984. As a result, the Adams report on the feasibility of a national competition—which was well constructed and presented to the commission at the end of 1985—pretty much cast the same light over what was happening and what was to come.

Adams' report did say that a "complete national football competition including teams from Victoria, Adelaide, Perth, Sydney, Brisbane, Tasmania and Canberra was not feasible", but that a competition "evolving from the Victorian Football League and including teams from Adelaide and Perth would be viable provided that the number did not exceed twelve". That might seem easy to put down with the benefit of hindsight, but none of it was favoured by public opinion. Adams made points that were certainly visionary, including "the control of the competition (when developed) should be vested in a body evolving from the commission of the Victorian Football League" and (cheekily, considering what we were to discover later) "the name of the competition should initially be the Victorian Football League but should be changed to the Australian Football League when firmly established". He also noted something that would become part of the League's marketing strategy some 30 years later: "There should be an extended promotion of the competition as 'The Australian Game'."[1]

The NFL had been effectively sidelined and its functions were gradually

---

1   All quotes in this paragraph from VFL Board minutes, October 1985.

subsumed by the VFL, which established its own rules committee that other Australian football leagues and associations gradually adopted. The VFL also assumed total responsibility for the development and promotion of the game and acquired the NFL name in the process.

However, "Australian Football League" was now the name that pushed all the right buttons—clearly it was a perfect fit. But sadly, someone else owned it. That person was Adams, who had been smart enough to register the name. As it turned out, it was much better in his hands than in the hands of someone who did not have a deep love of the game and was not involved as Adams had been over the years. His name was associated with many of the important reports that had made up the football intelligence of the 1980s, he had provided considerable assistance to the West Coast Eagles during their development phase, and he was steeped in football's traditions.

There was little doubt that Adams would eventually provide the name to us should we wish to rebrand our national football league, albeit not without some to-ing and fro-ing. I believe his delay in doing a deal was more about recognition for his protecting the name than wanting to profit substantially from it, although he did ask for some recompense. The commission felt that Adams should gain some reward for what was a fairly canny piece of name registration, but we didn't want to be held to ransom.

Peter Scanlon and I were delegated to sort the thing out and we played a reasonable version of good cop/bad cop. Scanlon was the hard man. "I went to see Adams," he recalls, "to tell him fairly strongly that I thought it was not very good form. He didn't see it my way. It took a couple of bottles of red to change the conversation."[2]

For my part, as the good cop, I offered to cover his costs and threw in a pair of AFL memberships for good measure. That did the trick, and in 1990 the Australian Football League was born, now in the hands of the game itself. I often wonder what might have happened had those discussions been with a different character who had different motives. NFL? You would hope not.

With our new identity came a new logo that removed the big "V",

---

2   Peter Scanlon, interview with the author, 2014.

a symbol of state dominance. The best submission we had received was from designers Russell Kennedy and the late Mark Perillo from Greatgraphics. They went with a heraldic style of logo: on a blue background similar to the colour of the Australian flag, they had a big "A" based on the Union Jack from the flag with a stylised Australian Rules ball below.

Through the 1990s the AFL Commission was past most of the hairy issues with the competition itself and was seeking to take a broader role in the development of the game Australia wide, emboldened by the faith of the clubs, which, following the handing-down of David Crawford's review of the administrative structure of the game, had vested full control of the League's governance in the commission. This was, in effect, the game's official corporatision—a completely independent board overseeing all parts of the game. Over time, that would also develop into the AFL taking control of state bodies and developing the game under one umbrella.

The national competition was established by then, and barring the odd hiccup it was ticking over nicely. The early issues surrounding territory, rights and the division of power between the clubs and the League were subsiding, and non-Victorian teams were bringing home the bacon for their supporters and, by extension, confirming that a national league was the way of the present and the future.

The West Coast Eagles lost their first attempt to win a flag in 1991, but did the job with great purpose and class in 1992 and 1994. Adelaide played in a preliminary final in 1993, Brisbane played finals for the first time in 1995 and Sydney, the ultimate yardstick of our national success, played in a losing Grand Final in 1996, having been wooden spooners in 1992, 1993 and 1994.

There was a shift in attitude occurring at the League. Having established this new national game, we began to openly take responsibility for its present and future strength as a code. The League was no longer insular: we saw ourselves as responsible for the many broad social responsibilities that flowed from our game's position of influence.

We adopted the position of "keeper of the code", making the AFL the one body responsible for the nurturing and development of the game. Gathering financial strength allowed us to adopt this role but we had to walk the talk: it would be our deeds as a League that ensured that all parties in the football world were able to accept the AFL's new sense of itself.

In line with this responsibility we addressed and developed many new stances and operating codes, not just for Australian football but for sport generally in Australia.

First came our faltering engagement with the players who put on the show every week. Today I look back and wonder how things happened as they did. I remember being distinctly uncomfortable in 1988 when, for the first time, the commission voted to ignore the approaches of the Players Association. Our view was that the players were getting ahead of themselves and, as the commission saw it, "throwing their weight around" at a time when the game was still getting itself into shape. To this end, the commission sent Alan Schwab and me to talk to the players' representatives but not to engage with them.

This was the first time I had not been in favour of a commission decision, and I know my ambivalence was reflected in our discussions with the Players Association. I'm a fair salesman, but our "say and give nothing" policy was the sales job from hell. It was the most unproductive meeting I had ever experienced and played on my mind for some time afterwards.

The commission soon realised the strategy was flawed and that we were on a hiding to nothing, so when we met the Players Association again and were able to engage, the relationship became more businesslike. How could it not, with the charming Peter Allen[3] in charge and the two Madden brothers, Justin and Simon, involved?

By 1990, the VFL had renamed itself the Australian Football League (AFL). The Players Association duly renamed itself the AFLPA, and

---

3   Peter Allen, who ran his own sports marketing company providing admistrative support for several sporting bodies (including the National Basketball League of Australia), was appointed as the Players Association's administrator in a part-time role in 1979, after being interviewed by a panel including current AFL Commission chair Mike Fitzpatrick. He would remain in that role until he was replaced by Andrew Demetriou in 1998.

eventually signed its first collective bargaining agreement (CBA) after complicated negotiations with the League. When the CBA was finalised, it was called a "deed of agreement" to avoid the use of the title CBA—as we saw it, the clubs were the employers and the players should be dealing directly with their employers.

In October 1992, the AFLPA, through its chief executive, Peter Allen, and president, Justin Madden, met the commission and indicated they wanted to work in harmony with the AFL and did not want to deal directly with the clubs. I confirmed the commission's position by relating that their submission to us could be split up into club matters, AFL matters and non-negotiable matters; the latter included a position on the commission for the AFLPA, abolition of the salary cap and player draft, and a share of revenue. Madden indicated that the salary cap and draft were not "major" items and that the AFLPA was more interested in a minimum wage, health cover, injury payments and option clauses.

The minutes note Graeme Samuel as saying, "centralising certain of these items removes the individuality of employer/employee relationships when in fact industry generally is tending towards enterprise bargaining."[4] It also seemed that a major stumbling block was recognition of the AFLPA, as the commission was of the view that the only form of recognition needed was the execution of the proposed agreement.

After some to-ing and fro-ing, on 28 January 1993 the commission considered a letter containing some 15 issues and confirmed its view that contractual conditions between the clubs and their players should be negotiated between those parties and should not be the subject of any form of collective agreement with the AFL. To further assist the players, the commission agreed to withdraw the standard player contract and stated that its contents should be negotiated between the club and players individually.

On 2 February, I reported that at a meeting with the club general managers on 29 January most GMs had indicated that, although some clubs had not yet spoken to their players, the players had no dispute with their individual

---

4   AFL Commission minutes, October 1992.

clubs, and the clubs were generally in favour of the proposal to withdraw the standard player contract. The commission agreed that "there was no point in talking to the AFLPA at this stage as the Association should now be dealing directly with the clubs".[5]

This prompted a historic meeting at the Radisson Hotel in Melbourne at which the players decided to threaten strike action. The AFL sought the assistance of Michael O'Shaughnessy from the Victorian Employers' Chamber of Commerce and Industry (VECCI), who met with the AFLPA and each of the clubs to discuss the dispute. The clubs then asked O'Shaughnessy to act on their behalf as the matter was set to go before the Australian Industrial Relations Commission (AIRC).

In March 1993, the AFL and AFLPA appeared before the AIRC and it was determined that a dispute between the parties existed and that the AIRC had jurisdiction to determine an award. The AFL and AFLPA were instructed by the AIRC to attempt negotiations away from the AIRC environment; these negotiations led to the CBA of 1994-95.

In 1995 a new CBA was negotiated with the players in which they gained an increase in the share of revenue from marketing activities and an increase in injury and illness benefits. By this time, 99 per cent of all players were members of the AFLPA.

With the authority of the commission now set in stone, we were able to do what most businesses do regularly: it was time for a strategic plan that would take us through to the turn of the century and beyond. This was a whole-of-AFL plan. In fact, Mike Sheahan, now well and truly back in the media as chief footy writer of *The Herald Sun*, took up most of the middle section of Saturday's paper on 20 August 1994 by previewing the launch of our much-anticipated five-year plan, to be let loose the following Monday.

The story was headed "Oakley's architects", with the kicker "Only a dozen people know the full story".[6] The newspaper had arranged a photo of the dozen all seated most uncomfortably in Bay 20 at the MCG. This

---

5   AFL Commission minutes, 2 February 1993.
6   Mike Sheahan, "Only a dozen people know the full story", *The Herald Sun*, 20 August 1994, pp. 48-9.

"preview" had Tony Peek written all over it, providing Sheahan with access to the mechanics behind the plan before we released it—just as governments leak bits and pieces before the big hits. We released the plan on the Monday and the next day took out full-page ads in metropolitan newspapers to make sure our message was presented as we wanted it to be. Just as well: among all the positives, Sheahan chose to write his review of the plan under the heading: "AFL puts guillotine to Fitzroy's neck".[7]

The leading points were the five bases of the plan. First, we would take a national view of football, not simply an expanded VFL view—nothing new there, but it had to be stated as it really was the fulcrum around which the rest of the plan would turn. Then came equalisation, "rather than the survival of the fittest"; 20 years later, that's still a work in progress. Third came the pronouncement that the AFL was not just the manager of the national competition but the "keeper of the code"—remember that at this stage the states were running their own agendas as far as development went, the draft still had refining to do in regard to where players could be chosen, and Auskick was still very much a Victorian product for kids. Fourth, the AFL was to be "a generator of income, but not a banker to the clubs"—hmm, that has twisted and turned somewhat in the years since. Perhaps it always will be the case that the overall AFL brand will be the feeder that keeps the clubs alive and well (and flourishing—back to equalisation). And finally, commercial sponsorships would keep admission prices at acceptable levels.[8]

I am proud to look back on that 192-page document and the impact it had—not just on the years immediately following, but right into the modern era. I am astonished at the detail, and am reminded of the energy we all put in to get it into shape. Of course, circumstances change—who could have foreseen a $1.2 billion TV deal not much more than 10 years after we produced the document?—and other plans supersede the basic model, as the AFL has done many times since and will continue to do. But I can always look back and say that, of the many plans that have underpinned the game we have today, this was the first produced by the executive. It was

---

7 Mike Sheahan, "AFL puts guillotine to Fitzroy's neck", *The Herald Sun*, 23 August 1994, p. 39.
8 All quotes in this paragraph from *AFL Strategic Plan 1994*, AFL Commission, 1994.

also the first time the rights of the players, as the basis of the game, were listed in great detail and with great strength of purpose and expectation.

The Final Eight was also introduced in 1994, expanded from various versions of a final six (1991-93). As a concept it was loudly derided at its introduction, but it has become a fundamental of the game, particularly as the competition has grown. Sometimes, as we have seen so often during the game's history, unpopular decisions become the norm, and we look back and wonder what the fuss was all about.

As I noted, circumstances are constantly changing, and a year after the five-year plan had been presented and as it was rolling along, the commission felt the need for an urgent update. This was forced upon us by movements across the Murray, where rugby league was being split apart by the Super League challenge. The commission presented a 20-page document to the clubs that addressed the Super League matter directly, with the question: "Could it happen here?"[9]

The answer was somewhat equivocal. The paper said, "While a takeover of our game is possible, it is unlikely", but noted that "if an outside party was prepared to commit legal effort and huge dollars—in the tens or maybe hundreds of millions—in pursuit of an Australian Football Super League, their chances of success would be more than reasonable". The report went through the same model as had been presented the previous year to support its view that we were, if not impregnable, close to it—meaning that the competition had to be balanced competitively and fiscally, and that in all major markets incomes had to be maximised outside attendances and players had to be well paid and receive "a fair share of any increased income generated by the game", and that the commission, not the media, governed the game.

Tough talk, but extremely well supported by the detail in those 20 pages, much of it to do with making sure that players were looked after and that clubs that were in difficulties seriously considered merging. The commission's stated view was "we want Port Adelaide in, and one less

---

9   Proposals to the AFL clubs from the AFL Commission, 19 June 1995.

in Melbourne". Sheahan's headline of a year earlier was more true than we might have thought at the time.

One area that was constantly before us—before and after the introduction of the five-year plan of 1994—was the problem of drugs in sport. Before the 1990s there was no drug code in any of Australia's professional sports leagues. To put this in perspective, this was the time when international athletes were constantly being found to be in breach of the laws of competition, with perhaps the most infamous infraction being that of Canadian sprinter Ben Johnson at the 1988 Seoul Olympics.

We were concerned about the potential of performance-enhancing drugs entering our sport and were therefore proactive in developing a pioneer drug code outside the world of Olympic sports.

In 1989-90, Senator John Black headed up the groundbreaking Drugs in Sport Senate inquiry that lifted the lid on "endemic drug use" in sport in Australia. The inquiry received evidence that up to 60 per cent of elite athletes were using banned drugs that, at the time, were not being effectively tested. The inquiry, which focused particularly on the Olympic sports, resulted in huge changes, including the formation of the Australian Sports Drug Agency (ASDA) and the introduction of random testing.

The AFL had been quick to see the problems it could face if it let the drug problem go unchecked, and in April 1989, before the Black inquiry had even commenced, I went with Tony Capes, the AFL's medical commissioner, to WA to meet Dr Ken Fitch, the West Coast Eagles team doctor and chairman of the Olympic Medical Committee of Australia, to seek his advice on what we should do as a League to be proactive in protecting our players against the scourge of drugs. As a result of our discussions we developed our own anti-drug code, based on the Olympic drug code.

Later I was summoned to the Black inquiry to give evidence and surprised them with the progress we had already made with our anti-drug code, which prompted Senator Black to heap praise on the League for its leadership in fighting drugs in sport.

Indeed, the AFL was the first football code in Australia to adopt an anti-drug code; it soon became a model for other Australian sporting associations and leagues. Our anti-drug code involved compiling a list of banned performance-enhancing drugs (PEDs) and implementing both in-season and out-of-season testing procedures using the facilities of ASDA. We also restructured our Tribunal system to hear breaches of the code, and imposed sanctions for the use of prohibited substances. Along with the anti-drug code we introduced a comprehensive player-education program.

Our anti-drug code was further developed over the years to reflect the existence of new drugs and new methods of doping, to include social drug use and to introduce the three-strike rule that applies to the use of illicit drugs today.

Attacking racial and religious abuse was our next target. The League's racial and religious vilification rule was landmark legislation for its time. It was designed to deal with not only failings on the field, but just as importantly, behaviour in the grandstands. As David Nadel wrote in *The Australian Game of Football*, one of our biggest challenges was still ahead of us: "The role of Oakley in this steady development of the national competition was significant. It was under his watch that the AFL, and by extension its clubs and affiliates, understood the scourge of racism in the game—on and off the field."[10]

And a scourge it was. Racial abuse was endemic to football in the 1980s and early 1990s, no doubt about it. It was a tactic designed to unsettle often brilliant Indigenous players. Collingwood's Tony Shaw is quoted famously from 1991 saying, "I'd make a racist comment every week if I thought it would help win the game."[11]

Nicky Winmar provided a watershed moment in 1993 when he lifted his jumper at Victoria Park and proudly pointed to his skin after an afternoon of racist taunting from the Collingwood faithful. Few single moments in the

---

10 Geoff Slattery (ed.), *The Australian Game of Football*, Geoff Slattery Publishing for the Australian Football League, 2008. p. 88.

11 Quoted in *The Sunday Age*, August 1991.

history of our game are so famous or so significant. I knew something had to be done, and I knew, too, that while racial vilification would be a tough thing for the AFL to address, if we were serious about our responsibilities as "keepers of the code" and as a dominant sporting body, we simply had to tackle it and show leadership.

As pioneers in this effort, it took us some time to grapple with the complexities of the situation. I spent many hours in discussion with Jeff Browne and his staff working through the detail, but it took another flare-up—the abuse of Essendon's Michael Long by Collingwood ruckman Damien Monkhorst at the Anzac Day match in 1995—to finally throw the switch.

Following the incident, a mediation session between the two players was organised. It failed, primarily because we had no experience in how to handle such a matter and also because, despite the advice of the two clubs that the matter be resolved privately and that Monkhorst make a formal apology to Long, Monkhorst had received legal advice that an apology would be tantamount to an admission of guilt.

It all went wrong from that point. When the two players came out of the room, after what seemed ages, to face the impatient media, our assumption was that the matter had been resolved and an apology had been offered. It later emerged that this was not the case, and Long was seething. Monkhorst had not apologised. Long made no comment to those of us waiting outside the room. Without further discussion, Long, Monkhorst and I went to a press conference. It turned out to be an embarrassment for all present. Long remained deeply angered by what had happened and it clearly showed on his face, although I could not see this from where I was seated.

Later Long told the media that Monkhorst had not apologised but had simply retorted: "You took it the wrong way, mate." Long suggested that the AFL wanted to "hush it up" but insisted that the public had a right to know what had happened and why he had been so deeply hurt that he had taken it to the League, and to the public. This outcome was far from what all of us in the commission had hoped for. I was deeply concerned about our failure to resolve the matter, not only to Long's satisfaction but also to uphold the moral values of the competition.

I wanted to convey my feelings to Long personally. With Tony Peek, I made my way to Essendon to talk to Long and to all the Indigenous players on the Essendon list at the time, including Gavin Wanganeen and Che Cockatoo-Collins, who had been in earshot of the on-field abuse. I wanted to apologise to Michael for letting him down, and I think he appreciated the gesture. But we knew we had to get it right in future.

Eventually, some weeks after the incident, Monkhorst apologised. In a 2011 interview he said he still deeply regretted his role in the 1995 Anzac Day race row but was pleased that some good had come from the incident, in that it was the catalyst for sweeping change. Admitting he had taken a long time to get over it, Monkhorst—who has had a distinguished coaching career since his retirement from playing, most recently as a ruck coach at Hawthorn—said he "faced a reminder of it every year on April 25". He said he was happy to "carry the can", especially since the ramifications played a part in providing a better environment for Indigenous footballers in the AFL and at lower levels. "It was a huge mistake on my part," Monkhorst pronounced. "But it has made a great difference to the AFL and to the Indigenous boys running around at the moment, and that's fantastic."[12]

Long's actions set in motion a profoundly transformative chain of events. The League's Indigenous players were beginning to demand action, and we met a delegation at the AFL. Immediately afterwards I organised for Peek to interview every Indigenous player in the League. I wanted to understand first hand the scope of the problem and get a sense of how we could handle any future racial abuse. It was clear the Monkhorst incident was not an isolated moment.

I was shocked when I learned that Peek's conversations revealed there were at least 10 serial offenders from half a dozen clubs. From these meetings and interviews came cross-cultural programs with the Victorian Aboriginal Education Association. Long and Cockatoo-Collins, along with the Saints'

---

12   Glenn McFarlane, "Racist row still hurts me", *The Herald Sun*, 22 April 2011.

Gilbert McAdam and Brisbane's Michael McLean, provided significant input into the development of the League's policy, with assistance from Jeff Browne and Ron Merkel QC. The players stressed that any policy had to be based on education, so that if their sons became AFL players, they would not be subjected to the abuse their fathers had received—on and off the field. To ensure the code covered all potential areas of abuse, and all of the many cultures that were part of the AFL game, we also sought advice from players from immigrant families, including Melbourne's Jim Stynes and Footscray's Tony Liberatore and Ilija Grgic.

A code of conduct regarding racial vilification, with religious and sexual vilification provisions, all of which had been in the making since the 1993 Winmar incident, was refined and included in our rules. Education was a key plank of the code, with confidential mediation a fundamental part of any complaints made either by players or by umpires, but players could be heavily fined or even suspended, and clubs could also face sanctions. Should mediation fail—meaning the vilified player was not satisfied with the outcome—the matter would be sent to the Tribunal.

The code, which extended beyond the playing field to include club officials and administrators, would go on to win a United Nations Association of Australia Special Peace Award, which still hangs proudly in AFL House. Within a few months of the Long-Monkhorst controversy, the AFL launched anti-racism advertising campaigns that included the threat of ejecting racist fans from matches. There were other consequences, including the launch of the AFL KickStart program, which aims to provide resources for education opportunities in Indigenous communities; it continues its good work today, with significant corporate support.

Nadel noted another outcome of the code's development:

> Although the complaint [from Long] was initially handled clumsily, Oakley made it his role to ensure that racism would be eradicated from the game. After AFL staff had interviewed all listed Indigenous players, and Oakley had made a personal apology to Long, the AFL introduced its groundbreaking Racial and Religious Vilification policy. The massive

increase in the numbers of Indigenous players on AFL lists ... can be traced directly to this policy.[13]

Massive increase indeed. In 1993 there were 19 Indigenous players of a total of 865 (2.1 per cent) on AFL lists.[14] In 2007, when Nadel wrote his essay, there were 61 of 702 (8.7 per cent), and in 2014, 70 of 811 (8.6 per cent). In percentage terms these numbers are far beyond the ratio of Indigenous to total population.[15]

It may have taken some time, but I think we got it right in the end. We delivered a groundbreaking code that was the first of its kind in Australian sport, and well worthy of its United Nations Association award. The code and its accompanying education programs—for the fans as well—has made a significant difference. Racism will always be a scourge of society, but there is no doubt the AFL's actions—and the bravery of Long, Winmar and others—have created an environment second to none in world sport.

Other changes were afoot. For the first time a female manager was appointed to a senior position in the League. Jill Lindsay had been working through the system since joining the League in 1970 and was appointed to manage the VFL membership department in 1986. Five years later she took on the significant and growing task of ground operations manager, dealing with all the hard nosed ground managers around the competition.

At long last the boys' club was beginning to shift, though gender diversity in the AFL remains a work in progress.

One of the other big issues at the time was that we were still not in control of the television footage from our games—our ultimate intellectual property. Channel Seven held most of our historic footage but had destroyed a great proportion of it in an austerity drive in the late 1980s when they wanted to reuse the tapes that contained these valuable records. It was

---

13   Geoff Slattery (ed.), *The Australian Game of Football*, 2008.
14   Total player numbers included reserves.
15   In August 2013, the Australian Bureau of Statistics announced that Australia's Aboriginal and Torres Strait Islander population had reached 669,900 (3 per cent of the total population).

imperative that the League control and retain footage of all our games for future generations.

Enter David Barham and AFL Films. Barham had been the producer of the international highlights program that was distributed to overseas television stations during the late 1980s, and felt he needed to keep these tapes for posterity; he stored them in a cupboard in his bedroom. Not long after he started producing the programs, he came to see me and I agreed to provide him with $30,000 to build a library. Once Barham had built it, he told me, he was sure it would be self-funding.

With our assistance, Barham dedicated himself to putting together the most important asset the League possesses: the images of its players on film and tape initially, now digitally stored for all future generations. The set-up included a computer system that allowed Barham's staff to tag games and thus find plays easily; this was clearly useful for sponsors and advertisers for use in commercials for a fee. In 1996 we decided to do a documentary on the history of football for the centenary year. The documentary, called *One Hundred Years of Australian Football*, was produced by Barham with the assistance of journalist Neil Kearney, and took a year to make.

Channel Seven had provided us with rights to their remaining footage, and it was then we found they had kept only two hours of the long-running Sunday sports show *World of Sport*! We did find footage that focused on Hawthorn's Dermott Brereton being hit and subsequently throwing up in the famous opening to the 1989 Grand Final—it was sitting on a shelf in a Channel Seven office. I also put an ad in the *Footy Record* to ask supporters if they had footage at home that we could use. Barham remembers the outcome well:

> One guy rang and said he had 35 cans of film and he had filmed John Kennedy in a Grand Final. I thought he was a lunatic, but then I spoke to you and the League agreed to give the guy $1000 to obtain the films. Thirty-four of the cans were ruined but after two days of looking at nothing the film miraculously started to flicker and up popped 40 minutes of John Kennedy.

I told Kennedy I had this film of him sounding off in the 1975 Grand Final and he said, "It's not me."

I said, "You'd better come around and have a look."

"No, no," he said, "it's not me."

I said to him, "Well, you should come and have a look."

He remained sure it couldn't be true, saying, "You know me—I wouldn't have done that."

He watched the film for about 10 minutes with his head in his hands and said, "I completely forgot I did that."

On the same tape was Barassi giving a couple of sprays to players, and that famous line of Tom Hafey's calling Sheedy, "a back-pocket plumber" shone through.[16]

The Kennedy film unearthed that famous line "Don't think—do" as the coach exhorted his players for one last gasp. It was not to be, as North Melbourne went on to win its first flag.

At the end of the year we had a good idea of what was still in existence, and this formed the backbone of our football history. The AFL now has the greatest library of all Australian codes and the other codes recognise this to be the case. We can only imagine what might have been if Channel Seven hadn't dumped all those archival tapes. Unfortunately we can't watch all the great champions of the past, but we can rest with the knowledge that the exploits of every player in the modern era will be retained for posterity. It's sad that there are but seconds of moving images recalling the balletic skills of legendary players such as Haydn Bunton and Dick Reynolds, when even a one-gamer these days can see every stat he has gathered!

We owe David Barham a great debt for his vision and dedication in building this superb asset for the League, which is now totally owned by the AFL.

The climax to all the change and achievement was the League's centenary in 1996, which was also the year I chose to mark the end of my time at the helm.

---

16 David Barham, interview with the author, 2014.

We had come through more trauma during the 10 years from 1986 to 1996 than any other time in the League's 100 years of existence, but now here we were. The commission had not just saved the game, but had grown and secured it. It seemed to be the right time to celebrate our great game, our survival, our development, and the success that this 100-year-old code—the oldest codified sporting competition in the world—had achieved in its time.

Initially there was the usual media criticism that 1996 was not our birthday year. Some said, "You have to finish 100 years before you celebrate a birthday"—the League had been formed in 1896 but played its first games in 1897. We wanted to celebrate many events that were the 100th of their kind. The 100th Grand Final, with its unique gold cup, would be the culmination of our 100th year.

The celebrations began with a launch at the MCG that featured an appearance by a George Burns lookalike. The legendary actor's doppelganger arrived in a helicopter, much to the amazement of the crowd. Burns turned 100 on 20 January and died not long after, on 9 March, before the start of the football season.

We had decided that the year would be a great time to honour past players, coaches, umpires and administrators by introducing an Australian Football Hall of Fame, and on this launch night we announced the first 100 inductees. It had all begun some years earlier, during a trip that Jeff Browne and I took to the USA in the early 1990s. We visited Cooperstown, the ancestral home of American baseball, and were captivated by Doubleday Field, where the first game of baseball had been played, and the Hall of Fame museum that had been built to honour baseball's greats. To walk into that Hall of Fame and stand silently in the chapel-like "plaque" room, face to face with life-size sculptures of 'Babe' Ruth, Willie Mays, Joe DiMaggio and Mickey Mantle instilled in me a reverence I had never experienced in a sporting sense. It was an almost spiritual feeling. I knew we had to replicate the experience in Australia.

Our centenary year was the perfect time to honour our past greats. There was the usual controversy over the selection panel and their choices, but most people thought they got it pretty well right. I saw it as one of the most important new developments in football because for the first time we could truly recognise the best of the best for their total package of skills. Unlike the Brownlow Medal, the game's most prestigious award for a great season's play, or AFL Life Membership, which recognises meritorious service, Hall of Fame induction recognises an individual's exceptional impact on the game.

Other key features of the celebration year were:

- We staged a re-enactment of the first-ever League round, for which four matches had been played on 8 May 1897. Commemorating that historic moment, on Wednesday 8 May 1996, Geelong and Essendon played each other on the MCG before a capacity crowd. It was a great spectacle, with the players wearing replica antique jumpers and even coming on to the ground wearing the caps that were all the go in the past century. We had the fireworks display to end all fireworks displays before the match, and then, the icing on the cake, a boy soprano sang the national anthem with a pipe-band backing. It was a hauntingly beautiful moment as the band marched through the fireworks haze.

- A football exposition was held at the National Tennis Centre featuring the most complete collection of VFL/AFL memorabilia—and original art commissioned by the League for the occasion—seen in one place during the code's lifetime. Unfortunately not enough people made time to see the expo. The foyer of AFL House today contains evidence of the great artworks created for the centenary year, including pieces by the late artists David Larwill and Ginger Riley Munduwalawala.

- The Centenary Ball on the MCG was conducted under the biggest canvas tent in the world and attended by 3500 people. It was a resounding success. Unfortunately, as often happens on these occasions, it rained just as we were erecting the tent. The centre wicket area (there were not yet drop-in pitches) became a quagmire, which had repercussions for the games played after the tent had been dismantled. It also rained on the night—at one stage water poured down one of the massive poles holding the tent up—but no one seemed to mind. It was a celebration that could only be held on the G. Spotless did a fantastic job serving the crowd food from mobile kitchens, and champagne flowed. Feature artists included John Farnham and Kate Ceberano and a highlight of the night was a medley of club songs sung by a large group of football personalities.

- For the players, the night of nights was a celebration at the Tennis Centre for 1200 who had played 25 senior games or more. We inducted and immortalised the 10 original Legends of the Hall of Fame, with impressions of their hands cast for posterity.
- We selected a Coach (Norm Smith) and Team of the Century, and a Player of the Century (Leigh Matthews). These honours were always going to be controversial regarding both who was on the selection panel and who was chosen, but it was a great occasion at Her Majesty's Theatre, and another celebration of the beauty of the game and its champion players.
- The 100th Birthday Grand Final, where North Melbourne and Sydney played for the one and only gold Premiership Cup, was a wonderful celebration with a galaxy of stars appearing. Naturally the legendary Mike Brady sang the all-time football anthem, *Up There Cazaly*, with the crowd joining in with gusto. It was a great show produced by Kerrie Hayes under the supervision of the AFL's Dean Moore; for the first time Kerrie was given a reasonable budget with which to work—she had been involved in most of the Grand Final entertainment and other ground presentations in my time and had displayed great creativity despite having little funding.

For all the great things that happened through 1996, there was one unforeseen moment that cast a deep shadow over the game—cast it into darkness, in fact. That was that infamous Saturday night at Waverley Park when the lights went out in the match between St Kilda and Essendon with just under five minutes to go in the third quarter. Essendon was leading by 20 points and Ryan O'Connor was about to have a shot at goal. We thought the problem would right itself but it never did, allowing fans the opportunity to dash on to the field and pinch a point post. There was no precedent for any decision as to the unfinished match, so we conducted a hasty meeting and decided it would continue the following Tuesday, with two 10-minutes "halves" to decide the result. Essendon ended up winning by 22 points.

Watching that moment all these years later courtesy of YouTube,[17] I'm bemused to note that the commentators, Malcolm Blight and Ian Robertson, thought it was rather funny. We certainly didn't, but there's not a lot you can do when somebody runs their car into a power pole and cuts all the electricity to the region. The same thing happened at the NFL Super Bowl in 2013, which made me feel a little better! At the time of our blackout, of course, there were all sorts of conspiracy theories. The best takes on the incident were created by the cartoonists, who so often put the good and bad into perspective. I purchased a cartoon by Andrew Fyfe of *The Footy Show* (reproduced in the photo section of this book) and it still holds pride of place on my wall at home.

The same week, I decided the time was right for me to hang up the boots. The Centenary Season was the perfect opportunity not just to leave but also to celebrate a turbulent 10 years in the big job, and I told the world on 17 June. *The Age* reported that my decision "shocked the football world".[18] Maybe so, because I had kept my thoughts close to the chest. I have always believed a decade is about as long as any executive should sit in the top chair (Andrew Demetriou made the same comment when he resigned in March 2014, after just over 10 years in the job). It was a good time to retire and let a new person take on the ongoing challenges—positive and negative—that come with a position that was now perhaps the one with the highest profile in business and sport.

When it all became public I was gratified by the response, not just from the media but from the fans, many of whom had been affected by decisions the commission had made during those amazing 10 years. I had endured

---

17 "Lights out at Waverley—AFL" [online video], 2013, http://youtu.be/ScWHmSl3CnU (accessed 22 May 2014).

18 Stephen Linnell, "Footy's top man reaches 'use-by date'", *The Age*, 18 June 1996, p. 1.

plenty along the way, but those last months in the job—I wouldn't be leaving until after the Grand Final—were a time of great pleasure and reflection.

I guess I was relaxed, but I was also buoyed by commentary from all sides as to the success of my time in the job. *The Age* even devoted an editorial to it headed "Ross Oakley's legacy". It was nice to wake up that morning and read:

> In the light of its cultural and financial importance, Mr Oakley's 10-year stint as AFL chief warrants appraisal. An objective assessment of his time at the helm of what became the AFL suggests that, overall, Mr Oakley served the game well. He was a zealous CEO and that zeal was occasionally a double-edged sword. From the outset, he was right in his conviction that Melbourne's clubs would have to be rationalised for the competition to become truly national. But he stumbled badly with the proposed merger in 1989 of Fitzroy and Footscray, a ham-fisted move that diminished the relationship between the competition and some of its fans.[19]

The piece wasn't all about zeal and ham-fistedness. Although it gave me a couple of whacks about the notion of a night grand final (watch this space!) and scheduling games at odd times through the week, it also said that:

> [T]here is no question that Mr Oakley will leave the competition at a financially more sustainable level and with a much stronger sense of forward-looking professionalism than he found it.
>
> Mr Oakley saw that the game had to become a more marketable piece of entertainment if it was to survive and, with a single-mindedness that some football lovers found frustrating, he managed to realise his vision. It was a single-mindedness that, on balance, Australian rules football needed ... The next AFL chief will, it is hoped, be mindful of Mr Oakley's experience. A beloved institution such as League football must change– but not too quickly, and not too much.[20]

---

19   "Ross Oakley's legacy", *The Age*, 19 June 1996.
20   Ibid.

As I noted, I was gratified by those words, but the writer missed out on one key point: it wasn't all about me. Without the commission's and my staff's strength, wisdom, support and vision and, eventually, the support of the clubs, none of those points could have been achieved.

The writer also failed to mention that revenues for the entire competition had risen from $51 million in 1986 to more than $200 million in 1996, but that's being picky.

For me, this was the perfect time not just to leave but also to celebrate a turbulent 10 years in the job. I had promised the commission I would stay for at least five years, and at the end of that period they had asked me to stay on indefinitely. But it had become a massive job—seven days a week, working in the office Monday to Friday and then attending two or three games each weekend. There was little time for rest: most days would start at 6am with the media on the phone and finish between 10pm and 1am, depending on what commitments had to be met. I could easily have been out every night of the week, but thanks to my ever-caring PA, Ros Desmond, two nights a week were kept free from engagements.

I took the occasional break during the season when things were rolling along nicely, and was sympathetic to Demetriou's policy of taking time away with his family through the season when he was in charge. Despite what the media thinks, this is not a modern phenomenon. I remember enjoying a week's holiday—just father and son—in Central Australia during the season and getting lost some 30 kilometres up a road blocked by a gate. We were listening to the ABC radio call of the Saturday game, and as Tim Lane was mulling over a problem in the match he said, "We need to hear what Ross Oakley has to say about this. If anyone knows where he is, get him to please give us a ring." My son and I both broke into laughter because even we didn't know where we were!

To look back now, what a sheer pleasure and honour it was to be asked to take on such a role in 1986. I could not have wished for a more wonderful 10 years, despite all the drama—which I listed in the *Footy Record* at the time I announced my retirement. All of these incidents have been covered variously in this book, but it's interesting to note the order in which I placed them in 1996.

These were "Oakley's top 10 news stories 1986-1996":

1. The mergers—one that worked, one that didn't
2. The removal of TV rights from Seven
3. Alan Schwab's death
4. The battle for Adelaide's first AFL licence and the issuing of licences to interstate clubs
5. The building of the Great Southern Stand, and the reconciliation with the Melbourne Cricket Club
6. The shifting of the Brisbane Bears' home ground from Carrara to the Gabba
7. The demise of the entrepreneurs, and the return of football management to clubs
8. Ground rationalisation.
9. The conclusion, and implementation, of the AFL's five-year plan
10. The lockout of AFL members at the 1992 Grand Final

And ... the Waverley blackout.[21]

A re-read of that list almost 20 years later remains satisfying, and I'm pleased I was prepared to list a couple of booboos at the tail of it. I will go to my grave content that I did my best and left the game in a better state than I found it—the ultimate mark of any executive or chairman. And, thankfully, I am greatly enriched by the memories.

But it *was* time for new blood and new ideas to take our game into the fast-approaching new century.

---

21   *Football Record Almanac*, August 1996, p. 55.

CHAPTER 21

Leaders of the pack

This book has described the near-death experience and rebirth of Australian football—a phoenix rising. But who deserves the credit?

Truth is, there was no single saviour of Australian football, no one hero. Indeed, as is normally the case in such revivals, it was more a case of fortunes colliding, sometimes planned and often not; it was a convergence of people and deeds, of many passionate people prepared to work long hours to massage the game and its foundations back to robust health. So many good people with ideas and drive make things happen. I was fortunate to have many, many good people to lean on.

Recalling and recording history as we all experienced it, putting that history in perspective for a generation born to an AFL only knowing success and seemingly limitless growth, and giving due credit were my motivations for writing this book. Bringing so many diverse strands and contributions together in one volume has been an enthralling task. There may never be another reflection on these formative years, so I hope I have provided a true and fair representation of what happened, as well as a clear view of the role of the many characters who played an important part in saving our game and positioning it in its current dominant place in Australian sport. These were characters large and small who often worked without favour or fanfare but provided the foundations, the colour and the excitement that make the indigenous game so appealing.

I have taken the controversial step of naming and ranking the 10 people I believe contributed most during the seminal period from 1980 to 1996, when the game had to be saved and then put on the road to success. Here are those remarkable people:

1. Graeme Samuel
2. Richard Colless
3. Peter Scanlon
4. Allen Aylett
5. Jeff Browne
6. John Elliott
7. Colin Carter
8. Dick Seddon
9. Mike Sheahan and Tony Peek
10. All private equity contributors

Let's look at them in a little more detail.

Graeme Samuel was my right hand during my early years on the commission. Samuel was and is a highly intelligent man with great financial skills. During a negotiation he could move from charming to hard-nosed—some might call it bullying—at a moment's notice. Personally, I would call it getting every last ounce out of a deal. This was often required during the early years, and I was most fortunate that Samuel was able to spend the time he did to assist me in those days of turmoil.

Samuel did nearly as many flying miles as I did in year one and provided the high-level strategic assistance that was not available or forthcoming from the few experienced staff I had under me at the time. Where would we be—where would I have been—without Graeme? It is impossible to imagine. He was the longest-serving commissioner, working for the game from the commission's foundation in 1985 until his retirement in 2002.

Richard Colless was the ultimate saviour of the Sydney Swans and therefore the linchpin of the success of the national competition we know today. If Sydney had failed after its private investors pulled back, we would have neither the truly national competition nor the revenue-generating power we have today. A healthy and competitive Sydney was and is vital to the growth and development of our national League.

After being financially burnt when he was involved in the first year of the West Coast Eagles, Colless was prepared to accept my challenge to chair a basket case in Sydney at a time when the wheels had just about fallen off—a time that also included the untimely death of the then interim chair of the club, Alan Schwab. Colless did what no one else could have done: he took a club that was in "enemy" territory and re-established its football credentials, made some great personnel decisions, and developed revenue streams and, most importantly, a culture of success that became the envy of every other club in the League. And he did all of that with a passion and devotion that was to the detriment of his own business.

Colless was passionate about football in NSW and understood better than anyone how important it was to the AFL's national ambitions. No one in football should underestimate the importance of his role as Sydney's chairman for 20 years (1994-2013). Under his leadership, Sydney became a club that players wanted to play with and for. I believe Sydney's status within the AFL community today is very much to do with Dick Colless, and the recognition he has received to date has fallen well short of his contribution.

Colless commenced his involvement in the early days of the Eagles, when he was one of the handful of investors who each put in $1 million to ensure that the young Eagles got to join the fledgling national League. Along with Colless, early financial contributors were Neil Hamilton, Murray McHenry, Robert Armstrong and Mark Hohnen, and we are duty bound to say thank you to them for their great contribution to West Australian football and the birth of the Eagles. I want to also recognise the role

Dr Peter Tannock played in engaging with the AFL Commission positively and guiding football in Western Australia through the late 1980s out of troubled waters to its position of strength today.

Peter Scanlon was an indispensable commissioner, extremely intelligent, a great strategist and, like Samuel, the sort of hard-nosed operator who would never accept no for an answer—a quality we needed on the commission. I can remember often sitting around the table and asking each of the commissioners for his view on an issue. Because Scanlon usually sat to my left, he would be last. I would watch him out of the corner of my eye scribbling barely decipherable notes to himself, and when it was his turn he would pause, look at his notes and say, "I might be dumb, but ..." Out would come a gem of an idea that often left me wondering, "Why didn't I think of that?" He had an ability to communicate with people and get a deal done from which everyone around the table could benefit. Scanlon was not one to seek attention, but his behind-the-scenes manoeuvring with regard to club ownership, TV networks and club mergers was legendary around the commission table. He did more than most people will ever know to make the League work.

Allen Aylett realised something had to change back in the early 1980s if the game was to survive, but he had great trouble getting the VFL Board to accept the parlous situation the game faced. Eventually his persistence paid off and the board took action to save the competition. Aylett's was the vision that translated the VFL into a national League, the first step of which involved the failing South Melbourne being sent to Sydney. It was a bold move that was bound to struggle due to a lack of proper financial support—support the VFL could not give thanks to the League's dire financial circumstances. Aylett was a man of great energy and determination who against all odds got a parochial board to accept that if something was not done to change the decision-making structure of the VFL, then the code's days were numbered.

Jeff Browne, my left hand for 10 years, was a pleasure to work with on our big projects. As the League's official legal adviser, he worked with four CEOs in his 20 years there. As the League developed, it became more and more important to have a person with his legal experience by our side. (Today the AFL has grown so much that it carries its own in-house legal counsels.) While Browne said he enjoyed immensely working on AFL projects, it limited him somewhat in expanding his own law practice into other commercial areas; the upside was that he was able to establish a practice specialising in sport that allowed him to drift into media, affording him other opportunities down the track. He became managing director of Channel Nine in Sydney after concluding his service to the AFL, and was appointed a Life Member of the League in 2004 for his great service to the game.

To me, Browne's greatest contributions were in labour market reform, including the development of the draft and salary cap over 20 years and the fine detail within the laws of the game, and also his involvement in most big deals undertaken by the League. His negotiation skills, particularly relating to the MCG deal (with me) and the Gabba deal (with Greg Durham and Andrew Ireland), were of the highest order. Jeff recently said to me, "There is no doubt that the importance of both these agreements has been underestimated in the game's history. Without an MCG agreement between the MCC and VFL, we would not have seen the development of the MCG as it is today and certainly would not have been able to achieve the level of ground rationalisation that has been possible."[1]

Of equal importance was Browne's ability to pretty much keep us out of court. When we did appear, we were generally successful.

John Elliott provided the motivation for change in the early 1980s. The parochial decision-making around the board table had to be addressed. Many reports and experts suggested structural solutions, but none of them came up with the ultimate answer. Elliott became fed up and proposed a breakaway super-league. As outlined in Chapter 1, he made a presentation at Sefton in Mt Macedon to selected club powerbrokers and some days later put a revised presentation to the board of the VFL that laid out a structure that no one to that point had had the guts to propose.

---

1 Jeff Browne, interview with the author, 2014.

That structure was pretty much the same as that of the AFL Commission and football competition we have today. The board accepted Elliott's recommendations and a gradual handing-over of power to an independent commission—probably the single most important decision in the history of the game. Thank you, John, for taking unilateral action—in the nick of time.

Colin Carter had an extensive involvement with the commission, first as a valuable consultant in the early days co-authoring the Blue Report and helping to facilitate the MCC deal, and later when he joined the commission after the 1992 Crawford review as a wonderful "blue skies" thinker. This was invaluable because things were moving so fast it was imperative to have someone who could look forward and envisage what might be possible 10 years down the track. That said, in 1986 no one—absolutely no one—could have imagined where we would be by the turn of the century. TV revenue moving from $3 million a year in 1986 to more than $50 million in 1996, sponsorship going from $1 million to $10 million, a redeveloped MCG and a new Docklands stadium on the books, two clubs each from Western Australia and South Australia, teams based in NSW and Queensland, non-Victorian club premierships, playing football pretty well every day and night of the week, massive improvements in player payments and conditions along with spectator comforts, and VFL Park members occupying space at the MCG. Woah!

Colin was a great help to me in putting the second AFL strategic plan together in 1994 and after I had retired he championed the development of the game in NSW with Dick Colless. Colin served the commission wonderfully well from 1993 to 2007, a period of extraordinary change, and continues to provide his wisdom to footy from his presidential post at Geelong (from 2011).

Dick Seddon was a great club man, but he was a lot more than that: he was the commissioner who understood best what structures were required to make the "new" League work. Seddon needed to change a few minds around the commission table about "mutual dependence" within a sporting competition in the early days. He championed the introduction of the licence agreement for clubs, which ensured the discipline required within the system to allow the commission to get things done. Jeff Browne wrote the club licence agreements with Alan Schwab, but they did so under Seddon's supervision. Seddon also convinced the hard-nosed free-market commissioners, particularly Graeme Samuel and Peter Scanlon, that it was fundamental to the survival of a multi-team competition to place some restrictions on clubs through the introduction of the draft and salary cap. His was an indispensible contribution to our game.

Mike Sheahan and **Tony Peek** carried the burden of media and public relations from 1985 and 1996 (and beyond, so far as Tony was concerned), a period of great drama and change in the VFL that has been described as the most turbulent in Australian Football's history.

In an inspired move by Jack Hamilton, Sheahan was recruited as the League's media director in 1985 with his declared task being to improve our public image. Seddon viewed his hiring as vital to improved media relations at the time, saying:

> Mike was a very respected print journalist who was held in high esteem by his peers. Not only was he an excellent exponent of his craft, but such was his reputation among his fellow journalists that he also gave the new commission a credibility it would not otherwise have had when providing background briefings to the media. His former colleagues trusted Mike not to "spin" them with propaganda but to "give it to them straight". This was vital for the new commission, three members of which were largely unknown, because it enabled us to get out into the public domain difficult messages that were not always going to be popular. Having Sheahan deliver the briefings ensured that at least the messages, although controversial, would receive a proper hearing so that they could be better understood.
>
> It was important that the commissioners did not abuse this special relationship Mike had with the media by asking him to do things he was uncomfortable with and risk compromising his integrity. I often

shuddered when some of the commissioners attempted to rewrite Mike's press releases. Fortunately, in the main he was able to resist them.[2]

On one of these "attempted rewriting" occasions, I heard Seddon say, "Gentlemen, you don't buy a dog and then bark yourself."

Sheahan possesses a strong "sense" of the game. His knowledge was invaluable and at times he was able to educate the more inexperienced commissioners on what was important to the football public, and why. He had a real affinity with the average supporter, and introduced many new ideas during his time at the League, particularly a more open approach with the media that involved, among other things, introducing briefings with senior journalists (a practice unheard of until that time) and thereby backgrounding people who could influence public opinion about our game. It was his insistence that the public had a right to know—a major change in League philosophy—that led to more exposure of the VFL's inner workings and thoughts to the average football supporter.

I really enjoyed Sheahan's enormous input to those heady days at the VFL. He certainly made a very worthwhile contribution to the development of the game, and continues to do so as Australian Football's most senior media operator.

Tony Peek replaced Sheahan in 1989 and walked straight into the Footscray-Fitzroy merger storm. This was a major test for our public relations and he used all his media skills to keep our head above water. I was in London when the licence was handed back to Footscray, which left Peek with the job of facing the glare of television lights to explain our stance to a media pack baying for blood. It was a baptism of fire, but he came through with flying colours.

Peek, who was a *Sun* journalist before taking on the media relations role at Tennis Australia, was all about introducing more and broader media access, restructuring it to include not just League executives but also players and coaches. Post-match interviews became a mandatory requirement for coaches and players—such interviews may seem mundane today, but were

---

2   Dick Seddon, unpublished personal notes and memoirs.

a major breakthrough in 1989. Coaches in particular saw this new part of their role as an imposition, but Peek convinced them all that we needed to enhance our TV and radio coverage with such inner-sanctum events. He organised a weekly spot on Neil Mitchell's 3AW radio show for me that disciplined me to make myself available no matter what issues were out there so that football supporters could be kept informed. There was no hiding, no preparation, no spin, and I was appearing with the most respected radio talkback host in Melbourne.

Peek not only dealt with the continuing issues confronting the AFL but was also a welcome source of wise counsel and a very good strategic thinker, providing many ideas during the preparation of the League's 1994 strategic plan. He has continued to make an incalculable contribution during his 24 years at the League, offering strategic advice first to CEO Andrew Demetriou and now to new CEO Gillon McLachlan.

Private equity provided the League with much of the money needed to advance its national growth. After much heated discussion and against our better judgment, the commission approved the concept of private ownership of non-Victorian clubs as a necessary evil and decided to charge the private owners of new clubs a $4 million licence fee to enter the competition. If we had not charged this fee, the existing clubs would not have agreed to the new clubs' entry. The private owners did more than keep a number of Victorian clubs alive, they also provided private capital to the new clubs to support their early extensive—and expensive—operational expenses. And so a new era was introduced, and with it some interesting new participants.

Many involved in the game today are not aware of how the game's growth occurred. At a recent luncheon at AFL House I was speaking to a group of young members of the League's planning department who were surprised and amazed that we actually charged clubs a licence fee to enter the competition. They didn't realise that we would not have had a national competition if this had not been done. I hope they read this book to get a sense of how much has changed since those foundation days.

Jeff Browne made an interesting observation recently when he told me that: "If it were not for Geoffrey Edelsten and Powerplay, Sydney would not have been as successful as early as they were. To think that the Swans would have been more stable and successful early on with the Sellers team is Melbourne thinking. Sydney needed more sizzle for the AFL to be seen. It needed to be introduced with pizzazz. It needed a flamboyant 'owner'."[3]

And we got one with Edelsten.

But when the Edelsten team failed and the licence ended up back with the League, we were able to convince the initially unsuccessful group of owners Basil Sellers, John Geraghty, Craig Kimberley, Peter Weinert and Mike Willesee to, belatedly, back the club. They worked hard at keeping the Swans operating, but did not get the financial backing from supporters—or, for that matter, from the AFL—that was necessary for survival. It was almost as if the supporters were not prepared to contribute as long as the owners were capable of delving into their deep pockets to operate the club. The game had been membership-based for as long as anyone could remember, and I don't believe the supporters were too enamoured with the concept of someone openly declaring ownership of a club that the supporters saw as belonging to them.

It was not until these investors handed Sydney back so that it could operate as a membership-based club from season 1993 onwards that enough supporters were motivated to contribute to its financial success. Despite the investors' willingness to return the club to the AFL in 1993—all of them financially the poorer for the experience—they still contribute to the Swans today, and as far as I am concerned we owe them an enormous debt of gratitude for the club's survival in those early days.

Again, no matter how repugnant his business practices were, we must recognise the financial support provided by the late Christopher Skase. More to the point, we must recognise the role played by shareholders of the failed Qintex, who ultimately were the contributing parties. Great personal support and sacrifice were also given by Paul Cronin, who made dealing with Skase almost bearable for me and the commission. I trust that out of

---

3   Jeff Browne, interview with the author, 2014.

the disaster that was Qintex, Cronin and the shareholders today get some satisfaction from understanding that they played an important part in the growth of the AFL in Queensland.

After Skase, it was Reuben Pelerman's destiny to contribute to the growth of the game. It was he who eventually handed the club back to the Brisbane football fraternity in 1994 and watched the team become successful before he passed on in 2004. Thanks, Reuben and Ann (along with Judah and Gerald Moses)—you were great football characters and contributed substantially to the growth of the game. History will not forget your contribution. Jeff Browne, who dealt with Pelerman with me, said, "He should be applauded for all the money he put into football without a clue what he was doing. He had two guys—Judah and Gerald Moses—advising him who were smart guys but also didn't know much about football. He bought us time and an opportunity to bridge the gap between Skase and the QAFL, who took over some years down the track when they were better placed to do so."[4]

In South Australia we can thank Max Basheer and Leigh Whicker for their passion for SA football, even if at times there were those in Victoria who thought their parochial positioning was not in the best interests of the development of the game nationally. Although they were not required to invest financially into the game in SA, as was necessary in other states, they put more than their share of time and effort into ensuring that the South Australians were properly represented in the national competition without the local game being affected. We owe them a great debt and this has been appropriately recognised by Whicker being made a Life Member of the League in 2003 and Basheer being inducted into the Australian Football Hall of Fame in 2005.

Limiting a list of significant contributors to 10 means I have had to leave out many people who played a key role in the growth of the AFL. At the top of that list (perhaps on top of the original list!) is my wife, Christine.

---

4   Ibid.

During those turbulent years, I experienced a lot of emotions—sadness, happiness, excitement, pride, anger and despair. I suffered with my family when they became concerned about their husband and father during the Footscray merger. I was upset for Christine when she later contracted chronic fatigue syndrome, most likely as a result of my work pressures, and had to give teaching—her life's love—away. Despite this setback, her emotional support to me was indispensable. She provided a shoulder to cry on when it was required—and there were plenty of times when it was—and the positive reinforcement I needed to do what I had to do. She still does.

We tend to underestimate how important our support networks are in life until we have to call on them. I called on mine on many occasions. Those networks extend beyond the family, of course, and the code has been very fortunate in selecting high-calibre part-time commissioners who have shown a remarkable commitment to the game. It all began with the early pioneers, and, along with those I have already mentioned, Peter Nixon played a major part in popularising the concept of an independent commission. It's assumed these days that we have an independent board overseeing the game, but such was certainly not the case in the early years. Not only was it new to the fans, who really had little sense of how things were managed internally, it was new to the clubmen and the League's directors.

Nixon is a thorough gentleman who came to the commission as a highly regarded politician, which was a vital CV to carry into his new role. He was also a great street fighter and knew his way around the media and political powerbrokers, so he was absolutely indispensable in those early years. He was always a willing participant when we needed to go after the hard ball. Browne saw him as a "cagey, politically savvy commissioner of the highest order; a wise adviser, a good sounding board, and one who was able to bring a discussion back on track if it wandered. I think he has been generally underestimated in his contribution."[5]

Later we were fortunate to have a pair of wise heads in Terry O'Connor and John Winneke on board. O'Connor had chaired both the Eagles and the

---

5   Ibid.

WA Commission before he joined the AFL Commission in 1993, and along with Winneke was of critical assistance when it came to fine-tuning the player rules and changes to the licence agreements for new clubs. Both men were QCs and had a no-nonsense approach to gaining the right outcome, and while Winneke was very good at ensuring both player and club rights, O'Connor championed the non-Victorian clubs around the table. Winneke was on the commission only in 1992 and 1993 before leaving to head up the Appeals Court in Victoria.

Albert Mantello replaced Dick Seddon in 1988, when Seddon was posted to the USA as an Australian trade commissioner. Mantello, a larger-than-life character steeped in club culture, provided the same first-hand club experience as Seddon had. An imposing big man in his 107 games for North Melbourne (1954-62), Mantello was a great source of "insider" knowledge that was otherwise missing around the table.

A key recommendation of the Crawford report in 1993 was to introduce a better governance structure that separated executive and board responsibilities and powers. The reason the original commission appointed only one person, me, as chairman of the League—with executive control—was to allow Alan Schwab to be elevated to the position of executive commissioner in order keep him at the League. There was not the same concern in 1993 about Schwabby leaving, so the commission then implemented a more appropriate structure that allowed only one executive, the CEO, to have a place on the commission—a system that is still in place today. I nominated John Kennedy as chairman because he was a legendary name in football and a person whose values and wisdom were off the scale. He was the right man at the right time and a great source of football understanding, influence and calmness at the commission table. I thank John for taking on the challenge.

Ron Evans also came to the commission in 1993, and was an immediate contributor through his detailed knowledge of club life and the acute business acumen he had developed during an illustrious career at Spotless. Evans showed a remarkable ability to move from the culture of being a club president (Essendon, 1988-92) to being able to see the big picture, particularly in game development and taking the national competition to maturity, and went on to contribute massively as commission chair after my time. He was not just a great leader of the commission, but also a mentor to Andrew Demetriou when the latter took over the CEO's job in 2003 from my successor, Wayne Jackson.

When Evans was president of Essendon and running Spotless, the League awarded the VFL Park catering rights to AVS Catering, who had the best bid. Evans came to see me asking that Spotless be able to put in a second bid as they understood this had always been possible in the past. I pointed out that his staff had been warned there would be only one go and that I couldn't allow that to happen. He left very disappointed with me, but quickly learned that Spotless had to change its game plan.

When he joined the commission I developed a great rapport with him—indeed, who could not? The way he led Essendon's relocation from Windy Hill to the MCG (in 1992) in an emotionally charged environment was a lesson for all other clubs. Essendon's move was not just a masterstroke for the club but showed all other clubs, and their fans, the truth of ground rationalisation. Evans was appointed commission chairman in 1998 and served in that role until shortly before his death in 2007.

Alan Schwab's story was one of triumph and tragedy. He was truly a larger-than-life figure in football, and before and after I joined the League he was the font of all knowledge insofar as the rules of the game were concerned. Browne spent a lot of time with Schwab and said recently:

> Alan had great passion for the game, and forming football mateships was really important to him—he told football stories with football people, got pissed with them. Football was his life. He was so caught up in its many facets that it was responsible, in many respects, for his excesses and personal issues.
>
> But after big nights he always came up in the morning; he would pop a few tablets and get into the new day. He would show his great passion for the game when he commented that "The greatest sound in life is the

sound of the siren when the umpire holds the ball aloft before a game and the leather slams down into the turf." He was clearly captivated by the prospect. For all that, Alan was a bit of a dinosaur lost in the old boys' world and had to be dragged along into the new world of football.[6]

I always enjoyed listening to Alan talk about the game with that passion that was deep in his soul. These were always captivating conversations, and his loss was met with great sadness by all of us who knew him well.

From the early days of the commission, when he was a relatively junior reporter for Channel 10, Eddie McGuire showed all the hallmarks of being a leader in the industry. He was polite, respectful and intelligent, and had common sense and a manner that ensured he received better information than the average reporter. It was certainly one of the better decisions of the Collingwood Football Club to elect him as president in 1999, and although he is passionate about his club he is able to see the broader picture and contribute powerfully. He has been extremely successful at lifting the fortunes of his club, which was in real strife when he took the reins. Collingwood is back as a true leader, not just in the usual metrics of membership and profitability but in its contribution to the game as a whole.

During that period of great change, particularly in the way the relationship between the AFL and the MCC moved from confrontation to collaboration, Dr John Lill and Don Cordner were both terrific leaders of the MCC. They need to be mentioned for their guidance in making the building of the Great Southern Stand happen and for making the process more than bearable.

There were many in the AFL's administration who made things work; many of them were young when I joined, and many worked for long periods to assist in the growth of the game. There was none better than Jill Lindsay, whose time with the League predated mine by 15 years. She worked her heart out until she could do no more. When she died in February 2011, Jill was the game's longest-serving administrator and only female Life

---

6   Ibid.

Member. Her League service began under Sir Kenneth Luke 41 years before her untimely death from cancer. A girl from NSW, she quickly fell in love with the game—and the Tigers—and once football was in her blood, she was in its grip for life.

"It's hard to imagine anyone who has made such a long-lasting impression on the game," CEO Andrew Demetriou said after Jill's death. "As a person her contribution was immeasurable. As a woman she was just an inspiration."[7]

As grounds operation manager Jill was a match for anyone, including some of the rough diamonds running our various grounds. She became one of the most respected managers in the code and had a great sense of fun, and you always knew when she was around. We all miss Jill immensely.

Jill was among the many AFL staff members who contributed much in difficult circumstances to the administration and development of the game during the period covered by this book. They were the front line who had to face often stiff opposition from the public, friends and acquaintances and explain why we were doing what we were doing. None of it would have happened without their commitment and belief.

---

7   Caroline Wilson, "Football loses its true first lady, Jill Lindsay", *The Age*, 8 February 2011.

CHAPTER 22

Reflections

Yes, the phoenix has well and truly risen. It was born again out of the destructive fires of the 1980s, a decade in which the Victorian Football League teetered on the brink of extinction.

Could anyone who knew the 1980s have imagined how far the phoenix would ascend?

Today's clubs share an enlightened vision. They understand how important they all are to each other, and have grasped the concept of "mutual dependence". Football's once-warring tribes have come to terms with being "an alliance of sworn enemies".

Two men from one club sum up this change. Allan McAlister, Collingwood's passionate president of the 1980s, was no less passionate about the fortunes of his Pies than their current president, Eddie McGuire, is today. But there is a subtle difference in philosophy. To Allan it was a simple equation: without the mighty Collingwood the League was nothing; for Eddie it's a slightly more nuanced view: Collingwood cannot be mighty without a mighty League.

And that, in essence, describes the change the commission brought to football from the late 1980s to its centenary in 1996 and beyond. A long and difficult road, but we did it, slowly influencing change over the years and dragging our constituents into the 21st century.

What a ride I had for 10 years on the back of the phoenix—Australia's passionate indigenous sport, now the dominant force in the Australian sporting landscape. A phoenix rising from the ashes, indeed.

Moving out of the corporate world into sport was a big gamble for me. Back in the 1980s I was eking out a very comfortable living in corporate Australia, but I was uneasy, restless, wanting something more for myself, looking for the next mountain to climb, something that would better utilise my creative energy—something that would stretch me to the limit.

Boy, did I find it. I moved from a comfortable England-based insurance company to the challenge that was the VFL. It was the job that every red-blooded young Australian who loved football would have given his right arm for.

This sport has been a major leisure interest of many in the southern states for more than 130 years. Before business, sport was my life, but particularly playing football. Not reading books, not the academic pursuits of my fellow students at school—I was a jock. Sport was everything. My ultimate achievement was winning triple honour colours before I left school at 19. (Yes, 19.)

And there I was in 1986, like a kid in a candy shop, at the helm of the sport that had been the bedrock and passion of my youth. It was a sport we were seriously at risk of losing altogether, with clubs deep in the financial and organisational mire that had enveloped football. Our sport needed more creative thinking as the environment around us changed with almost warp speed.

It was not a crusade for one man; it needed to be a team effort, and I was fortunate that the VFL Board provided me with that team. The foundation commission was a talented, diverse group who possessed the necessary skills to gain the football industry's confidence while dealing with the myriad complex issues confronting them, not the least of which was "Where will the money come from that can support all these teams?"

I initially found it difficult to separate myself emotionally from the job that had to be done and the life of football I had grown up with.

My childhood and adolescence had been spent in a sporting household and I had watched the game romantically as a boy, with my older brother Denis looming large in these memories as he played the game hard and tough and with great success. I played in many premiership teams as a schoolboy at Wesley College and at St Kilda in a career foreshortened by injury, coached in the amateurs twice, and have been both a sponsor and a director at Hawthorn. These were all strong emotional attachments, with great memories.

But now I needed to detach myself. This was a business under threat that needed dispassionate and logical attention, which is exactly what the commission was engaged to deliver and was prepared to deliver. And deliver we did.

Yes, it was a time in our game when it was make or break, when all the planets had to align for football to survive, let alone thrive. Thanks to hard work and a dash or two of good fortune, that's what happened.

Our game today dominates sport in this country, generating enough revenue to run a successful competition and support the financially weaker clubs. There's money enough to pay the players superior salaries commensurate with their professional status, spend increasing amounts on marketing and code development and launch new teams into virgin markets—and have some left over to do good in the broader community. And yet not so long ago there was a time many doubted that Australian football, at a professional level at least, would survive another season.

Today, those who were part of this era of "stabilise, then grow" can be proud of what has been achieved, especially with regard to where the game is positioned in Australian sport. This is not a game that benefits from vast international exposure or connections. It is "a game of our own", a game of the Australian people. We invented it. It is a good reflection of what we are as a people and that is why we are passionate about it and love it so much. It is part of our way of life.

Sometimes, when we look at what the game is today and reflect on those early years, we smile inwardly, and feel good about ourselves.

Acknowledgments

Writing this book has been a labour of love that has been made easier by many people whose contributions I would like to acknowledge.

Sincere thanks to those who supported the book. Firstly, the AFL for their support and encouragement and in particular retiring CEO Andrew Demetriou, who was rapid in providing the full resources of the League and generous access to the minutes of the game before, during and after my period in charge. Secondly, John Pearce, a great friend and supporter of sport in this country (much of which support is unheralded and not public knowledge), provided me with the resources to concentrate full time on this project through much of 2014.

I am grateful to Geoff Slattery, who, when approached with the idea for the book, enthusiastically embraced the concept and agreed to publish the result. Geoff understood the importance of the story to AFL history and the need for it to be told. I thank him and Jonathan Green for their help in writing the book and for the many interesting hours we spent in conversation despite their busy schedules.

Thank you to the staff at the Slattery Media Group, especially Katie Purvis for her editing and Kate Slattery for her design.

Special thanks to Tony Peek for his assistance in providing information and proofing the manuscript, and Col Hutchinson, whose knowledge of football events and statistics is second to none. Matthew Nicholson's doctoral thesis, *Print Media Representation of Crisis Events in Australian Football* (Victoria University, 2002), was an invaluable resource for information on the survival of the Footscray Football Club and the Fitzroy-Brisbane merger.

I thank former AFL/VFL commissioners Graeme Samuel, Colin Carter, Peter Scanlon and Peter Nixon for their considerable input and excellent memories, and Dick Seddon for allowing me to include sections of his valuable unpublished memoir—my thanks do not do justice to Dick's contribution. To the other 40 or so people whom I interviewed, my sincere thanks for contributing your time and thoughts to making this account more complete, informed and authentic.

Thanks to my family, Christine, Melanie and Gregory, who put up with much, including an often-absent husband and father, during the playing-out of the substance of this story. I am also very grateful for their support during the 18 months I needed to complete the book.

Particular thanks to my wife, Christine, who was probably happy that working on the book got me out of her hair during those 18 months! She will now have to find me another project to save her sanity.

Index

SYMBOLS

3AW 167, 230, 307

A

AAMI 85, 87, 164
Ablett, Gary senior 9
Active Marketing 18, 57, 162, 172
Adams, John 276-7
Adelaide Crows Football Club 246, 249, 271, 275, 278
Adler, Larry 57
AFL Coach of the Century 294
AFL Films 290
AFL Life Membership 293, 303, 309, 313
AFL Player of the Century 294
AFL Team of the Century 294
AFP Investment Corporation 132
Age, The 33, 43, 46, 58, 106, 138, 197, 271
Ahern, Mike 212
Akermanis, Jason 243

Alexander, Ron 247
Allen, Peter 279, 280
Anderson, Angry 191
Ansett, Bob 33, 35, 37, 39, 42, 45, 112
Ansett, Sir Reginald 33, 163
Ansett Airlines 121, 123, 163
Ansett subcommittee report 33, 38-9, 42, 49
Anti Football League 15
ANZ McCaughan bank 238
Arden Street Oval 185
Armstrong, Robert 206, 215, 301
Atkinson, Sallyanne 210
Austin, Rod 226, 236
Australian Airlines 121, 123, 163
Australian Broadcasting Corporation (ABC) 132, 145, 148, 149-51, 152-4, 156, 178, 184
Australian Capital Territory Australian Football League (ACT AFL) 181
Australian Football Hall of Fame 292, 294, 309

Australian Industrial Relations
    Commission (AIRC) 281
Australian Securities Commission..............252
Australian Sports Drug
    Agency (ASDA) 284-5
AVS Catering...312
Aylett, Allen 15, 16-18, 19-23, 26, 29,
    30, 33, 38, 42, 44, 45, 48-50, 52, 53, 56,
    188, 189, 192, 273, 276, 300, 302

B

Baker, Ian 231
Ballantyne, Peter 226
Barassi, Ron.......................17, 42, 155, 267-8,
    271, 273, 291
Barham, David..290-1
Barker, Anthony 204, 247
Basheer, Max......................... 243, 245, 249, 309
Beattie, Barrie...222
BHP...27, 85
Black, John..284
"Black Magic" newspaper
    advertisement......................................174
Blake, Martin 138
Blight, Malcolm...295
Blue Report (1985) 65-9,
    89, 117, 184-5, 187, 216, 269, 276, 304
Bolte, Sir Henry...188
Bond, Alan.............................57, 124, 139, 147,
    151, 163, 215
Bond Brewing...161
Bond Corporation 213-14
Borbidge, Rob..212
Bowes, Bill..193
Brady, Mike 172, 173, 175, 294
Brennan, Mike......................................253-4, 257

Brereton, Dermott...290
Brisbane Bears Football Club........10, 36, 95,
    118, 120, 124, 126, 131, 137, 141, 157,
    159, 176, 181, 202, 203, 206-13, 215,
    219, 237-43, 255-6, 258, 264, 266, 298
Brisbane Entertainment Centre....................207
Brisbane Lions Football Club 241-2,
    255-9, 278, 309
Broadcom.................131-4, 137-41, 149, 150,
    153, 160
Brooks, Des 159
Brown, Alan..190
Brown, John.. 119, 206
Browne, Jeff...62, 72, 75,
    79, 80, 108, 110, 169, 177, 194-5, 197,
    200, 203, 239, 244, 286, 288, 292, 300,
    302-3, 305, 307, 309, 310, 312
Brownlow Medal............................85, 154, 293
Brunswick Street Oval.............................35, 259
Buckenara, Gary..34, 267
Budget Rent a Car 33
Bunton, Haydn...291
Burgess, Grant..166
Burns, Creighton..58
Burns, George..175, 292
Busse, Neil..25, 171
Butcher, Mike..84

C

Cain, John.............................19, 188-9, 197-8,
    200, 203, 233, 234
Cain, John senior...188
Calwell, Arthur..188
Campaign Palace, The......................... 172, 174
Capes, Tony....................... 33, 88, 99, 100, 284
Capuano, Barry.. 227, 270

Carlton & United Breweries (CUB).........27, 161-2, 164, 178-80
Carlton Football Club..........................10, 26-7, 44, 77, 78, 81, 83, 94, 185, 187, 201, 209, 263-6
Carrara...........117, 120, 123, 207-9, 210-13, 238, 239, 298
Carrington, Gerry....................................136
Carter, Colin.................65, 195, 200, 300, 304
Carter, Ron..43
Casey, Ron..........110, 128, 134-8, 140, 141, 143-5, 151, 172
Cash, Pat..138
Ceberano, Kate......................................294
Channel 10................131, 129, 132, 145, 156, 155, 235, 313
Channel Nine........80, 129, 130-1, 139, 145, 147, 154, 172, 303
Channel Seven............110, 126-39, 141, 143, 145-7, 150, 151, 153, 155, 160, 161, 171-2, 174-5, 181, 289-91, 298
Chatfield, Irene.......................227-8, 230
Coca-Cola Company.............................181
Cockatoo-Collins, Che..........................287
Colless, Richard.......................203, 205-6, 215, 248, 267, 272-4, 300, 301, 304
Collingwood Football Club....................10, 26, 185, 76, 186, 201, 229, 249, 263, 265, 313, 315
Collins, Ian..............29, 37, 39, 83, 121, 123, 254, 264, 272
Columb, Nick.......................221, 222, 224, 228, 234
Cometti, Dennis....................................151
Cook, Brian..248
Cook, Ron................33-4, 45, 71, 81, 87, 88, 89, 99, 118-19, 143

Cordner, Don..........194, 197, 200, 202, 313
Cornes, Graham.....................................246
Cosser, Steve....................131, 133, 134, 139, 150, 153
Craigie, Rowen......................................197
Crawford, David.................23, 251, 268, 269, 270, 278
Crawford report..........268-70, 278, 304, 311
Cricket Australia.....................................69
Crockett, Justice William...................70-2, 79
Cronin, Paul............141, 142, 156, 206, 209, 211-12, 237-8, 240, 308-9

D

Dahlsen, John.......................................146
Daphne, Leon.......................................255
Dare, Norm..242
Davey, Noel...................................162, 164
Davis, Michael..42
De Bolfo, Tony......................................253
de Castella, Robert................................193
Dear, Paul...191
Demetriou, Andrew.........167, 295, 297, 307, 312, 314
Derry, Tom.....................................123, 121
Desmond, Ros................................114, 297
Dicker, Ian..261
DiMaggio, Joe......................................292
Docklands Stadium................187, 190, 195, 201, 304
Doubleday Field....................................292
Downie, Graeme.....................241, 243, 252
Drugs in Sport Senate inquiry................284
Duerden, Peter.......................................85
Dunn, David...253
Dunstall, Jason........................9, 191, 260

Durham, Greg 114, 124, 162, 214, 227, 303

E

East Fremantle Football Club 247, 248
Edelsten, Geoffrey 53, 56-9, 61-2, 64, 124, 215, 219, 240
Edgley, Michael 57, 119
Elders IXL 27, 77
Elliott, John 10, 26-32, 37, 42, 75, 77, 94-5, 187, 227, 264, 300, 303-4
Essendon Football Club 26, 81, 83, 185, 186, 201, 287, 312
Eustace, Ken 131
Evans, Ron 311-12

F

Fairfax Group 127, 129, 135, 137, 147, 151, 153, 155
Farnham, John 294
Feehan, Michael 233
Fenech, Jeff 191
Fenton, Gary 127-8, 132, 135-6, 145-6, 148, 155, 171-3
Fitch, Ken 284
Fitzpatrick, Mike 94, 98
Fitzroy Football Club 10, 34, 35, 118, 120, 121, 159, 210, 214, 216, 219, 220, 222, 224-6, 236, 243, 250-1, 253-9
Flower, Robert 9
Football Record 166, 290, 297
Footscray Football Club 10, 36, 128, 201, 219-30, 234-36, 250
Footy Show, The 154, 258

Fordham, Robert 234
Foschini, Silvio 24, 70-1, 79
Foster's Cup 78, 178
Fox, Lindsay 44, 70, 180
Foxtel 161
Fremantle Football Club 247-8, 259
Fyfe, Andrew 295

G

Gabba, the 120, 207, 210-11, 241, 258, 298, 303
Gaffney, Jack 170-1
Galimberti, Dennis 221-2, 228
Gannon, Ken 272
Gee, Peter 153
Geelong Football Club 26, 304
Geraghty, John 57, 62, 215, 308
Gibson, Don 222
Ginnane, Tim 229
Glendinning, Ross 9
Glenferrie Oval 86, 163, 185
Gordon, Noel 159, 242, 252, 258
Gordon, Peter 220, 227-35
Grant, Chris 236
Grant, Trevor 46, 106, 253
Greater Western Sydney Football Club 268
Great Southern Stand 197, 200, 202, 298, 313
Grgic, Ilija 288

INDEX

H

Hafey, Tom......................................62, 291, 315
Hamilton, Jack..............10, 15, 17-18, 21, 29, 38, 40, 43, 45, 48-54, 61, 65, 68-9, 71, 77, 85, 88, 90, 92, 93, 95, 98, 101, 104, 105, 107, 109, 110-11, 113, 117, 120, 128, 130, 164, 172-3, 188, 192, 194, 206, 243, 270, 305
Hamilton, Joan...271
Hamilton, Neil....................203, 206, 215, 301
Harada, Masahiko 'Fighting'............127, 191
Hardie, Brad..209
Hawke, Bob...104
Hawkins, Doug..226
Hawthorn Football Club.........33, 81-2, 86-7, 112, 128, 186, 201, 260, 317
Hayes, Kerrie..294
Healy, Gerard..9, 62
Hecron Ltd....................................118, 121, 214
Hennessy, John...18
Herald, The............68, 88, 91-2, 96, 106, 109, 112, 135
Herald and Weekly Times (H&WT)..136, 139, 144
Herald Sun, The..281
Hill, David (ABC)...............................145, 150-1
Hill, David (Channel Nine)...........................154
Hobbs, Greg.......................88, 91-3, 95, 104, 106, 109
Hohnen, Mark.......................206, 215, 301
Holmes à Court, Robert..27, 137, 139, 147
Hooker, John Lee..175
Hore-Lacy, Dyson..............251, 253, 254, 255
Hungry Jack's..78
Hutchesson, Errol.............................264, 265

I

ICI (Imperial Chemical Industries)..........220, 233
"I'd Like to See That" campaign..............174-5
Indian Pacific Limited (IPL).......................120, 204-6, 219
Ireland, Andrew......240, 243, 253, 256, 303
Ironmonger, John...154

J

Jackson, Daryl...197-8
Jackson, Wayne.......................167, 249, 312
Jacobs, Bill..230
Jacobsen, Kevin..119
James, Sandra..226
Jeans, Allan..84
Jetset..163
Johanson, Robert..44
John, Graeme...93
Johnson, Ben...284
Johnson, Bill..194
Johnson, Chris...259
Johnson, Ian...27, 194
Jolly, Rob..198
Jona, Walter..260
Joseph, Ron.....................17, 29, 99, 121, 267
Joyce, Alan...84
Junction Oval..35, 86
J. Walter Thompson agency....................160-1

K

Kardinia Park...27, 184
Kearney, Neil..290
Keating, Paul...146
Kelly, Ross..247, 248

Kennan, Jim 46
Kennedy, John senior 25, 95, 260, 269, 290, 311
Kennedy, Russell 278
Kennett, Jeff 200, 261
Kerley, Neil 'Knuckles' 244
Kerr, Bill 205
KickStart program 288
Kimberley, Craig 57, 62, 215, 308
King, Ray 85
Kirner, Joan 233
Knights, Peter 209
Krakouer, Jim 174
Krakouer, Phil 174

L

Lane, Tim 150, 152, 155, 297
Langford, Chris 260
Lappin, Nigel 242
Larwill, David 293
Lauritz, John 264
Lee, Bob 117
Lehmann, Kevin 123
Leighton Contractors 210
Leppitsch, Justin 242
Lewis, Gordon 96
Liberatore, Tony 288
Liddell, Carol 228
Lill, John 188, 192, 194, 198, 198-9, 200, 313
Lindsay, Jill 289, 313-14
Linnell, Garry 121, 134, 143, 151, 163
Linter Group 132, 139
Lockett, Tony 9, 240, 273
Locklear, Heather 175
Long, Michael 286-9

Lovett, Michael 96, 112
Luke, Sir Kenneth 52, 188, 191, 192, 314
Luscombe, Kevin 45

M

Macdonald, Ranald 31
Madden, Justin 9, 279, 280
Madden, Simon 9, 279
Main, Jim 53, 61, 264, 265, 288
Major League Baseball (MLB) 71, 79
Mandie, David 25
Mandie reports 25-6, 32, 37, 42-3
Mandie task force 25, 29, 42
Mantello, Albert 42, 88, 99, 100, 105, 114, 122, 224, 235, 311
Mantle, Mickey 292
Mariani, Wally 121-2
Matthews, Leigh 9, 243, 294
Mays, Willie 292
McAdam, Gilbert 288
McAlister, Allan 186, 229, 235, 265, 315
McAvaney, Bruce 127
McCutchan, Eric 17, 18, 52, 166, 188, 192
McDonald's 78
McEnroe, John 175
McGuinness, Tony 229, 235
McGuire, Eddie 235, 313, 315
McHenry, Murray 203, 206, 215, 301
McKay, Jim 18, 57, 74, 154, 160-1, 172
McKay, Michael 151
McKenzie, Ian 245
McKinsey & Co. 19, 21-2, 27, 65
McKinsey report 22-5, 42, 48, 214
McLachlan, Gillon 167, 307
McLean, Michael 288

Melbourne Cricket Club (MCC)........ 27, 52, 163, 188-90, 192, 194, 196, 197-201, 298, 303, 304, 313
Melbourne Cricket Ground (MCG) 18-19, 27, 52, 163, 184-91, 192, 195, 197, 201, 241, 260, 292, 293, 303, 304, 312
   MCG Trust 19, 188, 192, 197, 201
   see also Great Southern Stand
Melbourne Football Club 42, 201, 216, 251, 260
Merkel, Ron 57, 288
Miller, Bob 25
Miller, Greg 253-5
Mitchell, Harold 157, 164
Mitchell, Neil 167, 307
Monkhorst, Damien 286-8
Moorabbin Oval 86, 184, 186
Moore, Dean 294
Morphett, Drew 150, 153-5
Morwood, Paul 24, 71
Moses, Gerald 239, 309
Moses, Judah 239, 309
Muirhead, Justice James 111
Munduwalawala, Ginger Riley 293
Murdoch, Rupert 136, 139, 146-7
Murray, Kevin 259

N

Nadel, David 285, 289
Nathan, Sir Maurice 17-18, 45, 163
National Baseball Hall of Fame 292
National Basketball Association (NBA) 71, 79
National Football League of Australia 41, 154, 275-6
National Football League (USA) 71, 79, 177
National Hockey League (NHL) 71, 79
National Panasonic 178
National Tennis Centre 38, 199, 293
Nauru Insurance Company (NIC) 253
New South Wales Rugby League (NSWRL) 80
Niall, Jake 33
Nine Network *see* Channel Nine
Nixon, Peter 39, 42, 46, 49, 51, 61, 69, 76, 132, 142-4, 222, 235, 310
Nolan, Tony 229
Norman, Greg 158
Northey, John 54
North Melbourne Football Club 17, 33, 185, 189, 201, 214, 216, 219, 243, 253-7, 264
Norwood Football Club 131, 244

O

O'Connor, Ryan 294
O'Connor, Terry 273, 310
O'Neill, Kevin 158
O'Shaughnessy, Michael 281
O'Sullivan, Shane 240
Oakley, Christine 101, 232, 309
Oakley, Denis 193, 317
Oakley, Hec 192-3
One Hundred Years of Australian Football (film) 290
Osborne, Richard 226
Ovens, Jeff 247

P

Packer, Kerry 112, 130, 135
Palmer, Scott 245
Pappas Carter Evans and Koop 65, 195
Peat, Marwick and Mitchell 23
Peek, Tony 108-9, 123, 166-7, 282, 287, 300, 305-6
Pelerman, Ann 239, 309
Pelerman, Reuben 215, 239-42, 309
Perillo, Mark 278
Piesse, Ken 193
Pike, Martin 259
Piper, Alan 242-3, 252
Players Association (AFLPA) 32, 279-81
Port Adelaide Football Club 112, 244-5, 248-50
Poulton, Jim 214
Powerplay 264
Pratt, Bill 25
Pridmore, Allen 150
Princes Park 27, 35, 163, 184, 185, 187, 221, 226, 227
Pritchard, Bob 57
Punt Road Oval 163, 192, 255

Q

Qantas 121, 163
QEII stadium, Brisbane 206-7, 211-12
Qintex 57, 117, 120, 213, 237, 241, 308-9
Queensland Australian Football League (QAFL) 125, 124, 213, 234, 238, 240, 309
Quinlan, Bernie 9

R

Reynolds, Dick 291
Reynolds, Tom 200, 259
Rhys-Jones, David 171
Rice, Gary 154
Richmond Football Club 26, 65-6, 77, 124, 185, 201, 213-14, 243
Ridley, Ian 251, 260, 264
Rioli, Maurice 110
Roberts, Michael 42
Robertson, Ian 295
Roos, Paul 226
Rose, Lionel 127, 191
Rowland, Peter 158
Royal Insurance 63, 85, 88-9, 92, 166
Ruth, 'Babe' 292
Ryan, Phil 17

S

Samuel, Graeme 39, 42, 44-5, 51, 53-5, 56, 58-9, 61, 64-5, 76-7, 88, 90, 93-5, 98-9, 101, 105-6, 112, 118, 121, 123, 132-4, 139, 203, 206, 235, 247, 280, 300, 302, 305
Save the Dogs 227-9
Sawyer, Peter 158-9
Scanlon, Jack 45
Scanlon, Peter 39, 42, 45-6, 49-51, 55, 57, 59, 65, 76-7, 88, 90, 93-5, 98-101, 106, 108, 110, 112, 123-5, 130, 132, 134, 139, 152-3, 165, 194, 200, 203, 219, 235, 243, 264, 277, 300, 302, 305

INDEX

Schwab, Alan 'Schwabby'.................10, 32, 77, 79, 90-3, 95, 98-101, 103, 104-9, 112-13, 117, 123, 132, 137, 140-3, 154, 165, 182, 209, 244-7, 267, 269-72, 276, 279, 298, 301, 305, 311-13
Scott, Brett..267
Scott, Chris..243
Scott, Don...260
Seddon, Dick................22, 23, 28-30, 39, 42, 48, 51, 70, 72-3, 75-7, 79, 81-3, 88, 94-5, 98-100, 132, 300, 304, 306, 311
Sellers, Basil.............................57-9, 61-2, 215, 308
Seven Network *see* Channel Seven
Sewell, Greg..33
Shaw, David...264
Shaw, Tony...285
Sheahan, Mike...................50, 68-9, 103-4, 107-8, 114, 123, 125, 127, 138-9, 164-5, 166, 201, 281, 300, 305-6
Sheedy, Kevin.....................................268, 291
Sheehan, Tony..198
Skase, Christopher.........57, 117, 124-5, 151, 153, 155, 157-60, 177, 206-9, 212, 215, 219, 236-8, 241, 308-9
Skase, Pixie..157
Skilton, Bob..58, 62
Slade, Geoff..265
Smith, Daryl..58
Smith, Norm..294
South Australian National Football League (SANFL)...............119, 131, 243-5, 248-50
South Fremantle Football Club.................247-8
South Melbourne Football Club.........10, 19, 55, 70, 302
Speakman, Des..................................172, 174
Special Broadcasting Service (SBS)...........145

Sportsplay....................................132-3, 178
Spotless..311-12
Stimpson, Nicki..272
St Kilda Cricket Club..................................193-4
St Kilda Football Club............24, 44, 70, 84, 86, 91, 107, 186, 201, 214, 216, 219, 252
Stokes, Kerry...147
Stynes, Jim..288
Sun, The.....................135, 138-9, 142-3, 146, 221, 225-6, 229, 231, 236
Sunday Age, The..168
Sutherland, Doug...62
Sutton, Charlie..225
Sweeney Research..............................172, 174
Sydney Swans Football Club................10, 23, 31, 53-6, 59, 61, 64, 70-1, 89, 131, 176, 215, 219, 263-8, 270, 272-4, 278, 301, 308

T

TAA..163
Talking Footy...127
Tannock, Peter....................................247-8, 302
Teal Cup..80
Ten Network *see* Channel 10
Testro, Brenda..113
Thomas, Geoffrey..57
Thomas, Ted.........................129, 146, 148
Threlfall, Kevin..28
Timms, Daryl......................138, 141, 144
Tooheys Brewery...................................179-80
Touche Ross..58
Transport Accident Commission (TAC)..234
Trott, Stuart..264

Truth, The 155
Tutu, Archbishop Desmond 175

U

United Nations Association
 of Australia 288, 289
Up There Cazaly 172-3, 175, 294
"Up yours Oakley" sticker 231-2, 234

V

VFL Park 18, 52, 87, 161, 163, 171, 184-5, 187-92, 194-6, 201, 235, 271, 294, 298, 304, 312
VFL Travel 160
Victoria Park 35, 76, 169, 184-6, 285
Victorian Aboriginal Education
 Association 287
Victorian Cricket Association (VCA) 193
Victorian Employers' Chamber of
 Commerce and Industry (VECCI) 281
Voce, Bill 193
Voss, Michael 242

W

Walker, Bruce 166
Walker, John 203, 205
Walls, Robert 239, 242
Wanganeen, Gavin 287
Ward, Brian 57
Watson, Tim 9
Weber, Bruce 245
Weinert, Peter 264-6, 288, 308
West Australian Football Commission
 (WAFC) 247, 311

West Australian Football League (WAFL) 120, 206, 210, 247
West Coast Eagles Football Club 10, 78, 95, 118-20, 126, 131, 137, 176, 191, 202-4, 206, 210, 214, 219, 246-8, 272, 277-8, 301, 310
Western Bulldogs Football Club *see*
 Footscray Football Club
Western Oval 184, 226-7, 230, 232, 235, 250
 see also Whitten Oval
Wheeler, Terry 230
Whicker, Leigh 117, 244, 246, 249, 309
White, David 234
Whitten, Ted 244
Whitten Oval 35
 see also Western Oval
Wiegard, Keith 34
Wiegard, Leon 33-5, 118, 120-1, 222, 224, 226, 251
Willesee, Mike 215, 264, 308
Williams, Greg 9, 62
Williams, Mark 209
Wilson, Ian 27
Windy Hill 163, 184, 185, 186, 312
Winmar, Nicky 285, 288-9
Winneke, John 310
Winners, The 153
World of Sport 127, 290
Wynns Winegrowers 85-7, 166

X

XXXX beer 78, 161-2, 178

NEW VFL SUPREMO

Changes must be made — Oakley

At the end of the most momentous day in 100 years of football, the game is better placed than it has ever been.

PATRICK SMITH

UP YOURS OAKLEY

The Boss takes care of business his way

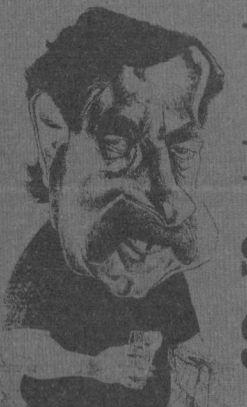

VFL TV rights sold for $24.5m